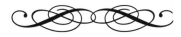

An Audience with
Queen Victoria

The Royal Opinion on
30 Famous Victorians

Ian Lloyd

To Julie and David Harsant,
true friends, with love

First published 2019

The History Press
The Mill, Brimscombe Port
Stroud, Gloucestershire, GL5 2QG
www.thehistorypress.co.uk

British Library Cataloguing in Publication Data.
A catalogue record for this book is available from the British Library.

ISBN 978 0 7509 8903 9

Typesetting and origination by The History Press
Printed and bound in Great Britain by TJ International Ltd

CONTENTS

ACKNOWLEDGEMENTS

A book that examines Queen Victoria's thoughts and opinions of her contemporaries would be nothing without access to her voluminous collection archive of written material.

I am therefore indebted to Her Majesty the Queen, the copyright holder, for her kind permission to quote from her great-great-grandmother's journals in the Royal Archives.

I would also like to thank the following individuals and also the representatives of organisations associated with the thirty iconic figures whose relationship with Queen Victoria is discussed in the book:

Angela Bamford (Linguist and Translator)

James Cornelius (Secretary of the Abraham Lincoln Association and Curator of the Lincoln Collection at the Lincoln Presidential Library)

Bruce Eldredge and Karen Roles (The Buffalo Bill Center of the West)

Steve Friesen (Director, Buffalo Bill Museum)

Merlin Holland (grandson of Oscar Wilde)

Robert Lacey (Royal Historian)

Helen MacEwan (The Brussels Brontë Group)

Christine McMorris (Commissioning Editor of The History Press)

Pamela Morton (NUJ Freelance Organiser)

Hugh Bell Muller (great-grandson of Alexander Graham Bell)

Michael Short, of the Liszt Society, UK, for answering detailed questions and for allowing me to quote from his forthcoming biography of the composer

Sarah Whale (Assistant Curator to the Marquess of Salisbury, Hatfield House)

Brian Wood (Curator, The Bell Homestead, Brantford, Ontario)

I am deeply grateful to Christine McMorris, Alex Waite and Jessicca Gofton for commissioning, producing and marketing this book for The History Press and finally I am deeply indebted to the friendly, hard-working staff of Cowley Library, Oxford, for dealing with my constant stream of enquiries and orders.

PREFACE

During her long life Queen Victoria met everyone from the opera singer Luigi Lablache, who was a pall-bearer at Beethoven's funeral, to the cellist Pablo Casals, who lived long enough to play for JFK at the White House. *An Audience with Queen Victoria* examines the contact between the Queen and is a veritable 'Who's Who' of her times. It draws on the honest character assessments in her journals and letters of those she met – for example, Alexander Graham Bell she thought 'pompous' while she found the composer Wagner 'short, very quiet, wears spectacles and has a very finely-developed forehead, a hooked nose & projecting chin'. Not all the meetings are up close and personal. Charlotte Brontë stood in the packed streets of Brussels to see the Queen drive past, though she did have enough time to see that her monarch was 'stout', 'vivacious' and 'plainly dressed'. Oscar Wilde claims to have been entranced by her sashaying walk at a garden party.

While those who did meet her face to face treated her with near reverence, once safely back on non-royal territory they could be entertainingly cheeky in their accounts to their nearest and dearest. Bell told his wife that the Queen was 'humpy, stumpy, dumpy' while the future Nicholas II of Russia referred to 'darling grandmama' as 'a round ball on unsteady legs' and even 'belly woman' in blokish letters to his brother George.

I have made an admittedly self-indulgent choice of famous Victorians whose lives one way or another came within the Queen's orbit, selecting those with amusing or rare anecdotes. In doing so I have omitted the well-documented accounts of those she knew best, such as members of her family, with the exception of two of her most charismatic grandchildren, as well as her friends, household and politicians.

Although the majority of chapters deal with the Queen's relationship with one of her contemporaries, two of the chapters deal with a married couple: first, Winston Churchill's parents Lord and Lady Randolph Churchill, and second Tsar Nicholas II of Russia and his wife Tsarina Alexandra, the Queen's favourite granddaughter.

I have also aimed to veer off-course now and then to bring in unusual aspects of the Queen's personality, such as her interest in modern technology. She was one of the very first in this country to try out (and later buy) a telephone. She recorded her voice on a phonograph as a present for an African king and was filmed in 'moving pictures' by Downey.

Above all I've aimed to search for lesser-known anecdotes, such as her account of seeing a polo match – 'a very fast game, something like Hockey on horsback [sic]' – and her dutiful sending of a gift of one of her widow's caps with streamers attached to an African chief, who wore it reverentially under his top hat. Added together they will hopefully give an insight into the Queen's multi-faceted personality, which continues to intrigue and entrance 200 years after her birth.

Ian Lloyd
Oxford
January 2019

1

OUT OF AFRICA
EXCHANGING GIFTS WITH KINGS AND CHIEFTAINS

Menelik II.

BRITISH MONARCHS have exchanged gifts with foreign leaders from the earliest times. Henry VIII and Francis I of France gave each other jousting horses at the Field of the Cloth of Gold in 1520, and the Ottoman ruler Suleiman I gave Henry two pet monkeys, which he took with him to meet the French king.

After the death of the Prince Consort in 1861, Victoria no longer travelled abroad on state visits and never visited any part of her growing empire. She did, however, receive visits from heads of state and delegations from her Indian and African territories. The presents they exchanged were often personal, and occasionally bizarre.

In her memoirs, Princess Marie Louise tells of a meeting between her grandmother and a chieftain from the Gold Coast, now Ghana. The be-robed visitor was the exotically titled holder of the 'stool' of Agbosome. After his audience at Windsor, the Queen asked if there was anything she could give him as a souvenir of their meeting. Pointing to the white 'lisse' widow's cap with its long streamers that she always wore in private, he replied, 'Yes, Mighty Queen: I should like to have a bonnet as Your Majesty is now wearing, and I would like to be the only chief entitled to wear it. I will pass it on to my successors.'

Both were true to their word. Victoria asked for a cap to present to the Chief and he and his successors wore it as proof of sovereignty. However, another local custom was for the leader to wear a top hat too. Years later Marie Louise was sent a photograph of the Chief in full regalia, with her grandmother's cap on his head surmounted by a top hat. As she herself commented, 'the effect is quaint to say the least!'[1]

Another visitor, a Chief of the Axim district (which again is in modern-day Ghana), was received by the Queen, who was accompanied by several uniformed courtiers. When asked what memento he would like he is supposed to have said, 'Your Majesty, I should like to have a medal bigger than any I see now,' and so Victoria obligingly had a specially large one struck just for him.[2]

The Queen and her government had a fraught relationship with Emperor Tewodros II of Abyssinia (now Ethiopia), later dubbed 'Mad King Theodore', the Ethiopian version of Russia's Ivan the Terrible. In 1863 he wrote to Victoria asking for skilled workers to come to Abyssinia to produce firearms and other skills. Unfortunately, the Foreign Office in London filed it under 'Pending' for a year before forwarding it to India, since Abyssinian affairs came under the remit of the sub-continent. Here it was filed under 'Not Even Pending'. The tempera-mentally volatile Tewodros, incensed at this snub by the Queen and her government, imprisoned the British Consul, Charles Cameron, as well as all the British subjects based in his country.

Eventually, after a three-year hiatus, the British sent a mission under the Abyssinian-born Hormuzd Rassam. The latter carried the much anticipated letter from 'your good friend Victoria R' written at Balmoral on her birthday, 24 May 1864. It offered Tewodros 'friendship' but denied him an embassy, ignored the request for help with arms, and asked for the release of 'Our servant' Cameron and the other British citizens.

This upset Tewodros even more and in retaliation he imprisoned Rassam and his mission with the other British and European prisoners, while he negotiated with the Queen. Writing to 'Victoria, who God has elected and exalted above all men', he once again asked for 'skilful artists … workmen' to help him establish a gun industry. 'Rejoicing in their coming,' he promised, 'I shall receive them with great honour, and give them good pay.' He included a list of equipment from a small blast steam engine to a gunpowder mill (with rollers).[3] The Emperor then released Martin Flad, a lay missionary with the London Jewish Society, whom he'd imprisoned with his wife and family, and tasked him to return to Britain with the letter.

The Queen received the missionary and her own Prime Minister at Osborne on 14 August 1866:

> Saw Ld Stanley* & a MrFladd [sic], a German Missionary, who was with those unhappy captives, confined by king Theodore of Abyssinia then released, & finally taken again. It is thought that my having seen MrFladd & asked him to tell the king that he must let these poor people go, may have a good effect. He is to say, that unless this is done, there can be no friendship between us.[4]

As the full story of Rassam's trial and imprisonment filtered through, all thoughts of a compromise involving the Queen were wiped out, and instead the government decided to send an expeditionary force under Sir Robert Napier. He defeated 9,000 troops loyal to Tewodros at the Battle of Magdala on 9 April 1868 with only two British casualties. The prisoners were released, but instead of negotiating, Napier went on to capture Magdala. Before this last ditch battle, Tewodros made it clear he would never allow himself to be taken prisoner by the enemy. As his remaining troops were slaughtered and his citadel was stormed by Napier's men, the Emperor seized a favourite duelling pistol, placed the barrel in his mouth and pulled the trigger. When the redcoats found the body minutes later, they noted the sunlight reflecting on a silver plate on the stock. The inscription read:

---

* Edward Smith-Stanley, 14th Earl of Derby, Prime Minister 1866–68.

PRESENTED
BY
VICTORIA
Queen OF GREAT BRITAIN AND IRELAND
TO
THEODORUS
EMPEROR OF ABYSSINIA
AS A SLIGHT TOKEN OF HER GRATITUDE
FOR HIS KINDNESS TO HER SERVANT PLOWDEN
1854[5]

Although the Queen never met Emperor Tewodros face to face, she was visited by several African leaders and delegations during the latter part of her reign. In her journal for May 1880 she records, with evident fascination, a meeting with Ugandan diplomats at Windsor:

Received the 3 black Envoys, from Central Africa, sent by the King of Uganda, who has been very friendly to the explorers & to Capt: Speke. They are very fine tall, dignified, youngish men, wearing a sort of loose blue coat & loose trowsers [sic] to the knee, with stockings & shoes, white shirts, & broad red sashes. Interpretors & Missionaries came with them.[6]

The most fascinating gift bestowed by the Queen was one that, sadly, never survived her lifetime. In her Diamond Jubilee year, 1897, Victoria received 'some presents from the Empress of Abyssinia, 2 necklaces, &c, one of them said to be exactly like that worn by the Queen of Sheba, from whom the Emperor Menelik claims to be descended'.[7]

The following year Menelik II – the third ruler of Abyssinia following the death of Tewodros II – asked if the Queen would record a message for him so he could hear her voice. 'After luncheon,' she noted in August 1898, 'Ld Denbigh brought a phonograph into which I spoke, as it was wished I should sent [sic] a message to the Emperor Menelik. It will be sealed up & destroyed, after he has received the message.'

Victoria's insistence that it should be destroyed may have been to stop it falling into non-royal hands after it was sent abroad. Another reason is embodied in a minute sent by Sir Thomas Sanderson, Permanent Under-Secretary of State at the Foreign Office, to the Prime Minister, Lord Salisbury. According to the former, 'the voice produced by a phonograph is rather nasal and squawky – a travesty of the original.' We have no transcript of Victoria's message, though a minute from Lord Salisbury to Sanderson observes, 'I think your formula will do admirably. If HM desires to add sentiment or admonition, she will do it better than we can.'

A delighted Menelik and his wife listened to the message with due ceremony. An artillery salute was fired and the royal couple stood in respect as it was played several times. The wax cylinder was then smashed to pieces as per the Queen's wishes. The Emperor and Empress recorded their own message, which was brought to Victoria at Osborne. She listened to it and read the translation, making the observation, 'it was very curious'.

There was one final gift from Africa in the summer of 1900. 'I saw the Zebra given me by King Menelik of Abyssinia, which has only now been brought down to the Shaw Farm from the Zoological Gardens,' the Queen noted at Windsor Castle on 13 July. 'It is a beautiful beast, very large, & wonderfully marked. Unfortunately the other one, which came at the same time, died.'[8]

Notes

1 Marie Louise, Princess: *My Memories of Six Reigns*: Penguin: 1956: pp.118–19
2 Ibid.: p.119
3 Marsden, Philip: *The Barefoot Emperor*: HarperCollins: 2007: pp.170–2
4 RA VIC/MAIN/QVJ (W) Tuesday 14 August 1866 (Princess Beatrice's copies). Retrieved 9 January 2018
5 Stanley, H.M.: *Coomassie and Magdala*: Sampson Low: 1874: p.251
6 RA VIC/MAIN/QVJ (W) Friday 14 May 1880 (Princess Beatrice's copies). Retrieved 9 January 2018
7 RA VIC/MAIN/QVJ (W) Tuesday 16 February 1897 (Princess Beatrice's copies). Retrieved 9 January 2018
8 RA VIC/MAIN/QVJ (W) Friday 13 July 1897 (Princess Beatrice's copies). Retrieved 9 January 2018

2

Two Degrees of Separation —
Victoria and Rita Hayworth
The Queen Meets the Aga Khan

Aga Khan III.

SULTAN SIR Mohammed Shah, known as Aga Khan III (1877–1957), succeeded his father Aga Khan II as imam (leader) of the Nizari Ismaili sect in 1885. He is most remembered today as a successful horse breeder and racehorse owner and for briefly being the father-in-law of the Hollywood actress Rita Hayworth.

In a 1954 television interview to promote his newly published memoirs, the Aga Khan remarked that the most notable person whom he had ever known was Queen Victoria. He would go on to be close to Victoria's five successors as monarch, and noted in 1954:

> When I was a young man I sat next to Queen Victoria at a dinner party and talked to her throughout it; the other day I sat next to Queen Elizabeth II at a tea party and talked to her throughout it. [1]

The Sultan's first encounter with the British Royal Family was with Victoria's third son, the Duke of Connaught. Named Arthur after his godfather the Duke of Wellington, he also served in the army and saw military service in South Africa, Canada, Ireland, Egypt and India. It was during his time in the subcontinent as Commander-in-Chief of the British Army from December 1886 to March 1890 that their paths crossed when the Aga Khan was only 9 years old. The boy ruler was a frequent guest of the Duke and his wife, the former Princess Louise Margaret of Prussia, who spoiled him with 'more toffee and chocolate than was altogether good for me'. He would also encounter the Duke riding each day, when Prince Arthur would always stop and talk to him. When he finally met the Empress of India at Windsor, 'she said at once, I remember, that she had heard all about me and my home from her son'. [2]

In 1898 the Aga Khan toured Europe and was twice received by the Queen at Windsor Castle, where, during the second visit, she personally invested him with the KCIE (Knight Commander of the Indian Empire). By then he had already glimpsed the Queen during her annual spring stay in the south of France. He stayed in the same hotel as Victoria in Cimiez and recalled, 'I had frequent opportunities of watching her go out to and return from her daily drives in her landau. She was helped in and out of her carriage by Indian servants from her personal household.' The Aga Khan condescendingly pointed out that the monarch's two Indian servants were 'distinctly second-class servants, of the kind that you find around hotels and restaurants', something he found 'highly odd'; and he mused that perhaps the pay was not high enough to attract men of a higher calibre. [3] Victoria's family and the Royal Household would have concurred with this viewpoint. The Queen, on the other hand, was neither racist nor class conscious, and her romantic view of India, its people and in particular her beloved manservant Abdul Karim overcame the many rumblings of discontent from those closest to her about her fondness for the low-born men.

On 6 May 1898 the 20-year-old Aga Khan finally had the opportunity to talk to the Queen when he was summoned to see her at Windsor. The Queen noted in her journal:

> After luncheon received, in the Audience Room, the Aga Khan, a young man, head of a big Mohamedan sect, called Khoja. He lives in India, but is really a Persian. He was dressed in a loose sort of Cashmere dressing gown, with a low turban on his head. He asked to kiss my hand, & was very shy, but speaks English quite well.[4]

In his memoirs the Aga Khan recalls the second meeting with the Queen when she invested him with the KCIE:

> The Queen, enfolded in voluminous black wraps and shawls, was seated on a big sofa. Was she tall or short, was she stout or not? I could not tell; her posture and her wraps made assessments of that kind quite impossible. I kissed the hand which she held out to me. She remarked that the Duke of Connaught was a close friend of my family and myself. She had an odd accent, a mixture of Scotch and German — the German was perfectly explicable by the fact that she was brought up in the company of her mother, a German princess, and a German governess, Baroness Lehzen. She also had the German conversational trick of interjecting 'so' — pronounced 'tzo' — frequently into her remarks.[5]

The Queen told him that, as he was a prince, she would not ask him to kneel and be dubbed by a sword in the conventional method of knighting but would instead hand him the insignia as an equal — a courtesy he found very touching.

He was asked to stay to dinner where he:

> sat at dinner between the Queen and her daughter Princess Beatrice.* The Queen was wearing her customary black — that mourning which, from the day after her husband died, she never

---

* Princess Henry of Battenberg (1857–1944), mother of Queen Ena of Spain.

put off. On her wrist she wore a large diamond bracelet set in the center of which was a beautiful miniature of the Prince Consort, about three inches long and two inches wide. The Queen was then seventy-nine; the vigor of her bearing and the facility and clarity of her conversation were astonishing.

The guests included the Lord Chancellor, the Earl of Halsbury, a small, squat, unimpressive-looking man. The Sultan remembered, 'I was both surprised and amused when the Queen murmured to me that Lord Halsbury, though not much to look at, was a formidable lawyer and statesman.'

They talked of India and the Queen was very concerned to find out if her senior officials and representatives in the subcontinent were 'civil or were they wanting in manners toward Indian Princes and gentry?' The Aga Khan assured her they all showed him 'impeccable kindness and courtesy'. Ironically there was nothing impeccable about his own kindness and courtesy to Victoria's Indian attendants, 'who were the same kind of rather second-rate servants whom I had noticed in her entourage at Nice'.[6]

The royal visitor has left us a valuable insight into the Queen's eating habits, and her rather good appetite even in her last few years:

> The dinner was long and elaborate – course after course, three or four choices of meat, a hot pudding and an iced pudding, a savory and all kinds of hothouse fruit – slow and stately in its serving. We sat down at a quarter past nine, and it must have been a quarter of eleven before it was all over. The Queen, in spite of her age, ate and drank heartily – every kind of wine that was offered and every course, including both the hot and the iced pudding.

Not everyone was impressed with Victoria's overindulgence. Her personal physician, Dr James Reid, tried to wean her on to Benger's Food, a wheat and milk food supplement designed to soothe the digestive system. Frustratingly for him she treated it as a food supplement and drank a nightly cup after gorging herself on her normal three-course late-night banquet.

After dinner she gave the Aga Khan a jewelled portrait of herself, decorated with the rose of England, the thistle of Scotland and the harp of Ireland – the latter in emeralds. More importantly to the equine-loving leader, she arranged for him to have a Royal Household badge for the Royal Ascot meeting — something that was re-bestowed on him in turn by Edward VII, George V, George VI and Elizabeth II.

Victoria's account of the investiture and dinner shows she was charmed by her young visitor:

> Invested the Aga Khan with the K.C. of the Indian Empire. He kissed my hand twice, pressing it to his forehead, & when saw him afterwards presented me with a most beautiful Tiara in pearls & diamonds, which can also be worn as a necklace … Dined in the large Dining Room … The Aga Khan sat next to me & is extremely intelligent & well informed, speaking beautiful English, which he learnt from his earliest youth. He was full of expressions of devotion to me & my family.[7]

The next morning Abdul Karim, known as 'the Munshi' or teacher by Victoria, was sent by the Queen to show the Aga Khan some of the texts she had copied in Urdu and Arabic characters. This time the Sultan made no scathing comments about the low-born Indian servant and instead opted to focus on Victoria's genuine concern that those who represented her in this part of the empire did so with sensitivity to local people and traditions:

> I particularly remember that at dinner she said to me with great earnestness she hoped that when British people in India visited mosques and temples, they conducted themselves with respect and reverence as they would in cathedrals in their own land.[8]

During his 1898 visit to Britain the Aga Khan attended two state concerts hosted at Buckingham Palace by the Prince of Wales* on behalf of the Queen. Edward acted benevolently to the younger man and enrolled him as a member of his own London club, the Marlborough Club. The Aga Khan was present at both Edward's coronation in 1902 and his funeral in 1910. Afterwards he became a close friend to Edward's successor George V and his consort Queen Mary, who were his near contemporaries, and he regularly dined with them whenever he was in Britain.

---

* Albert Edward, Prince of Wales, later King Edward VII.

The Sultan attended the lavishly produced Delhi Durbar (Court of Delhi) of 1911 attended by George V and Queen Mary to mark their accession as Emperor and Empress of India. He later recalled two disastrous evenings during the festivities. First:

> At the great state banquet, to which most of the notables of India had been invited, some disaster occurred in the kitchen, and the food that emerged was just enough to give the King and a handful of people sitting near him a full meal. For almost all of the guests it was the only chance in their lives that they would ever have of dining in the King's company, but most of them had no dinner.

Then a few days later George held an investiture, during which he made the Aga Khan a Knight Grand Commander of the Star of India. The event was held in a tent, brilliantly lit by electric bulbs, one of which near the canvas roof started to flicker and threatened to explode:

> Whistles were blowing, we could hear fire engines clanking up; behind their Majesties' thrones officers had already drawn their swords and were hacking at the hangings and the canvas to make a way out for the King and Queen. But the rest of us were trapped.

In the event both the King and the bulb remained intact.[9]

The Aga Khan had first met the future Edward VIII when the latter was a sailor-suited boy of 4 at St James's Palace. During Edward's ten-month reign in 1936 the two men met at several private parties where the Sultan was struck by Wallis Simpson's attempts to fit in with the besotted monarch's circle of friends: 'I found her as intelligent as she was charming, admirably well informed, devoid too of flippancy, and seriously and conscientiously striving to adjust her outlook to the King's.' He was also aware of the devastating effect the abdication crisis had on Edward's family, and in particular his mother, Queen Mary: 'Later in the year, in July I think, a great friend of Queen Mary's told me that every day she wept bitterly when she thought of this hidden, unspoken catastrophe which loomed for her dearly loved son.'[10]

The Aga Khan frequently visited George VI and, in his old age, was occasionally received by Elizabeth II. In July 1952, five months after her accession, the 26-year-old Queen watched the Aga Khan's horse

Tulyar win the King George VI and Queen Elizabeth Stakes at Ascot and afterwards she invited the Sultan to meet her in the royal box. The following year she invited him and Prince Mohammed Ali to tea during her Coronation year. Mohammed Ali had for a short time been Regent of Egypt during the minority of King Farouk. Like the Aga Khan he had dined with Queen Victoria at Windsor in 1898, was also a fan of racing and bred Arabian horses. Fifty-five years after her great-great-grandmother entertained these two men, Elizabeth II, whose knowledge of horse breeding and bloodlines would become encyclopaedic, must have relished her chat with two of the legendary names of horse racing.

Notes

1 Aga Khan, His Highness the: *Memoirs of the Aga Khan – World Enough and Time*: Simon and Schuster: 1954: Chapter 1
2 Ibid.: Chapter 3
3 Ibid.: Chapter 4
4 RA VIC/MAIN/QVJ (W) Friday 6 May 1898 (Princess Beatrice's copies). Retrieved 23 April 2018
5 Aga Khan: Op. Cit.: Chapter 4
6 Ibid.: Chapter 4
7 RA VIC/MAIN/QVJ (W) Wednesday 13 July 1898 (Princess Beatrice's copies). Retrieved 23 April 2018
8 Aga Khan: Op. Cit.: Chapter 4
9 Ibid.: Chapter 9
10 Ibid.: Chapter 12

'I HAVE SEEN THE WORLD'
AN ABYSSINIAN PRINCE CAPTURES
VICTORIA'S HEART

Captain Speedy with Alamayou.

ON THURSDAY 16 July 1868 Queen Victoria was in residence at Osborne House on the Isle of Wight. Unable to cope with the blistering heat, the Queen spent most of the day resting indoors before emerging for tea in the garden with her daughters Alice and Helena. The three stayed outdoors painting in the Italianate garden until 8 p.m., when word reached them that the young son of the Emperor of Abyssinia, whom they'd been expecting since yesterday, had arrived.

As she emerged on to Osborne's Lower Terrace the Queen came face to face with a bearded giant of a man and a frail, sad-looking child in Abyssinian robes. 'Little Alamayou is a very pretty, slight graceful boy of 7,' Victoria noted, 'with beautiful eyes & a nice nose & mouth, though the lips are slightly thick. His skin is a dark bronze. His hair, which has been shaved, is crisp & curly.'

This, of course, was a royal child, and Victoria treated him as she would one of her own:

> I kissed him, which he returned. He can say one or 2 words in English. Capt: Speedy, who has brought him, says the poor boy will never leave him for a moment, & always sleeps near him. They are an extraordinary contrast, Capt: Speedy being 6 ft: 6! & having red hair.[1]

Alamayou ('I have seen the world') was the son of Emperor Tewodros (or Theodore) of Abyssinia (modern-day Ethiopia). After the latter's suicide in 1868 the explorer and adventurer Tristram Speedy, who was in the country to assist the British expeditionary force under Sir Robert Napier, was given the task of escorting the Prince to England. Shortly after departing, Alamayou's mother, Empress Tirunesh, succumbed to tuberculosis, aged only 25, leaving Alamayou an orphan. Historians differ in their views on the removal of the Prince from his homeland. Some suggest the Empress lobbied Napier to keep Speedy away from her child and herself. The surviving accounts are nearly all British and paint another picture – one that was readily believed by the Queen.

Alamayou's plight was romanticised by Victorian England. One newspaper dubbed him 'England's Royal Foundling', and by the time he arrived at Plymouth in July 1868 he was a celebrity. Crowds gathered at his every appearance and blanket press coverage of his arrival was eagerly lapped up.

Victoria was no exception. The Prince moved in with Speedy and his wife Cornelia at their home, Afton Manor, Freshwater, on the Isle of Wight, just 15 miles from Osborne, and the Queen issued an immediate request to meet the new arrival.

After his first visit on the evening of 16 July, Alamayou and Speedy stayed on the royal estate at Osborne Cottage. The following day the Prince was brought to see Victoria. 'He was so nice & gentle,' she wrote in her journal. 'He took a peach, which I gave him, & seemed to enjoy eating it very much.'

The Queen was given an account of what Alamayou had been through: 'Capt: Speedy said that the poor child had a recollection of the horrible massacre of the captives by his father's hand & orders, having heard the shrieks.' Speedy also gave the Queen his version of how he came to look after the Prince, which clearly touched Victoria's heart:

There appears to have been madness in the family. When the poor mother was dying, she asked Capt: Speedy whether he bore her & Theodore any ill will. He replied no, & that he much regretted Theodore not having made peace, whereupon she said 'then will you be a father to my Boy?' which he promised he would. Nothing could be kinder than he has been to the child, quite like a mother. I have written strongly against Alamayou being removed from Capt: Speedy's care.[2]

After the two-day visit, a besotted Victoria sent a detailed account of Alamayou and his minder to her eldest daughter Vicky:*

The poor little boy a dear, gentle, pretty, intelligent little darling of seven years old, clings to him like an infant to its mother or nurse – can't bear him out of his sight, sleeps near him, and sometimes even in his bed – as he is very nervous, and seems to have dreadful recollections of the murder of those people whom his father killed.

To a modern mind the idea of Speedy sharing a bed with a vulnerable child raises all kinds of concerns, but the Queen saw only the purest of motives:

Captain Speedy is really like the tenderest mother to him and it is quite touching to see this great man of 6 foot 6 inches (!!) leading about this little child! The poor mother asked him to be a father to her child when she was dying.[3]

---

* Victoria, 1840–1901, Princess Royal of Britain, wife of 'Fritz', the future Emperor Frederick III of Germany.

During the first visit the Queen commissioned Jabez Hughes, a local photographer based at Ryde on the Isle of Wight, to photograph the Captain and the Prince, both wearing Abyssinian dress and with a round shield in front of them. The same month she invited the artist Reginald Easton to produce a watercolour miniature on ivory of Alamayou in his native dress. The sensitive portrait was exhibited at the Royal Academy's annual exhibition in 1869 and is still in the Royal Collection.

In May 1869, Victoria noted in her journal:

> Saw Capt: Speedy with little Alamayou, who is so much grown & improved, looking so nice & intelligent. Capt: Speedy is going to India, where he has got an appointment, and is going to take the dear little boy with him.[4]

Starting life anew in the subcontinent, the childless Speedys felt Alamayou had 'entwined himself around our hearts' and was 'the best boy in the universe'. What they hadn't banked on was the attitude of Gladstone's new Liberal government and in particular that of Robert Lowe, Chancellor of the Exchequer. Lowe felt the little prince's future was a matter for them and in a letter to the PM argued, 'We are in loco parentis and ought to look after his welfare as if he were our own child.'[5] He ordered Captain Speedy to send Alamayou back to England to start his formal education there. The Captain himself returned and pleaded in person to Gladstone and the Queen. A furious Victoria offered to pay for a private tutor so the boy could remain in India but found herself over-ruled by her ministers, and Alamayou was sent to a succession of private schools including Cheltenham and Rugby. Although he enjoyed sport he had little interest in studying and became depressed and isolated.

A series of photographs in the Royal Collection show Alamayou during his childhood and early teens. He is dressed to look a quintes-sentially British aristocrat in Lord Fauntleroy velvet knickerbockers and later in a woollen suit, clutching a bowler hat and gloves, and his sad expression in the photographs seems to testify to his confused emotions.

His Abyssinian grandmother wrote to him, begging for him to return, in letters he is thought not to have seen in case they distressed him. She also wrote, grandmother to grandmother, to Victoria: 'I humbly kiss your Majesty's hand. Three of my children have lost to death. Now only Dejazmach Alemayehu is left. I implore you look well after him.'[6]

The Queen continued to monitor the Prince's education and general development. Each summer she invited him to stay with her at Balmoral where he went out daily with the keepers and said the Highlands reminded him of his home. The Court Circular tells us he went to the local Braemar Gathering, which the modern-day Royal Family still attends.

In 1878 he was taken out of Rugby to begin an officer's training course at Sandhurst, but once again he was unhappy and asked if he could resume his studies with his old Rugby tutor Cyril Ransome, father of the *Swallows and Amazons* writer Arthur Ransome. By this time Ransome was a history professor at the Yorkshire College, now Leeds University, and Alamayou went to live with him at his home in Far Headingley, 3 miles north of the city.

The 18-year-old Prince had barely resumed his studies when, according to Ransome, he committed 'a foolish act (he went to sleep in the WC in the middle of a cold night)'. He contracted pneumonia, which developed into pleurisy, and despite the ministrations of several doctors, and after a six-week struggle, the Prince died on 14 November 1879.

The Queen, on the Balmoral estate, recorded Alamayou's decline in a series of entries in her journal from the end of October. She instructed Sir John Cowell, Master of the Household, to visit Alamayou and noted the courtier 'found him very ill, but quite pleased to see him'.

Victoria's sadness at the young man's death is clear from her entry for the 14th:

> Very grieved & shocked to hear by telegram, that good Alamayou passed away this morning. It is too sad! All alone, in a strange country, without a single person or relative, belonging to him, so young, & so good, but for him one cannot repine. His, was no happy life, full of difficulties of every kind, & he was so sensitive, thinking people stared at him on account of his colour, that I fear he would never have been happy. Everyone is sorry.[7]

The Queen arranged for Alamayou to be buried at Windsor, and Ransome accompanied his body from Leeds to Berkshire. The service was held at St George's Chapel, Windsor, with Ransome, Cowell, the Chancellor of the Exchequer Lowe and the Queen's son-in-law Prince Christian present. A floral tribute from Victoria with the message 'This wreath is a mark of affection and friendship from the Queen' was placed on the oak coffin. Afterwards the remains were interred in a specially built brick vault outside the west entrance in the Horseshoe Cloister.

On her return to Windsor the Queen visited the chapel and selected a spot for a brass plaque to be placed to commemorate the Prince with the words, 'I was a stranger and ye took me in.' At the same time she commissioned the sculptor Francis Williamson to create a brass bust of Alamayou based on a cast made after death. It is now in the Durbar Corridor at Osborne House.

In 2007 the Ethiopian Government requested the return of Alamayou's remains, to be interred in the land of his birth. At the time it was confirmed that Elizabeth II's representatives at Windsor were considering the request. To date, the young Prince of Abyssinia's body still lies on the royal estate, a quarter of a mile from where Victoria, his benefactress, was also interred.

Notes

1 RA VIC/MAIN/QVJ (W) Thursday 16 July 1868 (Princess Beatrice's copies). Retrieved 8 January 2018
2 RA VIC/MAIN/QVJ (W) Friday 17 July 1868 (Princess Beatrice's copies). Retrieved 8 January 2018
3 Fulford, Roger (ed.): *Your Dear Letter.* Evans Brothers: 1971: pp.202–3
4 RA VIC/MAIN/QVJ (W) Thursday 6 May 1869 (Princess Beatrice's copies). Retrieved 9 January 2018
5 Marsden, Philip: *The Barefoot Emperor.* HarperCollins: 2007: pp.342–3
6 Ibid.: p.344
7 RA VIC/MAIN/QVJ (W) Friday 14 November 1879 (Princess Beatrice's copies). Retrieved 9 January 2018

'This is Me!'
Barnum, the Greatest Showman, Fails to Impress the Queen

P.T. Barnum with 'General Tom Thumb'.
(National Portrait Gallery, Smithsonian Institution)

IN THE spring of 1844 Victoria and her family had three encounters with the American impresario P.T. Barnum (1810–91) and one of his legendary acts, Charles Sherwood Stratton (1838–83), better known as 'General Tom Thumb' – a dwarf who had achieved fame as a performer. While the Queen appears to have been besotted with the latter, she was less than impressed with the showman himself, especially after it became clear he had deceived her.

When P.T. Barnum arrived in London in 1844 with General Tom Thumb (billed as 'the Smallest Person that ever Walked Alone') this novelty act didn't enjoy the success the promoter hoped for. He soon decided he needed the ultimate publicity coup – an audience with the Queen. The 25-year-old monarch was a regular theatre-goer, and her presence at any performance guaranteed maximum publicity and a knock-on effect in terms of seat sales.

There was only one problem. The court was in mourning following the death of Prince Albert's father, Ernest I, Duke of Saxe-Coburg and Gotha, who had died on 29 January 1844. The Queen's rigid observance of mourning, including a ban on all forms of entertainment for the duration, helped mould an image of respectability for the monarchy, in contrast to the louche, hedonistic lifestyle of her Hanoverian predecessors.

Undeterred, Barnum called on the Hon. Edward Everett, the American Minister to London. The two men dined together and Everett was introduced to the boy Stratton.

While he waited and hoped for a royal invitation, Barnum concentrated on wooing the next best thing, the London-based aristocracy. A few days after his first meeting with Everett, Barnum and Stratton headed for the Piccadilly mansion of Baroness Rothschild, wife of the richest banker in the world. To his delight, Barnum was discreetly handed a well-filled purse on his departure, prompting him to reflect later, 'the golden shower had begun to fall'.

Then, just when he felt a royal summons was out of the question, Barnum was invited to breakfast at Everett's house. A second guest was Charles Murray, Master of the Queen's Household, who was no doubt testing the waters to see if Barnum was a suitable character to be presented to the Queen. Murray asked the impresario what his plans were. The latter shrewdly said he was off to France to show General Tom Thumb to King Louis Philippe, who would thus glimpse Barnum's young charge before the British Royal Family did. The showman added, 'though I should be glad to remain if the General could have an interview with the Queen … such an event would be of great consequence to me.'[1]

Barnum's ruse worked and the following day a uniformed messenger arrived with an invitation for the celebrity pair to see the Queen at Buckingham Palace on the evening of 23 March 1844. At Victoria's request, the General was asked to appear before her as he would for anyone else – in other words, without being restrained by royal protocol and etiquette. The royal appointment meant Barnum had to cancel one of his nightly performances at the Egyptian Hall, the venue in Piccadilly where his diminutive star was appearing. Not one to miss a chance for self-promotion, the impresario attached a placard to the theatre door, which proclaimed, 'Closed this evening, General Tom Thumb being at Buckingham Palace by command of Her Majesty.'

At the palace, the Lord-in-Waiting instructed them to address the Queen only via him and not directly, and that on leaving the audience they needed to walk backwards from the royal presence. In the event both instructions fell by the wayside.

The meeting took place in the Queen's Picture Gallery, where Victoria and Albert were gathered with her mother, the Duchess of Kent and twenty or thirty members of the Royal Household. 'They were standing at the farther end of the room,' recalled Barnum in his memoirs, 'and the general walked in like a wax doll gifted with the power of locomotion.' The royal party showed 'surprise and pleasure' at the 'remarkable specimen of humanity so much smaller than they had evidently expected to find him. The General marched forward, bowed and said: "Good evening, ladies and gentlemen!"'

'A burst of laughter followed this salutation. The Queen, dressed in a plain black mourning dress with no jewellery, then took him by the hand, led him about the gallery, and asked him many questions.' The General's direct responses to the questions amused Victoria. He told her the Picture Gallery was 'first-rate' and asked if he could meet the Prince of Wales. The Queen explained her 2-year-old son had retired to bed but that he could meet him on a future occasion.

After performing some of his songs, dances and impersonations, and having a quick chat with Prince Albert, the General and his mentor were permitted to leave. Meanwhile, after speaking to the Queen via an intermediary as requested, Barnum ignored protocol and spoke directly to the monarch: 'I suppose the Lord-in-Waiting was seriously shocked, if not outraged, when I entered directly into conversation with Her Majesty. She, however, seemed not disposed to check my boldness, for she immediately spoke directly to me.'

The American guests had then to perform the tricky manoeuvre of walking backwards from the royal party. The fact that the Picture Gallery is 47 metres long and quite narrow, and the royals were at one end, meant it was altogether a lengthy process. 'We had a considerable distance to travel,' recalled Barnum:

> and whenever the General found he was losing ground, he turned around and ran a few steps, then resumed the position of 'backing out,' then turned around and ran, and so continued to alternate his methods of getting to the door, until the gallery fairly rang with the merriment of the royal spectators.[2]

Victoria's poodle, excited by all the running around, started to bark. The General, 'however, recovered immediately, and with his little cane commenced an attack on the poodle, and a funny fight ensued which renewed and increased the merriment of the royal party.' While Barnum and Stratton enjoyed a buffet supper, the Queen sent a courtier to enquire if the child star had been upset by the battle with her pet dog.

Victoria's account of the visit in her journal shows her delight at the General and her disquiet about how Barnum treated him:

> After dinner we saw the greatest curiosity, I, or indeed anybody ever saw, viz: a little dwarf, only 25 inches high & 15 lb in weight. No description can give an idea of this little creature, whose real name was Charles Stratton, born they say in 32, which makes him 12 years old.

Barnum's duplicity is clear since Stratton was in fact born in January 1838, making him only 6 at the time of the visit:

> He is American, & gave us his card, with Gen:Tom Thumb, written on it. He made the funniest little bow, putting out his hand & saying: 'much obliged Ma'am'. One cannot help feeling very sorry for the poor little thing & wishing he could be properly cared for, for the people who show him off tease him a good deal, I should think. He was made to imitate Napoleon & do all parts of tricks, finally, backing out the whole way out of the Gallery.[3]

She would have no doubt been concerned to hear that Barnum sought out the courtier responsible for writing the daily Court Circular, detailing the Queen's activities. According to the showman, the member of the

Household 'promptly acceded to my request for such a notice as would attract attention. He even generously desired me to give him an outline of what I sought, and I was pleased to see afterwards, that he had inserted my notice verbatim.'

The Court Circular for Monday 25 March, which appeared in *The Times* (and in those days many regional newspapers also carried the entry), read:

> The American dwarf, 'General Tom Thumb', accompanied by his guardian, Mr P.T. Barnum, of New York, had the honour of attending at the Palace in the evening, when the General exhibited his clever imitations of Napoleon, & c., which elicited the approbation of her Majesty and the royal circle.

The Queen requested a second visit, which took place in the Palace's Yellow Drawing Room on 1 April. This time the General remarked to the Queen 'that he had seen her before', adding, 'I think this is a prettier room than the picture gallery; that chandelier is very fine.' The Queen took him by the hand and said she hoped that he was well, to which he replied, 'Yes Ma'am, I am first rate.' She added, 'General, this is the Prince of Wales.' 'How are you Prince?' said Stratton, shaking 2-year-old Edward by the hand, before standing alongside him and remarking, 'The Prince is taller than I am, but I feel as big as anybody.' The Queen also introduced him to her daughter, the Princess Royal, and to the Queen of the Belgians.[4]

Victoria mentioned Stratton in her journal with no mention of Barnum at all: 'Saw the little dwarf, in the Yellow Drawingroom, who was very nice, lively, & funny, dancing & singing wonderfully. Vicky & Bertie were with us, also Mama … Little "Tom Thumb" does not reach up to Vicky's shoulder.'[5]

On the General's third visit to the Queen, Victoria was joined by her uncle, King Leopold of the Belgians. She asked the General what song he would like to sing and he promptly replied, 'Yankee Doodle.' Despite its links with the American War of Independence, the amused monarch said, 'That is a very pretty song, General. Sing it if you please.'[6] This time the Queen's account of the meeting was cursory to say the least: 'at 6, we all saw the dwarf, whom our guests were much surprised at. He appeared in different costumes.'[7]

Victoria's interest in the American visitors began to attract criticism in the press. The radical journal *Punch* observed archly, 'It appears that the dwarf General Tom Thumb and his showman — "guardian" lisps the Court Circular — have been to Buckingham Palace, commanded thither by Her Majesty the Queen, whose admiration of genius, native or foreign, has passed into a proverb.' The same magazine viewed the second visit by Barnum and Stratton 'with due gravity' and it made great play of the report in the Court Circular that the Queen had given the General presents 'with her own hands', including a mother of pearl and gold pencil case. Even the Prime Minister, Sir Robert Peel, thought she was being indiscreet. There had been no dwarves at court since the death of Coppernin, who was employed by George II, and many felt the presence, even fleetingly, of a dwarf for entertainment was a disturbing image.[8]

If Victoria was aware of the criticism, she chose to ignore it. Over the next few years, in the wake of Barnum, a series of performances by those of restricted growth were held at various galleries across London. Victoria declined to see many of them, including the 'Boshie Men', bushmen from Africa. In May 1846 she did allow a family of Scottish dwarves, two brothers and a sister, named Mackinlay from the county of Ross, to dance for her, Prince Albert and the Duchess of Kent.

Three years later we hear of what may have been her final such encounter. On the evening of 21 February 1849 she wrote:

> After dinner we saw Jean Hannema, a most wonderful little Dutch dwarf, 10 years old & only 2 ft. & 4 inches high (3 inches smaller than Tom Thumb) weighing only 16 lbs!! He is a nice, well behaved, intelligent little creature, & speaks very funnily, & rather broken English. His father who was there is a respectable apothecary from Friesland, having had 3 other dwarf children, who are dead, but also 3 of a usual size, who are alive. The little boy danced, & performed all sorts of little tricks.[9]

Unsurprisingly, Barnum was delighted with the royal audiences, and the positive effect of the ensuing publicity. As a firm believer in the old adage that there is no such thing as bad publicity, he even welcomed the attacks in the press. For the rest of the spring he claims to have averaged $500 a day in ticket sales for the Egyptian Hall entertainment and that on some nights there were fifty to sixty carriages belonging to the nobility outside the building.

The Dowager Queen Adelaide, widow of Victoria's uncle, William IV, requested to see the General at Marlborough House. Barnum decked out his protégé in a specially designed court uniform of embroidered brown velvet, white silk stockings, a cocked hat on top of a wig and a dress sword. 'Why General,' exclaimed the Dowager, 'I think you look very smart today,' to which the young visitor cheekily answered, 'I guess I do.'

She took him on her knee, and noticing that he did not have a watch, asked him if he would like one. She later had a miniature gold watch and chain made for the boy Stratton. Never one to miss a PR opportunity, Barnum had Adelaide and Victoria's gifts prominently displayed on a pedestal in the entrance hall of the exhibition under a glass dome for all to see.

Queen Adelaide's fondness for the young General is poignant considering her own distressing attempts to produce a child. A daughter born in 1819, hastily named Princess Charlotte of Clarence, only survived a matter of hours, and a second daughter, Princess Elizabeth of Clarence, who would have succeeded her father to the throne as Elizabeth II in 1837, instead of her cousin Victoria, died aged 12 weeks in 1821. Adelaide also had three stillborn sons.

Barnum mentions in his memoirs:

While we were in London the Emperor of Russia, visited Queen Victoria, and I saw him on several public occasions I was present at the grand review of troops in Windsor Park in honor of and before the Emperor of Russia and the King of Saxony.[10]

The showman's account suggests he was very much in the thick of this VIP visit, which caught the public's imagination in a more powerful way than he or his General had. In actual fact he was just one of many thousands of onlookers at the parade in Windsor and he was disappointed not to have been able to perform for the autocratic Tsar. Even Victoria didn't have it her way. She decorated a suite of rooms for the Tsar at Buckingham Palace, which in the end he declined to use, perhaps because he famously slept on a straw mattress like any of his ordinary soldiers. (A legacy of the visit is the '1844 Room', still named in honour of Tsar Nicholas. It's been a backdrop to modern state visits including that of Barack and Michelle Obama in 2011, and it's where they were photographed meeting the newly wed Duke and Duchess of Cambridge.)

The publication of Barnum's autobiography in 1855, when he was only 45, damaged his reputation in Britain since he candidly admitted to deceiving the public. Among the revelations was that General Tom Thumb's age had been doubled, and that he had managed to wangle an invitation to the palace, as well as giving details of Victoria's embarrassingly enthusiastic reaction to Stratton and her gifts to him. While the American press adopted a 'Good on you' attitude, the British media were critical that Barnum had taken the Queen and her countrymen for a ride. 'The Thumb tour was the noblest ever done by an American freeman,' stated *Punch*. 'It was a death blow at kings and kingships.'[11]

There was a final meeting between Stratton and the British Royal Family at the end of 1864, when General Tom Thumb and his wife Lavinia performed for the Prince and Princess of Wales at Marlborough House.

Meanwhile Barnum continued to stoke the wrath of the Royal Family when, in February 1882, he purchased Jumbo, a popular elephant at London's Regent's Park Zoo, for £2,000. Arriving at London Zoo in 1865, Jumbo quickly became a firm favourite of Queen Victoria and her children and she made several visits to the zoo, even during her reclusive early widowhood, often to see animals gifted to the Royal Family. After her last tour in 1877 she wrote that she:

> saw the Esquimaux dogs (2 very fine ones, brought back by Capt: Young of the 'Pandora', — the splendid new lion house, with the lions, tigers, panthers, &c, belonging to Bertie, endless fine pheasants, deer of all kinds, & on the other side, Bertie's 4 young elephants all in a row. They are quite tame, & there were 2 quite little ones, who salaamed & were ridden about at an immense pace. There was also an ostrich belonging to Bertie.[12]

The public outcry about the purchase of Jumbo for the Barnum and Bailey Circus was intense. One hundred thousand schoolchildren wrote to the Queen to ask her to intervene. She protested, as did the Prince of Wales, but to no avail. Jumbo was shipped to America, and was later killed when he was hit by a freight train at a railway yard in Ontario, Canada. Barnum naturally turned even this sad episode into a public relations opportunity, announcing that Jumbo had been killed trying to lead to safety a young circus elephant called Tom Thumb.

Notes

1 Barnum, Phineas T.: *Struggles and Triumphs*: Warren, Johnson & Co.: 1872: p.175

2 Ibid.: p.175ff

3 RA VIC/MAIN/QVJ (W) Saturday 23 March 1844 (Princess Beatrice's copies). Retrieved 23 April 2018

4 Barnum: Op. Cit.: p.180ff

5 RA VIC/MAIN/QVJ (W) Monday 1 April 1844 (Princess Beatrice's copies). Retrieved 23 April 2018

6 Barnum: Op. Cit.: p.181

7 RA VIC/MAIN/QVJ (W) Monday 1 April 1844 (Princess Beatrice's copies). Retrieved 23 April 2018

8 RA VIC/MAIN/QVJ (W) Wednesday 21 February 1849 (Princess Beatrice's copies). Retrieved 23 April 2018

9 Fitzsimons, Raymund: *Barnum in London*: Geoffrey Bles Ltd: 1969: p.95ff

10 Barnum: Op. Cit.: p.184

11 Fitzsimons: Op. Cit.: p.161ff

12 RA VIC/MAIN/QVJ (W) Wednesday 14 March 1877 (Princess Beatrice's copies). Retrieved 23 April 2018

5

GETTING CONNECTED

VICTORIA IS TAUGHT HOW TO USE THE TELEPHONE BY ALEXANDER GRAHAM BELL

Alexander Graham Bell. (Library of Congress)

VICTORIA WAS the first European monarch to have a telephone installed, as well as the first to be taught how to use one.

In January 1878 she was given a lecture, a demonstration and a chance to practise using it by the man credited with patenting the newfangled device: Alexander Graham Bell.

Edinburgh-born Bell immigrated to Brantford, Ontario, in 1870 at the age of 23. The following year he moved to Boston, Massachusetts, where he taught at a school for the deaf. At the same time he began to research methods to transmit multiple telegraph messages simultaneously over a single wire – a development that would eventually lead to his invention of the telephone.

On 7 March 1876 Bell pipped his great rival Elisha Gray to the post, being awarded what would become one of the most valuable patents in history for 'the method of, and apparatus for, transmitting vocal or other sounds telegraphically'.

Three days later, at the workshop at 5 Exeter Place, Boston, his assistant Thomas Watson, with a receiver operated from a liquid transmitter, heard Bell's voice say from another room, 'Mr Watson – Come here – I want to see you.' Prosaic words for a profound moment in history, but ones recorded in Bell's journal on 10 March. They were the first intelligible words spoken over the telephone.

The following year the Bell Telephone Company was created and its founder began a series of public demonstrations and lectures in the USA and Europe. He and his new wife Mabel arrived in London in August 1877, where they eventually set up home at 57 West Cromwell Road, in South Kensington. While they were there a daughter, Elsie, was born in May 1878. (A second daughter, Marian, arrived two years later and narrowly escaped being named Photophone by her technology-absorbed father.) From the time of his marriage until his death in 1922 he signed himself 'Alec Bell'.

A series of well-publicised stunts ensured press coverage of Bell and his invention. At a colliery in Newcastle he set up a link between the coal-face and the pit-head. Back in London he donned a heavy rubber suit and copper helmet to descend to the bed of the Thames, where he conversed with assistants on the river bank; an experiment that nearly ended in disaster when he was brought to the surface too quickly and developed a bad attack of the bends. There was even an underwater cross-Channel link between Dover and Sangatte in France, though interference made speech unintelligible and both ends of the line settled on singing 'Auld Lang Syne' to each other instead.[1]

The greatest publicity coup was undoubtedly an audience with the normally reclusive and inaccessible Victoria. It is traditionally assumed that the Queen Empress, hearing of Bell's exploits throughout her realm, invited him to demonstrate his invention.

A letter in the Bell Family Archive at the Library of Congress suggests, however, there was a go-between: Lyon Playfair. The latter, a scientist who co-founded the Chemical Society in Britain, was well known at Victoria's court. As an expert in sanitation, he was recommended by Prime Minister Robert Peel to assist the Prince Consort in his new invention – the filtering of the royal sewage to fertilise the Osborne estate. He went on to become a special commissioner to assist Albert in his plans for the 1851 Great Exhibition.[2]

On 10 December 1877, Playfair forwarded to Bell a copy of the letter he had sent to Sir Thomas Biddulph, Master of the Household, 'suggesting that Her Majesty might like to see your telephone in operation'. As shrewd a publicist as Bell, he added, 'I thought that this would be regarded by you as the inventor in the light of a compliment and that in England it would promote the success of your undertaking.'[3] An appointment was arranged for the evening of 14 January 1878 at Osborne. Mabel, rather precipitately it turned out, hurried to Paris to buy a special gown from Worth, only to find on her return that she was not invited.

On 14 December Alec took the train to Southampton and the ferry across the Solent to Cowes. Once in situ at the royal residence he rigged up telephone wires from Osborne Cottage, Biddulph's residence, to the Council Room at Osborne House. At both ends he used a basic handset that the user had to move from mouth to ear to operate.

Later that evening he was conducted to the Council Room with Colonel William H. Reynolds, a cotton and cotton goods broker from Providence, Rhode Island, who in the previous summer had bought a portion of Bell's patent for $5,000 cash. Waiting to meet them were the Queen, her third son the Duke of Connaught, and her youngest daughter Princess Beatrice.

Victoria later recorded in her journal:

After dinner we went to the Council Room & saw the Telephone. A Professor Bell explained the whole process, which is most extraordinary. It had been put in communication with Osborne Cottage, & we talked with Sir Thomas & Mary Biddulph, also heard some singing quite plainly. But it is rather faint, & one must hold the tube close to one's ear. The man, who was very pompous, kept calling Arthur Ld Connaught! which amused us very much.[4]

43

'Pompous' Alec's description of the Queen was equally unflattering. In a letter to Mabel he described her Majesty as 'humpy, stumpy, dumpy', and was amazed to note that her ungloved hands were 'red, coarse, and fat as a washerwoman's and her face also fat and florid'. Nevertheless he found her personality 'was genial and dignified and, all in all, quite pleasing'.[5]

Bell was later told by one of the Royal Household that the Queen had been much pleased with him personally, and the fact that she was willing to stay from 9.30 p.m., sitting through several faulty connections, until the lines to Cowes and Southampton were up and running at midnight, suggests it was a success.[6]

The event began with a brief presentation by Alec on the origins and development of the telephone. He then picked up the instrument and spoke to Sir Thomas before handing it to the Queen who also spoke to both Biddulph and his wife.

The royal party then listened to a selection of songs sung by Kate Field, an American writer hired by Reynolds to publicise the telephone. Miss Field sang 'Kathleen Mavoureen', Shakespeare's 'Cuckoo Song', 'Comin' through the Rye' and, as a finale, the epilogue from 'As You Like It'. At the end of the mini-performance 'her Majesty returned gracious thanks telephonically through the Duke of Connaught' – clearly intent on keeping her own voice for courtiers' ears only.[7]

As Field's performance was about to start, the Queen happened to be looking away, so Alec, used to dealing with his wife's complete deafness, touched her arm and offered her the instrument. Thanks to Bell's efficient PR team, it was reported in the press that the Queen was smiling sweetly as Bell pulled at her arm.[8]

To demonstrate the telephone's use to callers further afield than a cottage on the estate, Bell had set up links with Cowes, Southampton and London. It seems he also set up a forerunner of the Royal Variety Performance as the three venues entertained the Queen with a cacophony of trumpets, singers, an orchestra and an organ.

Supervising the line at the West Cowes Post Office was Major Webber of the Royal Engineers, one of the heads of the Post Office telegraph system. He linked the royal party with Southampton, where Sir William Preece, Chief Engineer of the British Post Office, was overseeing events. Preece is today remembered for one of the worst technical predictions of all time. Asked in 1876 about Bell's invention he sniffed, 'The Americans have need of the telephone, but we do not. We have plenty of messenger boys!'

According to a journalist from the *Isle of Wight Observer*, 'we heard a bugle blow several Light Infantry calls and a cornet-a-piston playing "The Bluebells of Scotland" most beautifully, every note being perfectly distinct'. More impressively, a Mr Wilmot, 70-odd miles away in London, eventually treated the Queen to a long-distance rendition of 'Home Sweet Home' and 'God Save the Queen', both played on the organ. Back in Cowes, Webber had assembled a quartet of singers comprising his daughter Bessie, Miss Louise Strohmenger, Mr Hamilton and the splendidly named Mr Spedding Curwen. They sang 'Sweet and Low' so well that the Duke of Connaught asked for an encore.

After another bout of bugling from Southampton, and a faulty first wire which delayed everything, the four parters sang 'Sir Knight, Sir Knight Whither Away'. The royal party, however, was staying put and Connaught asked over the phone, 'Please give another one.' They responded with 'Stars of the Summer Night' and the second National Anthem of the evening. 'The singing at Cowes is lovely,' said the Duke, adding that he 'wouldn't have missed it for anything; it was more like singing on water'.[9]

Intriguingly, Preece's biographer paints a less rosy portrait of the evening. In this account, Preece had assembled an orchestra and choir in Southampton to perform a selection of similarly sentimental hits followed by the ubiquitous National Anthem. Sadly the telegraph relay failed and Victoria was the first royal user in this country to experience a dead line. By the time contact was once again made at around midnight, the performers had packed up and gone home, so an enterprising Preece decided to hum 'God Save the Queen'. At the other end of the line, an unimpressed Victoria, with the receiver still in her ear, said, 'It is the National Anthem, but it is very badly played!'[10]

The experiment was repeated the following morning, this time without the Queen's presence. Osborne House, Osborne Cottage and Cowes were once again linked. Bell was at the latter while the Council Room was packed with the great and good – Beatrice, Connaught, the Duke of Richmond, the Earl of Ripon, Lord John Manners, the Biddulphs, the Royal Librarian and an honorary chaplain. Conversation with each party was followed by more fa la la-ing as the Cowes quartet was obliged to sing 'Sir Knight, Sir Knight' four times in a row.

Victoria was so impressed with the telephone she decided to invest in two. Biddulph wrote to Bell on 16 December:

My Dear Sir, — I hope you are aware how much gratified and surprised the Queen was at the exhibition of the Telephone here on Monday evening. Her Majesty desires me to express her thanks to you and the ladies and gentlemen who were associated with you on the occasion. The Queen would like, if there is no reason against it, to purchase the two instruments which are still here with the wires, &c., attached. Perhaps you will be so kind as to let me know to whom the sum due should be paid.[11]

Bell replied two weeks later, offering Victoria a free upgrade:

Dear Sir, — I feel highly honoured by the gratification expressed by Her Majesty and by her desire to possess a set of Telephones.

The instruments at present in Osborne are merely those supplied for ordinary commercial purposes, and it will afford me much pleasure to be permitted to offer to the Queen a set of Telephones to be made expressly for Her Majesty's use.

Your obedient Servant, Alexander Graham Bell.[12]

Bell was true to his word and sent the Queen two upmarket telephones with ivory and gold receivers. There is no evidence he charged her for them but the letter from Biddulph and his reply was leaked to *The Times* and regional newspapers, thus telling the whole country that the Queen endorsed the invention, and giving Bell maximum publicity for free.

Victoria was not the first head of state to have a telephone. American President Rutherford B. Hayes had a telephone installed in the White House telegraph room on 10 May 1877 (however, it wasn't until 29 March 1929 that President Herbert Hoover had a telephone installed in the Oval Office). In Canada, the first telephones were leased to Prime Minister Alexander Mackenzie in September 1877. They were placed in the Prime Minister's office at the Department of Public Works and the Governor General's residence.[13] The first monarch in the world to receive a demonstration of the telephone by Alexander Graham Bell was Dom Pedro II of Brazil, with the demonstration taking place at the Philadelphia Centennial Exposition in June 1876.

In the same month that Victoria received her personal tutorial, it was reported in *The Times* that the Persian Ambassador had ordered telephones for the Shah of Persia. Also in January 1878 King Alfonso XII of Spain married Mercedes of Orléans. A telephone link between his rooms and those of Mercedes allowed them to keep in regular touch during the days of elaborate ceremonial. Five years later the King of Portugal had the Ajuda Palace, his official residence in the capital, connected with the Lisbon telephone exchange, making him the first European monarch to become a subscriber to the public telephone exchange. He also had private lines linking him to the various ministries and the Opera.[14]

It was the autumn of 1896 before Victoria had all her residences on a telephone network. In mid-September it was announced that the Queen had ordered telephonic communication to be laid between Balmoral Castle and Aberdeen, where her private wire would be connected to the new Government trunk cable linking the city with London. At the same time Balmoral was connected to the local estates at Birkhall, Mar Lodge and Abergeldie Castle, as well as to nearby Ballater Station.[15]

The *Westminster Gazette* reported, 'The Queen delights in telephonic communication.' On the other hand it proved to be a mixed blessing for some of her relations. Alexandra, Princess of Wales, complained that whenever she stayed on the Balmoral estate, the phone linking her at Abergeldie to her mother-in-law's castle never stopped ringing.[16]

In October 1896 it was announced that Windsor Castle would be linked to government departments via the telephone centre at the Treasury.[17] When the Windsor link was announced one newspaper recalled the occasion when 'the Queen "rang up" personally the other end, and the operator responded with the customary salutation of "Hello! Who are you?"' The unfortunate person rapidly backtracked and responded with a meek 'Hello, Your Majesty', but by then the affronted monarch had already hung up.[18]

Although Alec only met the Queen face to face on one occasion, she was a constant in the lives of both him and his wife. When the 'Grand Old Man' of British politics died in May 1898, Mabel wrote to Alec:

> So Gladstone is dead. He and Papa and Queen Victoria were the three strong fixtures in life for me, no there's Mamma too, I realize now as never before that we are mortal, living one little span, presently to banish and the world will go on and on and on until when and where?[19]

As an 11-year-old, still living in Edinburgh, Alec had entered the Royal High School. A surviving scrap book of poems includes this patriotic, if uninspiring, paean to his sovereign:

VICTORIA
Victoria, Queen Victoria,
She rules a mighty band.
Who'll stand by her for ever
To guard their Native Land.
A. Bell / 58 [20]

Alec's father Melville Bell himself petitioned for an audience with the Queen in 1864 to demonstrate his own invention: 'Visible Speech'. This was a system of phonetic symbols to represent how the organs of speech articulate sounds. It was used to help the deaf learn how to speak. Unfortunately, less than three years into her prolonged widowhood, Victoria made it clear she had no desire to interrupt her melancholy seclusion at Balmoral to sit through his lecture.

Victoria is a recurrent theme in Alec's love letters to Mabel. Several times he refers to her becoming 'a loyal subject of Queen Victoria' by preferring 'a Scotchman to an American'. On one occasion he writes:

I suppose it will not be long before we have a woman wanting to be President of the United States! Well it is not for me to say to her 'Nay' – seeing that I am a subject of Queen Victoria – a woman-sovereign – and one of the best the world has seen – so my best wishes go with her.[21]

As their personal fortune soared, Alec was amused at exaggerated press reports that his wife was almost as wealthy as the Queen Empress. He wrote to Mabel in 1889 that:

The Cosmopolitan for October contains an illustrated article entitled 'Wealthy Women of America'. The statement is made that 'there are two dozen women in the United States who have more money than any of the Crowned heads of Europe, except Queen Victoria, the richest of Sovereigns and half a dozen who have as much as she.'

The article then proceeds to details and gives the names and etc., Among them occurs the name of 'Mrs. Alexander Graham Bell, the wife of the inventor of the telephone, who not only shares her husband's millions, but is the only living child of Gardiner G. Hubbard from whom she will inherit several millions more.'!![22]

Increased wealth allowed the Bells to travel widely. August 1900 found them in Europe, where Alec left Mabel in Paris while he visited London. He was made aware on both sides of the Channel of anti-British feelings from the French as a result of the ongoing Boer War, especially the anti-Victoria propaganda. 'My English travelling-companion,' Alec wrote to Mabel:

> informed me that England had boycotted the Paris Exhibition on account of the outrageous cartoons of Queen Victoria published in France. He said one of them represented Kruger spanking Queen Victoria in the old school-boy fashion without particular regard to the way her clothes were arranged!! Other cartoons were still worse and of such coarseness as to defy description.[23]

In February 1901 Mabel was in London to witness Victoria's funeral cortège pass through the capital en route to Windsor, and has left us an atmospheric account. 'We had good seats for the procession at the Queen's funeral and saw everything splendidly,' she wrote to her daughter Elsie:

> At the slow, slow tread of the soldiers marching with guns reversed, all stood so still and motionless and presently all heads were bared. Daisy [Mabel's other daughter] said you could almost have heard a pin drop … in all that great multitude. The soldiers passed, the gun carriage rattled [by], the King followed grave and anxious-looking with the Kaiser reigning in his horse so that the King could ride a neck ahead … And then a brilliant mass of variegated coloured uniforms passed which we knew covered the persons of almost every reigning sovereign or sovereign's heir in Europe.[24]

Alec died aged 75 in August 1922, followed five months later by Mabel. They would have been surprised to learn that seventeen years later their love story would be one of the twin themes – the other being obviously his invention – in a Hollywood movie. In 1939, the year Darryl F. Zanuck produced *Gone With the Wind*, he also produced *The Story of Alexander Graham Bell*. It starred Don Ameche and Loretta Young as the Bells and Henry Fonda as Thomas Watson. It also included the historic meeting of Bell and Queen Victoria, and Alec's daughter Elsie was able to offer an interesting anecdote about the demonstration at Osborne.

In a letter written to Lamar Trotti, the film's scriptwriter, Elsie recalls her father contrasting the relaxed informality of his meeting with Brazil's Emperor Dom Pedro with the rigid protocol of Victoria's court: 'Dom Pedro went around everywhere by himself, while Queen Victoria didn't even address a single question to my father herself, but spoke to him through her son, her daughter or her secretary. So formal was the audience.'[25]

In the film biopic, Victoria was played by 63-year-old Beryl Mercer who, at 4ft 11in, was the same height as the Queen. She also portrayed her on stage in 1924 and in an unrelated film, again released in 1939, *The Little Princess*, starring Shirley Temple.

Victoria proved it was good to talk by telephone, and her use of the invention was the greatest marketing tool Bell could have wished for. Sales of phones rose steadily in the following decades and by 1931 the Royal Family helped mark another milestone. *The Times* reported:

> one of the latest hand-micro telephones, finished in old gold, has just been accepted by the King for use in Buckingham Palace. It bears a decorative plate, surmounted by a Crown, and is inscribed: 'This instrument installed for his Majesty King George V, is the 2,000,000th telephone connected with the Post Office system, June 1931'.

The same day in a statement the Post Office declared, 'We are launching a campaign in the hope of persuading the general public to look upon the telephone as a general requisite and not merely a business machine.'[26]

George's granddaughter Elizabeth II has also given royal backing to the development of telecommunications. On 5 December 1958 she inaugurated automatic trunk dialling by making a phone call from Bristol Central Telephone Exchange to the Lord Provost of Edinburgh, more than 300 miles (482km) away. Her call lasted two minutes five seconds and cost (pre-decimal) fourpence.

Three years later the Queen officially opened CANTAT, the transatlantic telephone link between Canada and Britain. Elizabeth began a stilted conversation with the words, 'Are you there, Mr Prime Minister?' John Diefenbaker, the said Prime Minister, was 'there' in an Ottawa Hotel with 150 eavesdropping dignitaries. 'I am delighted to speak to you on this new cable from my home in London,' the monarch continued. The line marked the first leg of a round-the-world Commonwealth link-up.

The Royal Collection has a gilt-copper medal given to the Queen in 1976 on her state visit to the USA. The tour was to mark the bicentenary of America's independence, but it was also of course the centenary of Bell's invention, and the medal was presented to her by the Bell Telephone Corporation.

There was another meeting of Bell and Regina in 1997 when Alec's great-grandson Hugh Bell Muller met Victoria's great-great-granddaughter Elizabeth II at the Bell Homestead in 1997. The Queen was there to unveil a cairn which officially designates the inventor's home as a National Historic Site of Canada.

In 2016 Muller recalled:

> My family did have the honor and pleasure of meeting the Queen at the Bell Homestead in 1997. During our meeting the Queen did mention that our great grandparents [sic] had met some time ago and that it was nice to meet a Bell descendant.
>
> As you would expect she was charming and spoke to each member of the family including my first grandchild, Andrew Joseph Bell Muller, who was under a year old and slept through the entire event. The Queen spoke with Andrew's mother and looking down at the sleeping baby remarked, 'He's not likely to remember much about this event.' Imagine meeting the Queen of England at the age of 1, a memorable event, and not to remember it![27]

As a memento, the Queen was given a brass 1924 50-Type (or daffodil-style) telephone, known as a candlestick telephone, by Bell Canada.

Victoria would have been impressed to hear that her descendant has gone on to own a mobile phone, an iPod and a laptop, has sent emails, and has Twitter, Instagram, Flickr and Facebook accounts.

Notes

1 Mackay, James: *Sounds Out of Silence*: Mainstream: 1997: p.1727

2 Gooday, Graeme J.N.: 'Playfair, Lyon, first Baron Playfair (1818–1898)', *Oxford Dictionary of National Biography*: Oxford University Press: 2004: online edn, January 2016, www.oxforddnb.com/view/article/22368, accessed 4 July 2016 Lyon Playfair (1818–1898): doi:10.1093/ref:odnb/22368

3 Library of Congress Letter from Lyon Playfair to Alexander Graham Bell, 10 December 1877 //www.loc.gov/resource/magbell.30000102

4 RA VIC/MAIN/QVJ (W) Monday 14 January 1878 (Princess Beatrice's copies). Retrieved 18 November 2016

5 Mackay: Op. Cit.: p.173

6 Bruce, Robert V.: *Bell – Alexander Graham Bell and the Conquest of Solitude*: Gollancz: 1973: p.241

7 'The Telephone at Court': *Nottinghamshire Guardian* (London, England): Issue 1695: Friday 18 January 1878: p.7

8 Bruce: Op. Cit.: p.241

9 'The Telephone at Osborne': *Isle of Wight Observer* (Ryde, England): Issue 1312: Saturday 19 January 1878: p.8

10 Baker, E.C.: *Sir William Preece F.R.S: Victorian Engineer Extraordinary*: Century Benham: 1976

11 Letter from Sir Thomas Biddulph to A.G. Bell dated 16 January 1878: *The Times* (London, England): Issue 29161: Friday 25 January 1878: p.10

12 Letter from Alexander Graham Bell to Sir Thomas Biddulph: 1 February 1878: Library of Congress www.loc.gov/resource/magbell.30000106

13 Wood, Brian, Curator, Bell Homestead, Ontario: Email dated 3 July 2016

14 *The Times* (London, England): Issue 30707: Wednesday 3 January 1883: p.6

15 Pall Mall Gazette Office: *The Pall Mall Gazette* (London, England), Issue 9820: Tuesday 15 September 1896

16 Hardy, Alan: *Queen Victoria Was Amused*: John Murray: 1976: p.129

17 *Lloyd's Weekly Newspaper* (London, England), Issue 2812: Sunday 11 October 1896

18 *Reynolds's Newspaper* (London, England): Issue 2412: Sunday 1 November 1896

19 Letter from Mabel Hubbard Bell to Alexander Graham Bell: 24 May 1898: Library of Congress www.loc.gov/resource/magbell.04000601

20 Bruce: Op. Cit.: p.28

21 Letter from Alexander Graham Bell to Mabel Hubbard Bell: 5 October 1875: Library of Congress www.loc.gov/resource/magbell.03400202

22 Letter from Alexander Graham Bell to Mabel Hubbard Bell: 14 October 1889: Library of Congress www.loc.gov/resource/magbell.03700625

23 Letter from Alexander Graham Bell to Mabel Hubbard Bell: 27 August 1900: Library of Congress www.loc.gov/resource/magbell.04100116

24 Bruce: Op. Cit.: pp.421–2: Letter from Mabel Bell to Mrs G. Grosvenor: 11 February 1901

25 Letter from Elsie Bell Grosvenor to Lamar Trotti: 6 January 1939: Library of Congress www.loc.gov/resource/magbell.24700119

26 '2,000,000th Telephone': *The Times* (London, England): Issue 45856: Tuesday 23 June 1931: p.13

27 Email to the author from Hugh Bell Muller: 18 September 2016

6

FRENCH LEAVE
QUEEN VICTORIA MEETS SARAH BERNHARDT

Sarah Bernhardt. (Library of Congress)

THERE IS a famous anecdote of the Victorian matron who remarked to her friend as the curtain fell on Sarah Bernhardt's impassioned and erotic performance as Cleopatra: 'How different, how very different from the home life of our own dear Queen.' While the latter's court and family life was a model of rectitude and morality, Bernhardt was the polar opposite, actively leading a passionate and bohemian life in the full glare of publicity, while neatly juggling it with a highly success-ful acting career. The two women met when they stayed in the same hotel in Nice and they were both clearly moved by the experience.

Sarah Bernhardt was born in the Latin Quarter of Paris in 1844, the illegitimate elder daughter of Julie Bernhardt, a Jewish courtesan from Amsterdam. She became, according to her entry in the *Oxford Dictionary of National Biography*, 'not simply the most famous actress the world has seen; she was among the most gifted'.

Her mother's 'professional' contacts helped. One of her lovers, the Duke de Morny, Emperor Napoleon III's half-brother, arranged for her to train at the Paris Conservatoire, the government-sponsored acting school. Later de Morny pulled more strings to have Sarah enrolled at the national theatre company, the Comédie-Française. Her contract was ended the following year when she slapped the face of a senior actress who had been rude to Bernhardt's younger sister.

She found her true vocation working with the Odéon theatre, where she was critically acclaimed for playing the role of Anna Damby in the 1868 performance of *Kean* by Alexandre Dumas. More success came the following year when she starred as the minstrel Zanetto in a new one-act play, *Le Passant*, by the young dramatist François Coppée – a role she was asked to perform for the Emperor Napoleon III.

As her career became increasingly varied, intense and stellar, so too did her love life. Aged only 19 she had an affair with the Belgian aristocrat Henri, Prince of Ligne, who fathered her only child, Maurice Bernhardt, born on 22 December 1864. She would never seriously discuss her son's parentage other than to say, 'I could never make up my mind whether his father was Gambetta, Victor Hugo or General Boulanger.'[1]

Joining the prestigious list of paramours was the Prince of Wales, who became enthralled by Sarah during her 1879 visit to London to perform the title role in Jean Racine's *Phèdre*. Thanks to her passionate performance and her gift for self-publicity, Bernhardt took the British capital by storm. She turned her rented home in Chester Square into a menagerie, with a newly acquired cheetah and wolfhound joining her pet monkey and parrot. She happily posed for photographers with her red frizzy hair tumbling over a dramatic ensemble of white pantaloons and matching jacket. Even more theatrically, she was known to lie in a coffin to learn her lines or occasionally to sleep. Naturally, red-blooded Bertie was besotted. He saw her *Phèdre* performance night after night and visited her gallery in Piccadilly. After they were finally introduced the attraction was instant, so much so that Bernhardt had to leave a note for her director Edward Got, giving a very clear reason for missing a stage call: 'It is 1.20 and I cannot rehearse at this hour. The prince has kept me since 11 … I shall make amends tomorrow by knowing my part.'[2]

The prince and the showgirl had met at the Royal Albert Hall earlier in the day at a charity bazaar. Bertie bought one of Sarah's self-portraits in oils. The Princess of Wales bought two blue-eyed white kittens. The Prince stayed at Bernhardt's stall until she raised £256. The Waleses also visited her at the William Russell Galleries in Piccadilly, where her art work was being exhibited. The Prince purchased a piece entitled 'La Dormeuse' and the royal couple commissioned a painting as well as a bust of Lord Beaconsfield.

After their liaison, the couple stayed in touch. A few years later Bertie saw her performance in *Fédora* in Paris, during which she wore a style of felt hat which would later be named after the play. The Prince revealed he'd liked to have been an actor. No sooner said than done, Bertie was handed a costume and led to an onstage couch. He lay there, playing dead for most of the final act, until Bernhardt came over to the deceased 'Vladimir', murmured something over his body and kissed him.[3] Presumably neither the Prince nor the audience would have known that during the run Bernhardt asked a procession of past and present boyfriends to play the corpse.

The Prince of Wales wasn't the only one of Victoria's sons to be infatuated by Bernhardt. His haemophiliac younger brother Prince Leopold was prevented from leading the libidinous life enjoyed by Bertie because of bouts of ill-health and his over-protective mother. When he did occasionally enjoy a stimulating visit to the West End, he attended every type of entertainment from high opera to burlesque. One of his favourite haunts was the Gaiety Theatre and it was here in June 1881 that he met up with Sarah who was starring in *Froufrou*. Afterwards he recorded in his journal that it was 'an interesting and affecting play, beautifully acted – went in the 1st entr'acte to see Sarah in her room (had not seen her since '79) she was dressing. We had a very pleasant talk.' A few days later he saw her in *La Dame aux Camélias*. Prior to the London run, the play had been censored because it 'ennobled immoral behaviour, glorified harlotry, and profaned the sanctity of death', which is presumably what attracted her to the role. She must have informed Leopold she was about to return to France since he visited her dressing room to say farewell.[4]

Not all of Victoria's children were admirers of 'the Divine Sarah'. In 1893 Vicky wrote to her daughter Sophie (later Queen of Greece and aunt to Prince Philip, Duke of Edinburgh). While acknowledging Bernhardt was 'an extraordinary actress from all I have heard', she added, 'I hope you did not make her acquaintance, as alas no lady can, she is so very bad, and has an awful reputation. It is a pity those immoral pieces are always given, such as you saw.'[5]

Prior to April 1897 Queen Victoria was of the same opinion. The Queen had left Windsor Castle on 10 March for what by then had become an annual six-week spring holiday on the continent. She was travelling under her usual alias of 'Madame de la Comtesse de Balmoral' – a disguise so thin it never fooled anyone – and huge crowds gathered at the various ports and railway stations along her route. During the last ten years of her life Victoria holidayed in France seven times. This, in her Diamond Jubilee year, was her fifth visit. The royal party stayed at the newly built Hotel Excelsior Regina, named in her honour, at Cimiez, one of the neighbourhoods of Nice. She paid 80,000 francs for her two-month stay in her own specially built wing, at a time when women working ten-hour shifts in the local perfume factory received 1 franc 25 centimes a day.[6] The Queen, of course, never travelled lightly. A staff of sixty to a hundred accompanied her abroad, the number fluctuating each time depending on how many royal relatives were accompanying her. She always took six dressers, a French chef, six cooks, her own carriages, horses and ghillies.

Everyone in Cimiez seems to have bent over backwards to ensure the Queen had a relaxing stay. To ensure her privacy the owners of adjoining estates linked their pathways to form a 6-mile route for her to drive around unobserved by the curious locals and tourists. She favoured the gardens of the nearby Villa Leserb as a *salon vert* in which to breakfast, lunch and work on her state correspondence. A new electric tramway abutted the estate, but its obliging directors took it out of service whenever Victoria was in the garden.

One Riviera resident resolutely uncowed by the legendary royal visitor was Alice de Rothschild. She was a member of the prominent banking family and had a personality as powerful and individual as the Queen's own. A passionate gardener, she was horrified to see Victoria leave the lawn by treading on a much-cherished flower bed, crushing a few prize exhibits along the way. Alice told her to 'get off' in no uncertain terms and she was thereafter referred to by the Queen as 'The All-Powerful One'.[7]

There were conflicts of another type within the Royal Household. This particular visit was tense since the Queen had insisted that her Indian servant, Abdul Karim, known as 'the Munshi' (teacher) to his royal mistress, should dine with members of the Household as an equal. To her credit, Victoria wasn't racist, though most of her Household was. It wasn't just the colour of his skin that offended the courtiers but the knowledge that the royal physician, Dr James Reid, had been treating Karim for gonorrhoea for several months — something he brought to the Queen's attention in February. In addition the elderly monarch's daily routine could be stultifyingly boring for those in attendance. They were obliged to stay in or near the hotel while the Queen worked on her state papers each morning. Senior members were allowed to accompany her on what little sightseeing she undertook. On the day of her meeting with Bernhardt, her itinerary included a visit from former diplomat Sir Edward Malet and his wife Ermyntrude as well as the 'all-powerful' Alice. After luncheon she took a carriage drive to St-Jean, where she took tea and received a bouquet from the Mayor of Villefranche before driving back. On the return journey they passed the 24th Chasseurs who were on manoeuvres at the Palace Villefranche. They presented arms, filed past the royal carriage and saluted its occupant. She also met a delegation from the International Literary Congress, which had been sitting in Monaco. The Court Circular noted, 'They cheered her Majesty enthusiastically.'

Also on 22 April, the Queen:

> conferred the Fourth Class of the Royal Victorian Order upon Dr Sturge who, during the construction and completion of the Queen's wing of the Excelsior Regina Hotel, was entrusted with the duty of superintending the sanitary arrangements, and ensuring its general fitness for habitation.

After six weeks of such fairly limited excitement, members of the Royal Household were excited to hear that the legendary Bernhardt had taken over the whole of the first floor of the Regina's east wing. She was in Nice from the 19th to the 27th to perform in several plays including *La Tosca, La Dame aux Camélias* and *Lorenzaccio.*

Several courtiers suggested the Queen should ask the actress to perform for her. At first she refused on the grounds of Bernhardt's questionable morality. Having rescued the monarchy from the depravity of what she called 'my disreputable uncles', her own moral compass was beyond reproach and she wasn't prepared to abandon it now she was in the relaxed south. For instance, when Canon J.N.B. Woodroffe held a Sunday service for the Queen in her hotel suite he took as his text for the sermon 'I have a sting of the flesh'. When a concerned Victoria asked him to explain what this meant, the quick-thinking cleric avoided anything to do with temptations of the flesh and explained it was simply to do with eye-strain caused by malaria. She was so pleased that she gave him a gold pen to thank him for his ministrations.[8]

For whatever reason, she changed her mind about Bernhardt. Perhaps a month and a half of Mediterranean sun had relaxed her enough to give in to the cajolery of her courtiers. It was a decision she didn't regret, as she makes clear in her journal entry.

At ½ p. 6 the celebrated & famous actress Sarah Bernhard [sic], who has been acting as Nice & is staying in this Hotel performed a little piece for me in the Drawingroom, at her own request. The play was called Jean Marie by André Theuriet, quite short, only lasting ½ an hour. It is extremely touching & Sarah Bernhard's acting was quite marvellous, so pathetic & full of feeling. She appeared much affected herself, tears rolling down her cheeks. She has a most beautiful voice & is very graceful in all her movements. The story is much the same as that of 'Old Robin Grey'. The 2, who acted with her were also excellent, particularly the one who took the part of Jean Marie. The scene is laid in Brittany. When the play was over, Edith L. presented Sarah Bernhard to me & I spoke to her for a few moments. Her manner was most pleasing & gentle. She said it had been such a pleasure & & honour to act for me. When I expressed the hope she was not tired, she answered. 'cela m'a reposé' ['it was a rest for me']. She leaves tomorrow for Marseilles. Thora, the 2 eldest Children, & the Ladies & Gentlemen were present with me.[9]

After dinner there was an audience to honour the sanitary arranger: '... received Dr & Mrs Sturge (both very nice people).'

During the visit to Nice, Frederick Ponsonby, the Assistant Private Secretary, was in charge of the Birthday Book. 'This most tiresome' volume, in Ponsonby's words, was a glorified autograph book in which 'everyone who visited her had to write their name, and it became a mass of names of celebrities and nonentities all mixed up together'.[10] Often mistaken for the Bible, as it was reverentially carried into ceremonies, the Birthday Book had several versions and only the Queen seems to have been fully au fait with which one should be used, as Ponsonby soon discovered. After Victoria left the Grand Salon he produced the book and asked the actress to sign it. She rather theatrically insisted on kneeling to write her name. Then with another theatrical flourish, she signed 'Le plus beau jour de ma vie, Sarah Bernhardt.'

The following morning the Queen sent a message to Ponsonby to see if he'd remembered to get an autograph. Rather pleased with himself, he sent the volume to her:

> To my surprise I got no marks. First of all it was the wrong book, and I ought to have used the artists' book, and secondly, I ought to have prevented her taking up the whole page. I was told that the Queen was much put out at this, but in any case I was to get Sarah Bernhardt's signature in the artists' book.[11]

Since the actress was leaving Nice for Marseilles immediately after that evening's performance, Ponsonby, clutching the correct Birthday Book, was obliged to buy a ticket and sit through the performance. During the first interval he hot-footed it backstage and was refused admission. During the next entr'acte he had no choice but to drop the Queen's name, which worked like a charm. He was admitted to Bernhardt's dressing room and asked her to sign. Sensing she couldn't understand why, the desperate man intimated that the Queen wanted an autograph for a second book, a rare honour – 'plus intime'.

Unfortunately there was no ink to be had in the theatre so Ponsonby had to sit through another act before heading backstage, where the manager had procured some. Before he had time to take the book back, Bernhardt insisted on looking at the other signatures. Spotting artist after artist, she soon realised why she'd been asked to join the list: 'The spell was broken. She handed back the book to me with a shrug of her shoulders. She understood.'[12]

A decade later Ponsonby was in attendance in Paris when Edward VII and Queen Alexandra attended a play starring Bernhardt. During the interval she came to meet the guests in the royal box. Recognising

Ponsonby, she immediately recalled his desperate attempts to get her signature in Nice.

The new reign strengthened Bernhardt's links with the British Crown. At Bertie's coronation in August 1902 she was one of several female guests in a gallery above the chancel where the princesses were seated. These were the new king's lovers, past and present, including Lady Randolph Churchill and his latest squeeze, Alice Keppel, the great-grandmother of Camilla, Duchess of Cornwall. Wags dubbed this special seating area 'the King's Loose Box'. Never one to hide in the shadows, Bernhardt caused a sensation by dressing conspicuously head to toe in white.[13]

Notes

1 Skinner, Cornelia Otis: *Madame Sarah*: Houghton-Mifflin: 1967
2 Ridley, Jane: *Bertie – A Life of Edward VII*: Chatto and Windus: 2012: p.220
3 Nelson, Michael: *Queen Victoria and the Discovery of the Riviera*: I.B. Tauris: 2001: p.112
4 Zeepvat, Charlotte: *Prince Leopold*: Sutton Publishing Ltd: 1999: p.158
5 Nelson: Op. Cit.: p.112
6 Duff, David: *Victoria Travels*: Frederick Muller Ltd: 1970: p.332
7 Nelson: Op. Cit.: p.55
8 Longford, Elizabeth: *Victoria R.I.*: Weidenfeld and Nicolson: 1964: p.572
9 RA VIC/MAIN/QVJ (W) Thursday 22 April 1897 (Princess Beatrice's copies). Retrieved 11 June 2018
10 Ponsonby, Sir Frederick: *Recollections of Three Reigns*: Eyre and Spottiswoode: 1951: p.36ff
11 Ibid.: p.38
12 Ibid.: p.39
13 Ridley: Op. Cit.: p.368

WHIP-CRACK-AWAY
QUEEN VICTORIA AND THE WILD WEST SHOW

Buffalo Bill.

VICTORIA'S 1887 meeting with William Cody, alias 'Buffalo Bill', was the nineteenth century's most unexpected encounter since Livingstone met Stanley. Their impact on each other was huge. He recalled 'a great occasion of which the mental photograph will remain long with me'. To the Queen the American showman was 'a splendid man, handsome, & gentleman-like in manner'.

Cody's 'Wild West Show' at Earl's Court in West Kensington must have had something special to induce Victoria to break her post-Albert exile from all types of London entertainment. She visited the show in the month before her Golden Jubilee and was so entranced she agreed to a performance at Windsor for her fellow monarchs, gathered to celebrate her monarchical half century. Five years later Cody brought his display of Cossack riders to the castle for a second command performance in front of the Queen.

Victoria was never averse to raw masculinity, as her infatuation with her loyal but often brutish manservant John Brown testifies. Her journal entry after meeting the Wild West hero shows her evident fascination with '"Buffalo Bill" as he is called having killed 3,000 buffaloes with his own hands'. She adds, 'He has had many encounters and hand to hand fights with the Red Indians.'[1]

Like many of her subjects, it appears the Queen fell hook, line and sinker for the often hugely exaggerated claims of Cody's press agent and publicity manager John Burke, who erroneously described himself as 'Major' Burke, and who is credited with trumpeting Buffalo Bill on to the world stage.

Cody had certainly been an action man of the American Old West. Born in 1846, he became a rider for the Pony Express at the age of only 14, once riding 384 miles in 21 hours and 30 minutes. He was also a stagecoach driver and, after fighting for the Union in the Civil War, was a civilian scout for the US army during the Indian Wars, and was awarded the Medal of Honor in 1872. He founded 'Buffalo Bill's Wild West' – the word 'show' never appeared in the title – in 1883, and four years later made the first of eight visits with this huge company to Britain and continental Europe. His first visit to London was in the Jubilee summer of 1887, when the show was part of the American Exhibition at Earl's Court.

Men numbering 1,200 worked around the clock to assemble the pavilions and Wild West stadium. The main exhibition building was 1,140ft long and 120ft wide. The amphitheatre for Cody's show was also impressive, with covered seating and boxes for 20,000 people, standing room for 10,000 and open-air standing room for a further 10,000.[2]

Meanwhile, on 31 March 1887, Cody, his business manager Nate Salsbury, and some 200 cowboys, Indians, squaws, children and Mexicans, set sail from New York on the steamship *State of Nebraska*. The Native

American group was a mixed tribe of Sioux, Cheyenne, Kyowa, Pawnee and Arapaho. Among them was Ogila-sa or Chief Red Shirt, billed as 'Chief of the Sioux nation' and, according to Cody, 'a redoubtable warrior and second only in influence to Sitting Bull himself'. Indigenous names were never used, and 'Red Shirt' was joined by the dramatically re-branded Little Bull, Cut Meat, Black Elk and Poor Dog.[3]

British public interest and constant press coverage, fuelled by Burke's efficient public relations team of twelve staff, ensured every detail of the American arrival in London was documented. The *Pall Mall Gazette* covered the visit of forty Indians 'bedecked with paint and feathers' to a service in the Congregational Chapel, West Kensington, where they sang 'Nearer My God To Thee' in their own tongue. The Native Americans were given a guided tour of Westminster Abbey, and enjoyed the Tower of London so much they asked to go again. They were taken on a boat trip to Hampton Court and a train ride to Windsor Castle. Others were spotted walking round Kensington fully garbed. In the evenings they enjoyed music hall at the London Palladium and several of them went to the Lyceum to see Henry Irving and Ellen Terry in *Faust*. For the latter, while the cowboys sat in boxes the Indians sat in the front row, eating sugar plums and presumably blocking the view of anyone in rows B to M as they were once again well-feathered. Much to the delight of the audience Irving even called them on stage to share a curtain call.[4]

Irving and Terry had already been to see the Earl's Court tented encampment soon after the Americans arrived. Other VIPs flooded in, headed by Grand Duke Michael of Russia and the former Prime Minister, William Gladstone. The latter's stilted conversation with a diffident Red Shirt was meticulously documented by a *Daily Telegraph* reporter:

Mr Gladstone asked Red Shirt what he thought of the English climate. The chief said he had not much to complain of so far. Mr Gladstone asked if he thought the Englishmen looked enough like the Americans to be kinsmen and brothers. Red Shirt wasn't sure about that.

According to Burke, Gladstone 'enjoyed himself like a veritable school-boy'. Red Shirt dutifully told the press, via his interpreter, 'though my tongue was tied in his presence, my heart was full of friendship.'[5]

Buffalo Bill himself wasn't bedded down under canvas but in a suite at the Hotel Metropole. He was very soon the toast of London, lunching at the Garrick Club, being feted at Mansion House by the Lord Mayor of London, and dining with Lord and Lady Randolph Churchill, where he met their son, 13-year-old Winston. His later meeting with the monarch was kick-started by his formal presentation at the Reform Club to her cousin, the Duke of Cambridge, and to the Prince of Wales, whom Cody plucked up the courage to ask to come to the Earl's Court spectacle.

Bertie, his wife Alexandra and their three daughters dutifully visited the Wild West camp on 5 May where they were treated to a full dress rehearsal three days before the official opening. The royal box was decorated with American and British flags – the first time in history the two had been combined in such a display. The Prince was so excited he remained standing throughout the entire show, shouting words of encouragement from the royal box, and he and his family gave the performers a standing ovation at the end.[6]

Afterwards the Prince of Wales met Red Shirt inside his tepee. Bertie was introduced as the 'coming chief of the Pale Face Nation' and asked the Sioux tribesman how he liked the British weather, which by now must have seemed a traditional white man's introduction.[7] The Prince was shown relics including tomahawks, bows and arrows, and scalps. Alexandra was then introduced as 'the Great Chief's wife' and made a fuss of a mixed-race papoose, patting it on the head.

Later Bertie inspected the stables, where he was particularly interested in seeing Cody's 21-year-old horse 'Old Charlie', which another royal visitor, Grand Duke Michael of Russia, would ride during one show, chasing a buffalo around the arena. He then entered Cody's deluxe 'Pahaska [long hair] Tepee' and was shown the gold-mounted sword presented by US army generals. The two men then sat in comfortable armchairs smoking cigars.

As the royal party prepared to leave Earl's Court promising to return to see the show as often as they could, Bertie noticed Red Shirt again, and walked over to him, opened his cigarette case and gave its contents to the Indian, who handed them round to his companions.

For the grand opening on 9 May, a capacity crowd filled every one of the 20,000 seats. Stewards showed them to their places and sold souvenir programmes at 6d each and a new sticky, salty confection called 'popcorn' at one halfpenny a cone-full. The only royal presence that day was a minor member of the House of Hanover, Princess Victoria Mary of Teck, who six years later would marry Prince George, Duke of York, and eventually become Queen Mary, grandmother of the present Queen.

Cody's next royal encounter would, in the words of Nate Salsbury, land Buffalo Bill 'at the foot of the throne of England' and the ensuing publicity would be 'enough to secure the attendance of every person in London who desired to be "it"'.[8]

On Wednesday 11 May 1887 Londoners had two opportunities to see Queen Victoria driving through the streets of the capital. At 11 a.m. she visited Westminster Abbey to inspect preparations for her forthcoming Golden Jubilee service. She walked 'into the Choir which is one mass of boarding & lumber, so that it looked dreadful'.[9] Thankfully her own seating arrangements won approval: 'The Dais has been put in the same place, where the Throne was, when the homage took place at my coronation, & the old Coronation Chair, with the stone from Scone, is placed on it, for me to sit in.'[10]

After a palace luncheon, a meeting with the Prime Minister, Lord Salisbury, and an afternoon concert – 'Tennyson's fine Ode, very beautifully set to music' – Victoria 'hurried back & took a cup of tea before to Earl's Court, where we saw a very extraordinary & interesting sight a performance of "Buffalo Bill's" "Wild" "West"'. (Her inverted commas, fired like gun shots, suggest she was as unfamiliar with the show as she was with the Wild West itself!)

Her request to see the show – 'lasting not more than an hour' – at 5 p.m. was an unmistakable 'royal command'. It caused havoc at Earl's Court since the 3 p.m. sell-out show for 40,000 had to be cancelled, and the choreographed routine hastily adapted for the select royal audience of twenty-six. Several newspapers lamented the Queen's decision to see the show privately, thus inconveniencing those who had pre-booked for the afternoon show. 'Seeing that it is Jubilee Year,' grumbled one, 'it would not have done any harm had her Majesty, just for once, tolerated the presence of her subjects in the same public building as herself.'

Punch also waded in: 'Why did the Queen go for a private view to B.B.s in Wild West Kensington, when Her Majesty could have commanded the buck jumping riders to have given their show at Buckingham Palace?'[11] The answer was simple enough, as Cody later recalled: 'as with Mahomet, the mountain was altogether too colossal to take to Windsor [or any other royal residence for that matter] and so the Queen came to the Wild West.'

Victoria's abbreviated Wild West would miss out on a train attack, Mustang Jack's leaping from horse to horse and an Indian scalping, but what was left of the package guaranteed an entertaining experience.

At five on the dot, the Queen's carriage procession cantered down Earl's Court Road, accompanied by a detachment of the 2nd Life Guards. One of the Indians, Red Elk, recalled she came in 'a big shining wagon, with soldiers on both sides'. Outside the arena 100 policemen were on duty to stop intruders, presumably including disgruntled ticket holders who'd been unable to access the matinee performance, as well as the many who came for a rare glimpse of their reclusive monarch.

Victoria's cavalcade circled the stadium, stopping in front of the royal box. 'We sat in a box in large semi-circle,' noted the Queen in her journal. 'It is an amphitheatre with a large open space, all the seats being under cover.' A dais with a single throne had been added for the monarch, who was accompanied by her youngest daughter, Princess Beatrice.

The show got off to a memorable start. After the National Anthem and 'Yankee Doodle', Frank Richmond, the Master of Ceremonies, gave the introduction, during which a horseman entered the arena waving the American flag above his head. Victoria instantly stood and gravely bowed in its direction. Cody later wrote, 'For the first time in history, since the Declaration of Independence, a sovereign of Great Britain has saluted the star spangled banner, and that banner was carried by a member of Buffalo Bill's Wild West!'[12]

After the Queen had resumed her seat, the cowboys, Indians and Mexicans all entered the arena for an introductory parade. Bennie Irving, 5-year-old son of 'Bronco Bill' Irving, endeared himself to the royal party by riding directly up to the front of the royal box, kissing his hands and then blowing kisses at Victoria. Cody entered the arena on 'Old Charlie' and magisterially proclaimed, 'Welcome, Your Majesty, to the Wild West of America.'

Victoria's journal takes up the story:

All the different people, wild, painted Red Indians from America, on their wild bare backed horse, of different tribes, — cow boys, Mexicans, &c. all came tearing round at full speed, shrieking & screaming, which had the weirdest effect. An attack on a coach, & on a ranch, with an immense deal of firing, was most exciting, so was the buffalo hunt, & the bucking ponies, that were almost impossible to sit. A young girl, who went through the 'haute école', certainly sat the most marvellous plunges beautifully, sitting quite erect, & being completely master of her horse.

The Queen was enjoying herself so much that she sent word backstage that she would extend her stay and see the programme in its usual entirety. This caused panic among Cody and the other organisers as they hastily re-jigged the presentation while Victoria happily watched the company dance the Virginia Reel on horseback. She enjoyed seeing the Deadwood stagecoach being attacked by Indians – perhaps reflecting on her own seven near misses from would-be assassins while she sat in her carriage.

Cody assembled the covered wagons for another attack and 'Mustang Jack' for his athletic leap over his horses while clutching dumb-bells. Then Buck Taylor wrestled a Texan steer to the ground before the entire cast gathered for a final salute. Taylor, 6ft 4in, was the heart-throb of the company and very popular with the ladies on the tour. He entered the arena on a snorting mule ominously named 'Suicide', proceeded to pick up a handkerchief at full gallop and was heading for the royal box with it when he was headed off by Nate Salsbury, the show's director.[13]

In the end only the Indian scalping was omitted, wisely it turned out, as the Queen wrote in her journal that she found 'their War Dance, to a wild drum & pipe, was quite fearful, with all their contortions & shrieks, & they came so close'.

After the performance the Queen asked to meet selected members of the company. She told Cody that she was very satisfied with all she had seen. He later wrote that she had said other complimentary things but 'modesty forbids me to repeat them,' not that modesty usually got in the way of a good story being leaked to the world by either him or John Burke. The Queen seems to have been impressed, noting in her journal, 'Col. Cody: "Buffalo Bill" … is a splendid man, handsome. & gentleman-like in manner. He has had many encounters & hand to hand fights with the Red Indians.'

Some of the Native Americans were also introduced, complete with war paint and feathers. '"Red Shirt" the Chief of the Sioux tribe, was presented to me,' Victoria recorded. According to the Burke PR machine, 'Red Shirt' told her, 'I have come a long way to see Her Majesty, and am glad to look upon the Great White Mother, who has greater power than any brave in the world.'[14] In his memoirs Burke later admitted, 'This was a fair sample of the Indian version of blarney, since the chief had never heard of Victoria until he crossed the ocean.'[15]

The Queen was also introduced to two squaws and their papooses. She shook hands with the former and patted the babies on their heads. According to one report, 'the squaws raced across the arena to see Her Majesty. Their notions of etiquette were of a somewhat startling nature, for they stretched out their hands in an excited fashion and dismounted the brown babies with remarkable alacrity for royal inspection' before they 'gathered their children and fled after their warriors'.[16] When, during the following summer, the squaw of Little Chief gave birth to a baby while the Wild West show was in Manchester, it was named Frances Victoria Alexandra after Mrs Cleveland, wife of the US President, the Queen and the Princess of Wales.

Victoria's procession left fifteen minutes later than planned, watched by a vast crowd as well as men and boys on the rooftops of some of the West Brompton houses. She took the Royal Train from Paddington Station, arriving at Windsor Castle at 7.15 p.m.

Both the Queen and Cody and his team spent the evening reflecting on the visit. Victoria wrote in her journal, 'The cow boys, are fine looking people, but the painted Indians, with their feathers, & wild dress (very little of it) were rather alarming looking, & they have cruel faces.' The Indians themselves were equally forthright in their accounts. 'Black Elk' was reported as saying:

> We stood right in front of Grandmother England. She was little but fat and we liked her, because she was good to us. After we danced, she spoke to us. She said: 'I am sixty-seven years old and I have seen all kinds of people, but today I have seen the best looking people I know.'

(In fact she was 68 and unlikely to have said anything like this at all. Perhaps more Burke spin?)

> She shook hands with all of us. Her hand was very little and soft. We gave a big cheer for her, and then the shining wagons came in and she got into one of them, and they all went away.[17]

A couple of days after the royal visit, an enormous parcel arrived at Earl's Court. It contained a Parian marble bust of the Queen on a plinth, sent as a gift from Victoria to Frank Richard. It remained in his tent for the rest of the stay in London and proved a talking point among the Native Americans, who frequently gathered to touch it.

The Waleses made a return visit on 15 June with their eldest son and three daughters. The royal party boarded the Deadwood Coach, and were driven round the arena by Cody while being 'attacked' by the Indians. Afterwards Alexandra toured the rest of the 'Yankeries', made two trips on the switch-back railway and went down a toboggan slide. This was repeated five days later to entertain visiting royal guests assembled in London to honour the Golden Jubilee at a service in Westminster Abbey on 21 June, the day before Edward and Alexandra took the kings of Greece, Saxony, Belgium and Denmark to Earl's Court along with three Crown Princes – including the future Emperor Wilhelm II of Germany and the ill-fated Crown Prince Rudolph of Austria. This time the monarchs shared the Deadwood Coach while Edward and Cody shared the reins as they hurtled around the arena, once again pursued by an Indian attack.

The poker-loving Prince of Wales said, 'Colonel, you never held four kings like these before,' to which Buffalo Bill joked, 'I've held four kings, but four kings and the Prince of Wales makes a royal flush, such as no man held before!'[18] Afterwards an exuberant Cody wrote to his mother, 'we sure did rock around that arena, with the Indians yelling and shooting behind us, fit to kill. And Mamma – I wouldn't want to say it out loud – but I'm pretty sure that before the ride was over, most of the kings were under the seat. It sure was fun.'[19]

Two days later Edward sent Cody a diamond pin bearing the Prince of Wales' emblem of three feathers together with his 'Ich dien' ('I serve') motto. He had also arranged for members of the company to watch the Jubilee procession from VIP seats on the route. Later 'Black Elk' recalled:

all the people in the seats were roaring and yelling 'Jubilee!' and 'Victoria!' Then we saw Grandmother England. She was sitting in the back of the wagon ... her dress was all shining and so were the horses. She looked like a fire coming ... We sent up a great cry and our women made the tremelo.[20]

The Wild West show returned to Earl's Court in 1892. The Queen was keen to see the Cossacks led by Prince Ivan Rostomov Macheradse, who claimed to be a direct descendant of the Ukrainian Cossack leader Mazepa. This time Mahomet came to the mountain as Cody agreed to show this equine act at Windsor Castle, though as it only took twelve minutes to perform he added enough material to make up a performance of an hour. Cody and his team visited the castle on Saturday 25 June. They travelled by a specially chartered train from London paid for by the Queen. Several hundred locals watched as Cody rode in to the castle grounds on his white horse 'Billy' followed by the Cossacks. That night the Queen noted in her journal:

> At 5, Lenchen [her third daughter, Princess Helena] & Thora [Helena's daughter, Princess Helena Victoria] having joined us, we went on to the East Terrace, & watched from a tent, open in front, a sort of 'Buffalo Bill' performance, on the Lawn below. It was extremely well arranged, & an excellent representation of what we had also seen 5 years ago at Earl's Court.

Victoria was joined by Nate Salsbury in the pavilion, taking his hat off to greet the sovereign. After a while she said to him, 'Mr Salsbury, please put on your hat, as I feel a strong draught here, and please take a chair.' Salsbury replied, 'Your Majesty, I am very comfortable,' only to be told, 'But I would be more comfortable if you took a chair.'

Victoria's journal gives a detailed account of all she saw:

> There were Cow Boys, Red Indians, Mexicans, Argentines, taking part & then a wonderful riding display by Cossacks, accompanied by curious singing, & a war dance by the Indians. There were extraordinary buck jumping horses, shooting at glass balls, by Col: Cody (Buffalo Bill), & display of cracking huge lunge whips.

The Queen asked Salsbury what gun Cody was using, and was told, 'It's a Winchester rifle, Madam, an American firearm.' She seemed impressed: 'Ah, a very effective weapon and in very effective hands.' Victoria's account ends:

> The whole, was a very pretty, wild sight, which lasted an hour. At the conclusion of the performance, all advanced in line at a gallop & stopped suddenly. Col: Cody was brought up for me to speak to him. He is still a very handsome man, but has now got a grey beard.[21]

Victoria was so taken with the American showman that she asked for a photograph of him wearing his fringed buckskins and a cowboy hat, leisurely leaning on his rifle. It was taken by society photographer Clarence Fry and it is still in the Royal Collection. The Queen also gave Cody a watch charm as a token of her appreciation.

Victoria's interest in Buffalo Bill was an unlikely factor during Cody's divorce proceedings in 1905. Cody had initiated a plea for divorce from his wife Louisa. The depositions before Judge Charles Scott in Cheyenne, Wyoming, grew increasingly absurd. When one of the witnesses for Mrs Cody, a Mrs H.S. Parker, claimed that Louisa was jealous of the attentions paid to her husband by Queen Victoria and Queen Alexandra, the judge acted with fury. He ordered the references to the two British Queens should be expunged from the record as 'manifestly unjust, preposterous, false and brutal'. Strangely the marriage survived, though the negative publicity of the near-divorce threatened to undo all John Burke's efforts to promote Buffalo Bill as a royal favourite.

Notes

1   Gallop, Alan: *Buffalo Bill's British Wild West*: The History Press: 2009: p.101
2   Ibid.: p.45
3   Ibid.: p.40
4   Ibid.: p.65
5   Weybright, V. & Sell, H.: *Buffalo Bill and the Wild West*: Hamish Hamilton: 1956: p.152
6   Ibid.: p.154
7   *The Morning Post*: 6 May 1887
8   Kasson, J.S.: *Buffalo Bill's Wild West*: Hill and Wang: 2000: p.77
9   RA VIC/MAIN/QVJ (W) Wednesday 11 May 1887 (Princess Beatrice's copies). Retrieved 30 August 2017
10 Ibid
11 Gallop: Op. Cit.: p.102
12 Russell, Don: *The Lives and Legends of Buffalo Bill*: University of Oklahoma Press: 1973: p.330
13 *The York Herald*: 14 May 1887
14 Gallop: Op. Cit.: p.101
15 Burke, John: *Buffalo Bill*: Cassell: 1974: p.176
16 *The York Herald*: 14 May 1887
17 Gallop: Op. Cit.: p.102
18 Weybright: Op. Cit.: p.331
19 Gallop: Op. Cit.: p.112
20 Ibid.: p.113
21 RA VIC/MAIN/QVJ (W) Saturday 25 June 1892 (Princess Beatrice's copies). Retrieved 30 August 2017

8

'STOUT ... PLAIN ... NOT MUCH DIGNITY'
CHARLOTTE BRONTË GLIMPSES THE QUEEN

Charlotte Brontë. (Library of Congress)

ON 18 SEPTEMBER 1843 Queen Victoria and Prince Albert arrived in Brussels shortly after 1 p.m. during their state visit to Belgium as guests of their uncle, King Leopold I. Watching the carriage procession pass through the aptly named rue Royale was a 27-year-old teacher from the nearby Pensionnat Heger.

Charlotte Brontë was halfway through her two-year stay in the capital and was lonely, homesick and had developed an infatuation with her employer, Constantin Heger. She could hardly fail to have been aware of the royal visit. The processional route and the palace were only a stone's throw away from the Pensionnat and the burgomaster had put out a proclamation to drum up interest in Victoria's arrival. Posted on public buildings throughout Brussels it trumpeted:

> Fellow Citizens! I have the great pleasure of informing you that H.M. the Queen of England will visit the capital of Belgium where she will make her entry by the Porte de Cologne on Monday at 1 p.m. and will drive to the Palace by the Boulevard du Jardin and the Rue Royale.[1]

Brontë can't have been too excited by the glimpse of her monarch, since it took her until 1 October to write an account of it after a prompt from her sister Emily, back in Howarth Parsonage:

> You ask about Queen Victoria's visit to Brussels. I saw her for an instant flashing through the Rue Royale in a carriage and six, surrounded by soldiers. She was laughing and talking very gaily. She looked a little stout, vivacious lady, very plainly dressed, not much dignity or pretension about her. The Belgians liked her very well on the whole. They said she enlivened the sombre court of King Leopold, which is usually as gloomy as a conventicle ...[2]

In her journal Victoria noted:

> To attempt adequately to describe Brussels, the prettiest town I have ever seen, our reception there & what passed, will be impossible. The heat was awful & driving along the streets, we were quite broiled by the sun ... The streets were crowded with people on foot, & the 'beau monde' were at the windows, – all, so civil & kind.[3]

Brontë was not the only person there that day who deplored the Queen's plain dress. Lady of the Bedchamber, Charlotte Canning, had looked through the royal dresses for the tour while waiting to set sail from England and noted:

they are decidedly very badly chosen and quite unlike what she ought to have. Her dresser never ceased sighing and lifting up her hands and eyes all the time I looked at them lamenting how little she cared about her dress.

A few days later Canning was still complaining, 'I am very much distressed that the Queen has not been better dressed on this journey for all the Belgians remark it.'[4]

Appearance aside, as one recent Brontë biographer explains:

Victoria was an object of wonder across the globe – so young, so powerful, so female – and the sisters in Haworth had been fascinated by her ever since she came to the throne in 1837, a newly minted monarch of their own age and gender, ushering in a new age.[5]

On a lighter note, the literary sisters named their pet geese Victoria and Adelaide after the monarch and her aunt, the widow of William IV. These were treated with less reverence than their namesakes. Emily writes in her diary in July 1841 that the pets 'are ensconced in the peat-house'[6] and they were given away when she and Charlotte left for Brussels.

Fifteen years later it was the Queen's turn to be fascinated with Charlotte. Just over a decade after its publication under the pseudonym Currer Bell, Victoria discovered the author's greatest work. One Sunday evening in March 1858, the Queen 'began reading "Jane Eyre" to my dear Albert, having finished Northanger Abbey, one of Miss Austen's admirable novels'.[7]

The Queen recorded her great admiration for Brontë's passionate writing in a series of entries in her journal for the spring and summer of 1858: 'Read to Albert out of that melancholy, clever interesting book "Jane Eyre"' (21 March); 'reading till past 11, in that intensely interesting novel (13 May); 'read afterwards in "Jane Eyre", in which we are so deeply interested (19 May); 'We remained up, reading in "Jane Eyre", till ½ p. 11, — quite creepy, from the awful account of what happened the night before the marriage, which was interrupted in the Church (21 May);[8] 'we read in "Jane Eyre", which proved so interesting that we went on till quite late. It was the part, in which comes the moment of her finding Rochester again, blind, & with the loss of a hand!'[9]; and finally, after a reception on the Royal Yacht at Cherbourg for the Emperor of France,

'At near 10 we went below & nearly finished reading that most interesting book "Jane Eyre". A peaceful, happy evening.'[10]

Throughout their forty-three-year correspondence, the Queen and her eldest daughter, the Princess Royal, frequently recommended both fiction and non-fiction titles to each other. The day after she began reading Brontë's most famous novel to Prince Albert, the Queen wrote to her daughter, 'We had your two brothers and Alice to dinner, à 5, and then when they were gone I began reading to Papa out of "Jane Eyre" which is very interesting ... It is given much in Germany as "The Orphan of Lowood".'[11]

The following year, the Princess reported:

I have finished 'Jane Eyre'. How awfully interesting it is − before I had finished the second volume, I could hardly sleep − that horrid, mad creature with her strange laugh haunts one. Do tell Miss Hillyard* I have read it, she said it would interest me so much.[12]

Apart from that one sighting in Brussels, Charlotte never again glimpsed the Queen, though their worlds collided several times. In early July 1850 the writer spent a couple of days sightseeing in Edinburgh with her publisher George Smith. She said it was one of the most enjoyable times she had had. The Scottish capital became 'mine own romantic city' and she contrasted the 'great rumbling, rambling, heavy Epic' of London with its northern counterpart. 'All the glories of architecture assembled together, you have nothing like Arthur's Seat,' she told the London-based publisher. Together they visited this volcanic outcrop by carriage driven by a Scotsman with a dry sense of humour whom Smith later recalled Brontë found amusing. They reached the summit by foot and Charlotte was in raptures at the stunning vista of the city and Victoria's Palace of Holyroodhouse in the foreground.[13]

A few weeks later the Queen arrived at this official Scottish royal residence and one of her first acts was to explore the same rocky peak:

At 10 we drove in 2 closed carriages with the 4 Children ... along the new drive, round the Arthur's Seat, & when we had gone some

---

* Miss Hillyard was herself the daughter of a clergyman and a governess, albeit to the royal children.

little way, we got out, & walked right to the top, a good height, which was quite hard work after a year's disuse of climbing. But it is nothing to the Highland climbing, the ground being so smooth. The view at the top is very rewarding. The beautiful town, with the Calton Hill, the Bay stretching out before it, with the Island of Inchquill, & the Bass Rock, quite in the distance, rising behind the coast line lay before us. Unfortunately, it was a little foggy & hazy. Coming down we had a small crowd following us. The view, when we rejoined the carriage near the small Dunsappie Loch, overhung by a Craig, with the sea in the distance was extremely pretty. Got home quite hot & stiff from our exertions, but the air was delicious.[14]

'The Queen, indeed, was right to climb Arthur's Seat, with her husband and children,' Charlotte wrote to James Taylor, a reader at Smith, Elder & Co., the company publishing her books. 'I shall not soon forget how I felt when, having reached its summit, we all sat down and looked over the city – towards the sea and Leith, and the Pentland Hills.'[15]

The following spring Charlotte stayed with George Smith and his family at their London home, 112 Gloucester Terrace. It was a handy base from which to visit that year's unmissable attraction, the Great Exhibition. This was the brainchild of Prince Albert and it showcased the best of British manufacturing, engineering and design, set in the magnificent Crystal Palace in Hyde Park. The writer made five visits to the exhibition and after her second wrote to her father:

It is a wonderful place – vast, strange, new, and impossible to describe. Its grandeur does not consist in *one* thing, but in the unique assemblage of *all* things. Whatever human industry has created, you find there, from the great compartments filled with railway engines and boilers, with mill-machinery in full work, with splendid carriages of all kinds, with harness of every description – to the glass-covered and velvet-spread stands loaded with the most gorgeous work of the goldsmith and silversmith, and the carefully guarded caskets full of real diamonds and pearls worth hundreds of thousands of pounds.[16]

Charlotte was particularly struck by the Koh-i-Noor Diamond ceded to Victoria the previous year along with the Punjab at the end of the

Second Anglo-Sikh War. Meaning 'Mountain of Light' in Persian, the massive diamond was displayed in London in its original lacklustre condition. Prince Albert ordered it to be re-cut as an oval brilliant that weighed 105.6 carats. The Queen once commented that she never liked the stone, and after her death it was bequeathed as a Crown jewel rather than a personal one. Now part of the Queen Consort's Crown it was last worn by Queen Elizabeth the Queen Mother at the Coronation of Elizabeth II in 1953.

Victoria had opened the exhibition on 1 May 1851 and was still proudly visiting it three times a week by the time Charlotte arrived in the capital on the 29th. Their paths never crossed, though there were other distractions as Charlotte mentioned to her father:

> I was in it [the Crystal Palace] again yesterday afternoon, and saw the ex-Royal Family of France – the old Queen, the Duchess of Orleans, and her two sons, etc., pass down the transept. I almost wonder the Londoners don't tire a little of this vast Vanity Fair – and, indeed, a new toy has somewhat diverted the attention of the grandees lately, viz., a fancy ball given last night by the Queen.[17]

Four years after her visit to London, Charlotte Brontë died on 31 March 1855, three weeks short of her thirty-ninth birthday, and nine months after her marriage to Arthur Bell Nicholls, her father's curate. Patrick Brontë, who had now outlived all six of his children, co-operated with the author Elizabeth Gaskell on *The Life of Charlotte Brontë*, which was published in 1857.

The biography was read to the Queen by her ladies in the spring of 1873. Her fascination with the tragic tale of the literary sisters is evident in her own writings. One journal entry records:

> The Dss of Roxburghe afterwards read & finished the most interesting, & sad life of poor Charlotte Bronte! who was so highly gifted & so good. It is one of the saddest lives one can imagine. Her 4 sisters died of consumption, which at last killed her also at the age of 35, when she had been happily married only 9 months![18]

Mrs Gaskell's book presumably inspired the Queen to read (or have read to her) another of Charlotte's works that same spring: 'The 3 Ladies dined, & Ly Erroll read to me afterwards, finishing "*Villette*", which is admirably written & very interesting.'[19] Six years later she chose *Shirley* 'which is very interesting'.

Although the Queen possessed the 1876 seven-volume *The Lives and Works of Charlotte Brontë and her Sisters*, there is no evidence that she read Emily Brontë's *Wuthering Heights* or either of Anne Brontë's classics, *Agnes Grey* and *The Tenant of Wildfell Hall*.

Victoria did however re-read 'that thrilling *Jane Eyre*' twenty-two years after first reading it to the Prince Consort. She completed it on the Royal Train en route from Ballater to Windsor after her annual autumn stay at Balmoral:

> Finished Jane Eyre, which is really a wonderful book, very peculiar in parts, but so powerfully – admirably written, such a fine tone in it, such fine religious feeling, & such beautiful writing. The description of the mysterious maniac's nightly appearances, awfully thrilling, – Mr Rochester's character a very remarkable one, & Jane Eyre's herself, a beautiful one. The end is very touching, when Jane Eyre returns to him, & finds him blind, with one hand gone from injuries during the fire in his house, which was caused by his mad wife.[20]

Clearly the Queen had lost none of her delight in the Gothic overtones and passionate romance.

Notes

1   Guerin, Winifred: *Charlotte Brontë – The Evolution of Genius*: Oxford University Press: 1987
2   Smith, Margaret (ed.): *The Letters of Charlotte Brontë, Vol. 1: 1829–1847*: Oxford University Press: 1995: p.331
3   RA VIC/MAIN/QVJ (W) Monday 18 September 1843 (Princess Beatrice's copies). Retrieved 15 March 2018
4   Surtees, Virginia: *Charlotte Canning*: John Murray: 1975: pp.110–5
5   Harman, Claire: *Charlotte Brontë – A Life*: Viking: 2015: p.5
6   Smith: Op. Cit.: p.262
7   RA VIC/MAIN/QVJ (W) Sunday 7 March 1858 (Princess Beatrice's copies). Retrieved 15 March 2018
8   RA VIC/MAIN/QVJ (W) Friday 21 May 1858 (Princess Beatrice's copies). Retrieved 15 March 2018
9   RA VIC/MAIN/QVJ (W) Monday 2 August 1858 (Princess Beatrice's copies). Retrieved 15 March 2018
10 RA VIC/MAIN/QVJ (W) Wednesday 4 1858 (Princess Beatrice's copies). Retrieved 15 March 2018

11 Fulford, Roger (ed.): *Dearest Child*: Evans Brothers: 1964: p.72: Letter headed Osborne, 8 March 1858

12 Ibid.: p.225: Letter headed Berlin, 17 December 1859

13 Fraser, Rebecca: *Charlotte Brontë*: Vintage: 2003: pp.374–5

14 RA VIC/MAIN/QVJ (W) Friday 30 August 1850 (Princess Beatrice's copies). Retrieved 30 March 2018

15 Gaskell, Elizabeth: *The Life of Charlotte Brontë*: Cosimo Inc.: 2008: p.413

16 Shorter, Clement K.: *Charlotte Brontë and her Circle*: Hodder and Stoughton: 1896: Letter to Rev. P. Brontë dated 7 June 1851

17 Ibid.: Letter to Rev. P. Brontë dated 14 June 1851

18 RA VIC/MAIN/QVJ (W) Saturday 15 March 1873 (Princess Beatrice's copies). Retrieved 30 March 2018

19 RA VIC/MAIN/QVJ (W) Wednesday 11 June 1873 (Princess Beatrice's copies). Retrieved 30 March 2018

20 RA VIC/MAIN/QVJ (W) Tuesday 23 November 1880 (Princess Beatrice's copies). Retrieved 30 March 2018

9

'A VERY MODEST YOUNG MAN'
PABLO CASALS PLAYS FOR VICTORIA

Pablo Casals. (Library of Congress)

THE LEGENDARY cellist Pablo Casals (1876–1973) is thought to be the only musician to have played for both Queen Victoria and President John F. Kennedy.

Although a lifelong republican, Casals' early career soared thanks to royal patronage, particularly in his home country of Spain. His career began modestly enough, earning 4 pesetas a day playing his cello in the family-run Café Tost. He played popular tunes as part of a trio and, still a schoolboy, he was dubbed by patrons 'el nen' – 'the little one'.

In 1893, after hearing Casals at the café, the Catalan composer and pianist Isaac Albénez gave Casals' mother Pilar a letter of introduction to Count Morphy, a patron of the arts and adviser to the Queen Regent, Maria Christina.

Casals' first performance at court was for the Infanta Isabella, sister of Maria's late husband King Alfonso XII. Señora Casals accompanied her son to the performance, where she hushed her screaming baby Enrique by breastfeeding him in front of the royals. 'Quietly without any fuss,' Casals recalled in his memoirs, 'or the slightest show of embarrassment, my mother unfastened her dress and proceeded to nurse Enrique. I continued playing …'[1]

He was introduced to Queen Maria Christina, who had been Regent of Spain since the death of her tubercular husband Alfonso XII just three days short of his twenty-eighth birthday. Their son Alfonso XIII, born posthumously in 1886, would only reach his majority in 1902.

The Queen presided over the most formal court in Europe, apart from the Vatican. Isolated in her loneliness, she grew attached to the diffident Casals and spent hours talking to him and listening to his music. He played the cello for her in her small library while she embroidered or did needlepoint. Occasionally they played piano duets, and he noted that Maria Christina played Mozart competently. Despite his anti-monarchist views, and his dislike of courtiers and court intrigue, he enjoyed his informal visits, when he also played with the young Alfonso, nine years his junior, though always referring to him as 'Your Majesty'.

The Queen gave Casals a scholarship with an allowance of 250 pesetas a month, and when he was still only 18, she decorated him with the Medal of the Order of Isabel la Católica. This was followed a few years later with a sapphire, which he had mounted in his bow, a Gagliano cello and the Order of Charles III. Unsurprisingly he lauded her as 'my protector', thought of her as his second mother and, even after being feted by nearly every other Queen in Europe, Maria Christina, to Casals, was always 'my Queen'.

Contacts had brought Casals to the attention of the Spanish Queen and similar good luck would bring the cellist to the Drawing Room of the British Queen. In the spring of 1899 Casals accompanied the American-born soprano Emma Nevada on her British tour. He played at the Crystal Palace in Sydenham under the direction of the conductor August Manns. *The Standard* noted, 'Señor Casals is a master of his instrument, his playing being marked by virility and perfect technique.'

His performance brought him to the attention of London society hostess Constance Eliot, and he performed for her at her Kensington home. In his old age Casals recalled, 'she asked me: "Would you like to play for her Majesty?" I said I would be happy to do so.' Constance was the wife of Colonel Charles Eliot, holder of the grandiose title 'Gentleman Usher and Groom of the Privy Chamber' to Victoria. Thanks to her undoubted use to his career, Casals was soon lauding Mrs Eliot as 'my English mother'.

On Wednesday 2 August Casals took the train from London to Southampton accompanied by Ernest Walker, the pianist who had performed with him at Mrs Eliot's house the previous month. They took the ferry to the Isle of Wight and dined at a hotel in Cowes, before the coach arrived to take them to Osborne House. Here they were met by a footman and escorted to a large room where they sat for half an hour surrounded by paintings of a kilted Prince Albert surveying some dead Highland prey.

Eventually the Master of the Household, Sir Edward Pelham-Clinton, escorted the musicians into the royal Drawing Room. In his 90s, Casals still recalled, 'an air of hushed solemnity in the small room ... and before-hand the guests – there were about thirty of them – conversed with one another in barely audible voices.' They were introduced to two future kings, Albert Edward, Prince of Wales, who would succeed his mother as Edward VII, and the Duke of York, later George V. Casals was more interested to meet his hostess:

I was curious to meet Queen Victoria, who was then eighty and a legendary figure. She was a small stout woman with soft wrinkled cheeks and prominent eyes. She wore a headdress of white lace that came down to her shoulders.

While Victoria chatted to a British admiral, Sir John Hopkins, Commander-in-Chief of the Mediterranean Fleet whom she had knighted earlier in the day, her other guests watched on in respectful silence. Casals began to wonder when he should start playing, but then 'an Indian servant in a green silk dress and yellow turban placed a stool under her feet and she raised a plump hand for the concert to begin'.

Victoria was handed a large hand-lettered programme, which seems a tad unnecessary for a recital of three short pieces. Casals had chosen an Italian sonata, the allegro from Saint-Saëns' cello concerto and Fauré's Élégie – all heard in total silence apart from the pedal squeaks of the American Chickering piano. 'There was no applause between the pieces,' recalled Casals in old age, although the Queen did make a few comments in German to her daughter Princess Beatrice, but when he finished the concert there was polite applause.

At the end of the performance 'two six-foot Indians came and grasped the Queen's arms, and helped her slowly, inch by inch … from her chair'. She was then escorted over to Casals and Walker. Victoria must have been told Casals didn't speak English since she addressed him in French when she thanked him for playing. She asked him about the red ribbon of the Spanish decoration pinned to his jacket and said that the Queen of Spain had spoken about him. She added that she hoped his artistic career would repay all the honour and trust that had been given to him.[2]

Then the Queen left the room, still leaning on her Indian servants. 'Before I left the Duke of Connaught [Victoria's third son] chatted briefly with me in Spanish and asked me to sign my name in the "Book of Honourable Guests".'[3]

Afterwards Pelham-Clinton gave Walker a silver cigarette case engraved with Victoria's cypher of 'VRI', as well as gold cufflinks for Casals. The cellist later claimed that Victoria also left him a medallion bearing a cameo portrait of herself which he gave to his mother.[4]

Before going to bed, Victoria noted in her journal:

After dinner a young Spaniard Señor Casals played on the violoncello most beautifully. He is a very modest young man, whom the Queen of Spain has had educated & from whom he received his fine instrument. He has a splendid tone & plays with much execution & feeling.[5]

Victoria also found time to dictate a message in German to the Spanish regent. 'Some time later,' recalled Casals in 1970, 'when I was in Madrid, Queen Maria Christina gave me as a present a telegram she had received from Queen Victoria following the concert.' The British Queen 'said she had found my playing *entzüchend – delightful*.[6] The same word echoes down through the years in a letter written on 5 August by another eye-witness, Harriet Phipps, one of Victoria's Women of the Bedchamber, to Marie Mallet, a Maid of Honour: 'His cello playing is *quite* delightful.'[7]

Despite his republican leanings, which never bothered Alfonso XIII – 'That is your privilege,' said the King – Casals had memorable meetings with most of Europe's Queens. In 1898, aged 21, he performed at the inauguration of the 18-year-old Wilhelmina of the Netherlands. At the Dutch border he was detained and interviewed at length, since he bore an uncanny likeness to a young anarchist who had been making assassination threats.

The same year he and the pianist Harold Bauer played for Carlos I of Portugal and his consort. Queen Amélie was reckoned to be the most beautiful Queen of her time. Casals found himself standing next to Carlos as they both gazed at his wife sitting on a couch surrounded by admirers. The King caught Casals' eye and gave him a huge wink.

Bauer joked about the contrast in size between the 6ft-plus Amélie and the pint-sized cellist. Casals retorted, 'It's not that I'm too small; it's that the Queen's too tall.'[8]

Apart from Maria Christina, it was the bird-like Queen Elisabeth, wife of Albert I of Belgium, whom he had the strongest bond with. Elisabeth was taught the violin by Eugène Ysaÿe – dubbed 'the King of the Violin'. What she lacked in talent she more than made up for in enthusiasm, bringing out her violin at many a private concert. Unfortunately her teacher couldn't make a silk purse out of a sow's ear, and while Casals loyally claimed Elisabeth 'plays like a Queen', Ysaÿe more accurately said 'she plays badly divinely'.

Casals had a later brush with British royalty when he played for the 18-year-old Prince of Wales, later Edward VIII, at the Royal Albert Hall in 1913. It was a charity concert given by the League of Mercy for its workers. Edward, like his father George V (who is reputed to have told the conductor Thomas Beecham his favourite opera was *La Bohème* because 'it's the shortest one I know'), was a philistine when it came to the arts. Referring to his opera-loving nephew and godson George Lascelles, he once said, 'It's very odd about George and music. You know his parents were quite normal – liked horses and dogs and the country.'

Sixty-two years after performing for Victoria, Casals played in front of another head of state, at the Camelot court of US President John F.

Kennedy. The one-hour programme on 13 November 1961 began with Mendelssohn's *Trio in D Minor*, and included five short pieces by Couperin, a Schumann allegro and the traditional Catalan 'Song of the Birds'. Afterwards, over supper, there was another reminder of Casals' longevity in the public eye when he was introduced to an elderly white-haired lady, Alice Roosevelt Longworth, who recalled another performance by the cellist in the same house, fifty-eight years earlier, hosted by her father, President Theodore Roosevelt.

Old age would also bring a coda to his relations with the Spanish Royal Family. While on a visit to Greece in 1966 to conduct a performance of his peace oratorio *El Pessebre*, Casals met Juan Carlos, grandson of Alfonso XIII and father of the present King Felipe of Spain. Casals told him, 'I have known five generations of Spanish royalty, beginning with Isabel II.' The following day the Prince and his wife Sophia called on the cellist in his hotel room. He later noted, 'they brought with them their two year old daughter [Elena]. And so I came to know the sixth generation.'[9]

In his late 80s he also paid a final visit to the UK where he told a correspondent from *The Times*, 'I am very moved to be here again. I have so many wonderful friends here. But many are gone – Tovey, Sir Henry Wood, Elgar ...' and with a gleam of mischievousness '... Queen Victoria.' 'To what extent was the Queen a music lover?' asked the youth from *The Times*. 'When I played for her she seemed to enjoy it!' replied the maestro, surely aware of the impact of his words, adding, 'She was enchanted with my playing.'[10]

Notes

1   Casals, Pablo: *Joys and Sorrows*: MacDonald: 1970: p.58
2   Kirk, H.L.: *Pablo Casals*: Hutchinson & Co.: 1974: p.120
3   Casals: Op. Cit.: p.88
4   Kirk: Op. Cit.: p.120
5   RA VIC/MAIN/QVJ (W) Wednesday 2 August 1899 (Princess Beatrice's copies). Retrieved 8 August 2017
6   Casals: Op. Cit.: p.88
7   Malet, Victor: *Life With Queen Victoria*: John Murray: 1968: p.xx
8   Kirk: Op. Cit.: p.112
9   Casals: Op. Cit.: p.66
10 *The Times*: Thursday, 3 October 1963: p.8

PITCH PERFECT

IVOR NOVELLO'S MOTHER AND FOUR WELSH CHOIRS IN FIVE YEARS

Above: The Welsh Ladies' Choir in their national dress. (Ceredigion Museum) *Right*: Clara Novello Davies.

IT TOOK decades from the death of the Prince Consort before Victoria felt able to resume her love of theatre, opera and concerts. Thirty years separated two Welsh choir performances in front of the Queen on her visits to the principality itself. In the last decade of her life she invited Clara Novello Davies and her female singers to Osborne. She enjoyed it so much that three Welsh male voice choirs were also asked to sing for her.

In October 1859 the Queen and Prince Albert spent the weekend as guests of Colonel Edward Tennant at Penrhyn Castle in North Wales. Tennant owned the local colliery and on the evening of Sunday 16 October the royal couple were entertained by a choir of a hundred voices made up of his tenants, as Victoria noted:

> [the] Quarry Men, with their wives & children sang most beautifully. They have such fine voices, sang in such good tune & such difficult things. Psalms, pieces from the 'Messiah', chiefly in Welsh, which is universally, & in many instances solely spoken by the people here.[1]

On her return to London the Queen sent a cup to be presented to the choir to mark the event.

Thirty years later, the Queen returned to North Wales and stayed at Palé Hall near Bala, accompanied by her granddaughter Alicky, the future Empress Alexandra of Russia. Once again local singers entertained her:

> After dinner, the choir of Llanderfel, 40 in number, sang in the Hall Welsh airs, quite beautifully. I remember in 59 at Penrhyn how well all the people sang, & how wonderfully the miners belonging to Col: D. Pennant sang sacred music & therefore much looked forward to hearing Welsh singing again. All the women or girls wore their nice national dress, with their hats on but without caps underneath. The Leader of the Choir, Mr Jones, a school master, came up & I spoke to him, also to 3 of the girls, to whom I said, I hoped they would never give up wearing their hats.[2]

Earlier in the day a deputation of Palé tenants presented her with 'a very handsome & useful walking stick, cut out of a tree on the estate ... I learnt from the fisherman & Keeper to say "I am much obliged" in Welsh, which pleased the people very much.'

Meanwhile on the south coast of Wales Clara Novello Davies (1861–1943) had in 1883 founded the Welsh Ladies' Choir, which toured America in 1887 and won the first prize for a ladies' choir at the Eisteddfod. Named after the famous soprano Clara Novello (1818–1908) who performed for Victoria many times during the first twenty years of her reign, Clara married David Davies, a solicitor's clerk with the same name as her own. Their son David Ivor Davies was better known as Ivor

Novello (1893–1951), famed for penning a host of sentimental hits from 'Keep the Home Fires Burning' to 'We'll Gather Lilacs' and for Ivor Novello Awards, named in his honour, for songwriting and composing.

At the beginning of 1894, while they were giving a series of concerts in Southampton, Davies was invited to bring her choir to perform for the Queen at Osborne. Private Secretary Henry Ponsonby issued the invitation, asking that the Queen would like to see the singers in their Welsh national dress, in particular the hats, which had fascinated her at Palé Hall.

On Thursday 8 February they sailed from Southampton at 6 p.m., arriving thirty minutes later at East Cowes, where thirteen royal carriages were waiting to transport the thirty-eight singers, Clara, her father and husband and other staff to the royal residence. An accompanying reporter from the *Western Mail* observed that they all wore 'a very subdued air'. They were shown to the Durbar Room, 'brilliantly lighted by electricity' noted the same chap, where a makeshift dressing room had been erected behind a stage. Presumably it was here that Clara, according to her later memoirs, 'carried off by mistake one of the Royal monogrammed hairbrushes'.[3]

Just before 10 p.m. the Queen walked slowly into the room using a walking stick and leaning on the arm of her Indian servant, Abdul Karim. She sat in a cushioned seat in the middle of the front row, with her eldest daughter, the Empress Frederick, on her right and her youngest daughter Beatrice on her left. Also present was her third son, Arthur, Duke of Connaught, and his wife Louise.

After an elongated, four-verse National Anthem in Welsh and English the Queen picked up her red morocco-bound programme with its white silver hangings. The choir sang eleven songs beginning with the patriotic 'Cymru Fydd' and ending with a Welsh air. The Queen had approved the programme herself, swapping 'God is my Guide' for a less ecclesiastical 'The Hawthorn Hedge', sung by Miss Bessie Evans and Miss Annie Jenkins. The Queen was noticed with tears rolling down her cheeks at the sentimental ballad 'Darby and Joan'. Usually concerts for Victoria were observed in respectful silence by the royal audience until the end, but here she, and therefore her Household also, loudly applauded each song, with the Queen beating her fan on her palm.

During the evening she spoke to Clara three times, telling her, 'You have got them so thoroughly in hand!' and enquiring, 'Did you take all these young ladies to Chicago?' She also acknowledged 'the two lovely contralto voices you have' (alluding to Dot Prosser and Bessie Evans) and at one point was heard saying to Vicky about Davies, 'Is not she a sweet pretty little thing?' After asking Clara what 'Cadw Hon' meant ('keep this') and telling the choir en masse, 'I am perfectly delighted with your singing!' the Queen stood through another lengthy National Anthem before leaving on the arm of the Empress.

In her journal for the 8th, the Queen recorded:

> We went over to the Durbar Room, where a Welsh Ladies Choir, 35 in number sang. They were placed on a low platform at the further end of the room. A lady accompanied on the piano, & a Mrs Davies conducted the Choir. They all wore their national dress, with those curious pointed hats over caps. They sang as the Welsh always do, most beautifully, in such perfect time & with such modulations. Some of the voices were very rich & fine, & there were some splendid contraltos. I spoke to Mrs Davies & her husband. All the Household were present, & some of the servants.[4]

As usual the relieved choir was given a lavish buffet supper before they set off for East Cowes at 1 a.m. on Friday morning. Clara had left a photograph of the choir in a walnut frame decorated with an imperial Crown, the date, a Welsh harp and two leeks.

The following day a telegram was sent from Osborne: 'The Queen hopes that the members of the Welsh Ladies' Choir party got back comfortably last night.' More significantly, henceforth they were to be known as the Royal Welsh Ladies' Choir.

Choral Competitors

As we have seen, the Queen's Welsh was limited to 'I am much obliged' and the bilingual National Anthem. It is doubtful she'd ever heard of 'Cythraul y Canu' ('Demon in Music') which neatly encapsulates the intense musical rivalry of two of the principality's finest choirs.

Singing was more than a passion; for a time it was everything that mattered in the coal-mining communities of the Rhondda. When England played Wales at a rugby match in Newport in 1891 they were watched by a crowd of 8,000. A few months later the National Eisteddfod's Chief Male Voice Choir Competition was watched by 20,000.[5]

The Treorchy (or Treorky as it was known to Victoria and many of her contemporaries) Choir began life in the Red Cow Hotel in 1883. A mile or so away in Ton Petre, its soon-to-be arch rival, the Rhondda Glee Society, had been singing since 1877.

Now neighbour was pitted against neighbour and miner against miner. Competition adjudicators took their lives into their hands as disgruntled supporters of the losing choir hurled tomatoes, books and chairs at the judges. The rivals spilled out into the streets and nearby fields to continue the punch-ups long into the night.[6]

Even the conductors Tom Stephens and William Thomas were rivals. Both began life in the Cynon Valley between Rhondda and Merthyr Valley. There the similarity ended. Stephens, a strict teetotaller and pre-centor of the Ton Petre Bethesda Chapel, conducted the Rhondda Glee Choir. Thomas was landlord of the Blacksmith's Arms in Treherbert as well as conductor of the Treorchy Choir.

A decade of intense rivalry started with the 1889 National Eisteddfod at Brecon. Their next meeting ended in a mass brawl in the streets and the constabulary dragging away bloody-faced competitors.

Queen Victoria's innocent invitation to perform before her at Windsor only fanned the flames.

The Treorchy Male Voice Choir: 29 November 1895

The eighty-four-man Treorchy Choir had won first prize at the National Eisteddfod at Llanelli in August 1895, with three of the four judges independently writing the word 'Wonderful' in their note, but it was the summons to appear before the Queen a month before Christmas that was the real icing on the cake of 1895.

What probably secured the invitation was the fact that the men and their families lived on some of the 40,000 acres of Welsh soil owned by the Earl and Countess of Dunraven. The Earl was Under-Secretary at the Colonial Office in Lord Salisbury's first and second administrations until he resigned in sympathy when his friend Lord Randolph Churchill also handed in his notice. Writing in her journal, Victoria, with her finger as always on the political gossip, put this down to 'disappointed personal motives'.

Dunraven was a passionate yachtsman, and a loyal attendee of the Cowes Week regatta. In his memoirs he recalls his horror at returning to land 'in wet-through flannels after a hard race, and finding a Command to dine at Osborne!' With only 'my shirt and undies ... all I had my own', Dunraven went round the fleet to scrounge stockings, frock coat, waistcoat, tie, etc. The pumps came from 'dear old Monty Guest', whose feet were elephantine. Summoned to have a word with the Queen, Dunraven flapped his way into the presence 'a fearful figure of fun ... The Queen was most gracious. I don't know if she was conscious of the plight I was in, but I do know that I was.'[7]

In August 1895 he was again a dinner guest at Osborne during the visit of the Queen's grandson Kaiser Wilhelm II, another yachting fanatic. It may have been then that Dunraven brought the award-winning Treorchy Choir to the attention of Victoria and her Household.

A date was fixed for a command performance at the end of November. On the 29th a special train was laid on from South Wales to Windsor, which arrived at 5 p.m. Accompanying them was Owen Morgan, the journalist from the *Western Mail*, who wrote under his bardic name of Morien, and who also documented the Clara Davies visit. The Treorchy visit received blanket coverage in the entire Welsh press, and seemingly most of those not in the Rhondda Glee Choir came out to wish the choir well as they set off.

At Windsor, the men split up into groups of six to twelve and headed off to find their various lodging houses in the town, reconvening at 8.30 p.m. at the statue of Queen Victoria that still exists on Castle Hill. Here they were each handed a black tie and told to march four abreast 'with military precision' through the castle's Lower Ward and on to St George's Hall. Here, at the eastern end of the room, was a railed-off screen underneath the organ loft, where a gallery had been erected for the singers to use.

As the clock struck ten the Queen entered and, as before, was leaning on the arm of her Indian attendant, the latter wearing a crimson costume and a fez. The Queen sat between her two daughters Beatrice and Louise and near to her second son, the Duke of Edinburgh. Just as the conductor, William Thomas, was about to begin proceedings, the Queen brought everything to a halt by criticising the lighting. 'I cannot see them very well,' she complained. As attendants scattered in search of hand lamps, she quickly added, 'I want to see their faces.'

Wielding his baton, Thomas began conducting 'Druid's Chorus' by Dr Joseph Parry. Sensing the choir was nervous, the Queen started the cheering and applause by clapping her fan on the programme. The Welsh hymn 'Aberystwyth', again by Dr Parry, received a subdued response, before 'The Tyrol' perked things up.

At this point the Queen asked to speak to Thomas, telling him, 'Your singing is beautiful and the training is exceedingly good. What refined voices they have!' She then asked Thomas if the men were all miners and was told, 'Yes, Your Majesty, all except a few tradespeople who are connected with the colliery district.'

Thomas resumed with a guaranteed royal tearjerker: a rendering of 'Gotha', a hymn tune composed by the Prince Consort and set to Welsh words, which, according to 'Morien' was received with 'profound and respectful silence'.

The choir was about to end with the National Anthem when the Queen asked her son-in-law Prince Henry of Battenberg to add another chorus or two. Thomas selected 'The Destruction of Gaza', which was effectively sung and the Queen cheered loudly, 'Beautiful! Beautiful' before asking who wrote it: 'Is he a Welshman?' 'No,' replied Thomas, 'he is a Frenchman', which made Victoria laugh. She then asked for 'Y Delyn Aur' and another chorus of 'Aberystwyth'.

The Queen later wrote an appreciative account in her journal:

> After dinner we went to St. George's Hall where a Welsh Choir, 94 in number, all miners from Ld Dunraven's estate & a few tradespeople sang. The Choir is called Treorky. Nothing can exceed the beauty of their singing, & the wonderful soft voices, so beautifully trained. They sang some Welsh songs, & other Glees. The conductor, Mr Thomas, a very homely sort of man, was presented.[8]

The Rhondda Glee Society: 22 February 1898

The other South Wales choir finally had its day in the sun when it was summoned to perform before the Queen some two and a quarter years after the Treorchy choristers.

Once again there was blanket coverage in the local media. That 'there is a thrill of delight throughout the frame of every Welshman in the principality' (presumably apart from the Treorchy choir and fans) was typical. As before there was a specially chartered Great Western train, cheering crowds and a brass band send-off.

The choir of 75 arrived in Windsor at 6 p.m. and had tea in the White Hart Hotel, where they were booked to spend the night. They too processed in quick time to St George's Hall where, once again, a performing area had been erected at the East End, with conductor Tom Stephen's rostrum set to the right to allow Victoria an unimpeded view of the choir.

The programme was a similar mix to the Treorchy one – Welsh classics 'Men of Harlech' to 'Land of my Fathers'; the sentimental 'Little Church'; the rousing 'Soldiers' Chorus' from *Faust*; and the loyal National Anthem in English and Welsh, and 'God Bless the Prince of Wales' in Welsh only.

The Queen entered on the arm of Abdul Karim and sat on a low black armchair, next to a small round table bearing her opera glasses, a magnifying lens and her red morocco-bound programme. This time, to make sure she could see the faces, a row of electric footlights illuminated the choir.

On this occasion there was no cheering from the royal party. The pro-Rhondda Glee coverage in the local press claimed this was because Treorchy had only worn 'Sunday clothes' and had therefore been received and treated as miners, whereas their rivals had turned up in evening dress and were treated as professionals.

This is clearly wishful thinking on the part of the writer since when Victoria said to the conductor, 'Mr Stephens, your singing is most magnificent. Are the members of your choir professionals?' She was told, 'No, Your Majesty, there is only one professional here. Three-fourths of the choir are miners.'

The Queen asked another guest, Mr W.O. Morgan, 'The Rhondda Valley is where there was a serious accident some time ago, is it not?' She was referring to the Tylorstown pit explosion of 1896 which had killed fifty-seven men and eighty ponies. It led to a change in safety procedure in mines, since autopsies revealed many of the men had died of carbon monoxide poisoning. Caged canaries, which were particularly susceptible to it, were brought into the mines after this. On a lighter note, the Queen asked him what the Welsh for 'Queen' was – something that appeared to faze him.

After the concert Stephens was presented with a souvenir jewelled tie pin bearing the Queen's VRI cypher, and she asked him to sign her Birthday Book.

The Queen noted in her journal:

> After dinner went to St. George's Hall, where the famous Rhondda
> Valley Choir sang, to the number of 75, conducted by Mr Stephens.
> They sang a number of fine choruses & songs, including some in
> Welsh, & quite beautifully. The Welsh are so musical & have such
> fine melodious voices.

She added, 'They were all miners', which isn't of course what Stephens
had told her.[9]

The following morning before leaving Windsor the Rhondda Glee
men were given a guided tour of the castle grounds, which appears to
have been one up on the Treorchy boys.

In Fiction and Film

In the 1939 novel *How Green was My Valley*, based on the Rhondda
mining community of Gilfach Goch, writer Richard Llewellyn depicts
a fictitious Welsh choir going to Windsor Castle to sing for the Queen.
Llewellyn, who actually lived in England, spent summer holidays with
his grandfather in the Rhondda and returned shortly before the war
to research his book. He must have been made aware of the Treorchy
and Rhondda Glee visits. In the novel Ivor, oldest brother of the narra-
tor Huw Morgan, is commanded to bring the choir to perform for the
Queen. In return he receives a signed photograph of Victoria and an
inlaid ivory baton as a present.

Hollywood rapidly turned it into a successful tearjerker movie, with
a non-Welsh cast, which won Academy Awards in 1941 for its director,
John Ford, and for Best Picture, controversially beating *Citizen Kane*.

The Final Welsh Chorus – Ervri Male Choir: 1899

A conductor who actually did receive a thank-you baton after performing at Windsor was John Williams (1856–1917), conductor of the Ervri
– or Royal Ervri as it became known – Male Choir, based in Carnarvon.

The choir had been asked to sing during the state visit of the German
Emperor, Wilhelm II, the news being conveyed to the secretary of the
choir, W. W. Lloyd Griffith, by the local MP, David Lloyd George. A list of

suggested pieces was submitted to the Royal Household. It included the ubiquitous 'Soldiers' Chorus' from *Faust*, which Victoria crossed off the list as she admitted she'd never liked it.[10]

The fifty-strong choir arrived in Windsor at 4.30 p.m. on 24 November. It was made up of men from Carnarvon and Llanberia, about half of them being employed at the Dinorwic Slate Quarries (closed in 1969 and now home to the Welsh National Slate Museum) and none of them professional.

On arrival at the castle shortly before 9 p.m., they received the disappointing news that the Queen would be unable to attend their performance due to mourning for Princess Marie of Leiningen. Victoria was one of the few who understood the complicated gradations of royal mourning. 'Marie L', as she referred to her, was the wife of the Queen's step-brother's son, but also a close friend to Victoria. The Queen carried on the programme for her grandson's state visit, including the banquet, but eschewed all other entertainment, including seeing the choir. For some reason William, although a grandson, as well as the Prince of Wales and the audience of 150 were exempt.

The Queen did however ask how the performance went, noting in her journal, 'Did not talk long after dinner, as there was some music for William – a Welsh Choir, which sang quite beautifully.'[11]

Notes

1 RA VIC/MAIN/QVJ (W) Sunday 16 October 1859 (Princess Beatrice's copies). Retrieved 24 August 2016

2 RA VIC/MAIN/QVJ (W) Friday 23 August 1889 (Princess Beatrice's copies). Retrieved 24 August 2016

3 Davies, Clara Novello: *The Life I Have Loved*: Heinemann: 1940

4 RA VIC/MAIN/QVJ (W) Thursday 8 February 1894 (Princess Beatrice's copies). Retrieved 24 August 2016

5 Powell, Dean: Rhondda Glee Club: retrieved 30 June 2018 from www.treorchyma-lechoir.com

6 Ibid.

7 Dunraven, the Earl of: *Past Times and Pastimes*: Hodder and Stoughton: 1922: p.50

8 RA VIC/MAIN/QVJ (W) Friday 29 November 1895 (Princess Beatrice's copies). Retrieved 24 August 2016

9 RA VIC/MAIN/QVJ (W) Tuesday 22 February 1898 (Princess Beatrice's copies). Retrieved 24 August 2016

10 *Llangollen Advertiser*: 1 December 1899

11 RA VIC/MAIN/QVJ (W) Friday 24 November 1899 (Princess Beatrice's copies). Retrieved 24 August 2016

A DICKENS OF A CRUSH
QUEEN VICTORIA AND CHARLES DICKENS

Charles Dickens. (Library of Congress)

HER VERDICT: 'He is very agreeable, with a pleasant voice and manner.'

His verdict: 'She is strangely shy … and like a girl in manner.'

On 9 March 1870 two of the iconic figures of the nineteenth century met, chatted and charmed each other for half an hour or so. He was the son of a one-time debtor and she was one of his greatest fans.

The following day's Court Circular dutifully recorded the historic event: 'Mr Charles Dickens and Mr Arthur Helps had the honour of an interview with Her Majesty this afternoon at Buckingham Palace.' For the host, Queen Victoria, it was fifth time lucky, as the author had turned down four earlier requests to be introduced; for her guest it was an embarrassing reminder of his twenty-something pretend crush on the young monarch.

The royal link dates from the 1830s. Despite being warned as a girl against reading novels by her mother, the Duchess of Kent, Victoria read the newly published *Oliver Twist* from cover to cover. She was clearly enthralled, as a long stream of references in her journal testifies. For example: 'Read in Oliver Twist, and the account of the murder of Nancy by Sikes [sic] – too horrid, and made my blood run cold, – but beautifully done – as also the man's feelings after the murder.'[1]

Aged 19, she recorded in her journal that she was much affected by 'its accounts of starvation in the workhouses'. Her Prime Minister, Lord Melbourne, kept her pitiably ignorant of the conditions so many of her subjects lived in, and was dismissive of the book. 'It's all among Workhouses and Coffin Makers and Pickpockets,' he lectured the impressionable monarch, adding, 'I don't like these things; I wish to avoid them; I *don't* like them in reality and therefore I don't wish to see them represented.' Victoria, protective of her literary hero, added, 'We defended Oliver very much but in vain.'[2]

Although she professed, 'I never feel quite at ease or at home when reading a novel,' Victoria waded through her fair share and was an assiduous, if pretty bland, reviewer. She found *The Last of the Mohicans* 'very interesting' and 'very horrible'; *The Mill on the Floss* was 'wonderful and painful'; 'the description of the mysterious maniac's nightly visit' in *Jane Eyre* 'was awfully thrilling'; while in *Adam Bede* she discerned a 'likeness to the dear Highlanders' in Adam. Her favourite writer was Sir Walter Scott, whom she dubbed her 'beau ideal of a poet'. There were apparently twelve copies of *Rob Roy* at Balmoral and thirty-two of his *Lady of the Lake*.

While the young monarch was thumbing through the latest bestsellers at Windsor Castle, she herself was unknowingly being perused by the ascendant Dickens, and becoming a bit of an in-joke between him and his arty friends. In February 1840 he wrote to his friend T.J. Thompson that he and another friend, the artist Daniel Maclise, 'are raving in love for the Queen – with a hopeless passion whose extent no tongue can tell, nor mind of man can conceive'. They had been to Windsor for a tour of the royal apartments and professed to be inconsolable that three days earlier she had married Prince Albert of Saxe-Coburg and Gotha, whom Dickens renamed 'the German Sassage [sausage] from Saxe Humbug and Go-to-her'.

He decided he would die for Victoria, either by throwing himself in the Serpentine or by 'heading some bloody assault on the palace and saving Her by my own hand'. Then, continuing in the same hyperbolic vein, he said he would like to be 'kept on the top of the triumphal arch of Buckingham Palace when she [was] in town, and on the north east turret of the Round Tower when she [was] at Windsor'. The pretend infatuation probably owed more to his fondness for what he dubbed 'fun and raillery' than a genuine crush, though Victoria's biographer Christopher Hibbert suggests her features 'bore a passing resemblance to his beloved sister-in-law Mary Hogarth'.

Certainly there were no chirpy mentions of her after he glimpsed her in the audience during his first royal command performance eight years later. Victoria and Albert were regular theatre-goers, heading into the West End sometimes three or four times a week and often seeing the same play or musical time and again.

The couple first saw Dickens acting in an 1848 production of Ben Jonson's *Every Man in His Humour*. In May 1851 she paid £50 for a ticket to see Sir Edward Bulmer Lytton's *Not So Bad As We Seem* at a charity fundraiser held at Devonshire House in aid of the Guild of Literature and Art, where guests included the Duke of Wellington. Afterwards she wrote in her journal, 'All acted on the whole well. Dickens (the celebrated author) admirably and Dr Jerrold, a funny little man, who writes in *Punch*, extremely well.'[3]

On 4 July 1857 the Queen attended another fundraiser: a performance of Wilkie Collins' *The Frozen Deep*, starring Dickens, his brother Alfred and eldest daughter Mamie (Mary). Victoria had invited Dickens to perform the play for her at Buckingham Palace, but in the first of several slights to the monarch he declined. His excused himself on the technicality that since his daughter hadn't been presented at court he didn't want her first palace appearance to be as an actress.

After the actual performance in front of the royal couple, the King of the Belgians and Hans Christian Andersen at the Gallery of Illustration in Regent Street, Victoria again tried her luck at meeting Dickens face to face, but to no avail. According to biographer Edgar Johnson, the author's 'almost bristling sense of his own dignity' was the problem. Dickens gave his own reasons for turning her down in a letter to his friend John Forster:[4] 'My gracious sovereign was so pleased [with the performance] that she sent round begging me to go round and see her and accept her thanks. I replied that I was in my Farce dress, and must beg to be excused.' Victoria sent for him again, saying, 'the dress could not be so ridiculous as that,' but Dickens wouldn't relent. He nevertheless earned a glowing review in the Queen's journal: she declared his acting 'beyond all praise and not to be surpassed'.

Victoria's theatre jaunts ended with Albert's death on 14 December 1861, when she plunged herself into a prolonged isolation that Dickens labelled 'very unsatisfactory'.

She did however gradually renew her literary interests. Exactly four months after the Prince's death she summoned the equally shy, morbid and unsociable Alfred, Lord Tennyson to tea at Osborne House. Although she found him 'very peculiar looking' and his *Holy Grail* left her 'quite bewildered', the visit perked up when the poet wept at the very mention of Albert's name, forging an immediate bond with the reclusive widow.

A few years later the American poet Henry Wadsworth Longfellow fared less well during his audience. After the Queen had complimented him on his work, he gushed that he hadn't realised how popular he was in England. Victoria reassured him, 'You are very well known. All my servants read you.'

By the late 1860s, fuelled by the publication of her own *Leaves from the Journal of Our Life in the Highlands* (described by the Prince of Wales as 'twaddle' but a runaway success with the public), Victoria began turning into a bit of a literary anorak. She asked the Dean of Westminster to arrange an academic gathering for her entertainment. The guests included George and Harriet Grote, Charles Lyell, Thomas Carlyle and Robert Browning. 'Rather amusing the literary line the Queen has taken up,' wrote her Maid of Honour, Mary Bulteel, sniffily to her husband.

She also asked favoured authors to send her signed copies, coming memorably unstuck with the Reverend Charles Dodgson, writer and mathematician. Legend has it that having admired *Alice in Wonderland* (penned by him under the name Lewis Carroll), she sent the message that she looked forward to reading anything else he produced. By return post she received a copy of his *Syllabus of Plane Algebraic Geometry.*

Meanwhile Dickens still remained tantalisingly out of her grasp. Yet another royal request, this time for a private reading of *A Christmas Carol,* was turned down on the grounds that as a performer he needed an audience and couldn't face reading it to her *à deux.*

Finally Dickens succumbed after the Queen sent a message to say she would like to thank him in person for some photos he had loaned her of the American Civil War. An audience was fixed for 9 March 1870, and Victoria even travelled up from Windsor to Buckingham Palace to suit the author, who'd been suffering from a painfully swollen left foot which he'd been having poulticed since the previous Christmas. Royal protocol dictated that Dickens should stand throughout their meeting, though in what was termed a 'gracious gesture' the Queen stood too, or to be exact, leaned against a sofa the entire time.

Beforehand the author wrote to Arthur Helps, the Clerk of the Privy Council, to say he would be 'proud and happy to wait upon Her Majesty'. Then, with a hint of that early facetiousness whenever the Queen came to mind, he wrote that if an honour was in the pipeline, 'We will have "of Gad's Hill Place" attached to the title of the Baronetcy, please' – a reference to his home at Higham in Kent.

By both their accounts the meeting was a success. They talked of everything from the servant problem and the high cost of food to Fenianism in America and Lincoln's foretelling his own assassination in a dream two weeks before his death. The Queen gave another sledgehammer of a hint that she would like a private reading but Dickens said his performing days were over, despite having another two to go in his final series of twelve readings.

Perhaps to prove her regal omnipotence Victoria asked for a complete set of his works to be delivered 'this afternoon'. Once again Dickens demurred and insisted on having time to order a specially bound red morocco and gold collection. (They were duly sent and made a reappearance in February 2012 when Elizabeth II held a reception at Buckingham Palace attended by Dickens' descendants to mark the two hundredth anniversary of his birth.)

Three months after their meeting Dickens died on 9 June 1870. On hearing of his death the Queen recorded:

He is a vy great loss. He had a large, loving mind and the strongest sympathy with the poorer classes. He felt sure that a better feeling, and much greater union of classes wld take place in time. And I pray earnestly it may.[5]

Notes

1 RA VIC/MAIN/QVJ (W) Monday 7 January 1939 (Princess Beatrice's copies). Retrieved 9 January 2018
2 RA VIC/MAIN/QVJ (W) Sunday 7 April 1939 (Princess Beatrice's copies). Retrieved 9 January 2018
3 RA VIC/MAIN/QVJ (W) Friday 16 May 1851 (Princess Beatrice's copies). Retrieved 9 January 2018
4 Johnson, Edgar: *Charles Dickens – His Tragedy and Triumph*: Viking: 1977
5 RA VIC/MAIN/QVJ (W) Saturday 11 June 1870 (Princess Beatrice's copies). Retrieved 9 January 2018

12

Thoroughly in Tune
Edvard Grieg Plays for Victoria

Edvard Grieg. (University of Bergen)

THE NORWEGIAN composer and pianist Edvard Grieg (1843–1907) was
a firm favourite of Alexandra, Princess of Wales, whom he met on his
1889 visit to England. He only met Queen Victoria once, at the end of
the Diamond Jubilee year of 1897, though she continued to have his
compositions played for her in her remaining years.

On 6 December 1897 an excited Victoria wrote to her eldest daughter from Windsor Castle, 'We are going to hear Grieg and his wife play and sing his beautiful composition this evening.'[1] The meeting was, as always, dutifully recorded by the Queen in her journal:

> After tea went to the White Drawingroom, where we heard the celebrated Norwegian composer Grieg, whose music I admire so much, play his own Compositions. His wife sang some of his songs, very well, with a pretty voice & much feeling & Wolff played twice with him. Grieg is elderly, very small, nice & simple, but he has very delicate health. He played with great expression & wonderful power. Some of the things were well known to me. Both he & Mme Grieg spoke German.[2]

Unusually the following morning's Court Circular gave details of the full performance. Grieg opened up proceedings, using the royal piano to play an extract from his third violin sonata accompanied by the violinist Johannes Wolff.

Nina Grieg then sang three songs before the composer played three pieces: 'Humoresque', 'Berceuse' and his celebrated 'Norwegian Bridal Procession'. After two more songs by Mme Grieg, the performance ended with extracts from the first violin sonata, once again accompanied by Wolff.

It wasn't the first time the Queen had heard the violinist. In September 1888, during her autumn stay at Balmoral, she noted, 'M. J. Wolff, a Dutchman, who is staying at Invercauld, played 2 or 3 pieces most beautifully on the violin.'[3]

She heard him again the following year at both Osborne and Balmoral, noting, again from her Highland residence, 'Afterwards Monsieur Wolff played most beautifully on the violin, accompanied by Beatrice, & Minnie Cochrane. I never heard him play better & for feeling & tone he is decidedly superior to Nachez.'[4]

Grieg gives a detailed account of his royal concert in a letter to his friend and fellow Norwegian, the writer Hans Brækstad:

> I'm not wild about court affairs, as well you know, but this was something quite different. The Queen is *sweet*, if one can say this about an elderly lady. She was full of enthusiasm. She knew practically everything in the programme, *enjoyed* Nina's singing in

Norwegian, and asked for more. I then played the 'Gavotte' from the *Holberg Suite*. When I was introduced to her, she said, 'I am a warm admirer of your music.' Everything was natural and genuine. She spoke about Peer Gynt and would have liked to have heard 'The Death of Aase' and 'Last Spring' for string orchestra. I declined all offers of a meal and took the next train home.[5]

A third account, written the same evening as Grieg's and the Queen's by Marie Mallett, a Maid of Honour, is effusive about the composer; less so about his wife:

Grieg came this evening at six and played his divine music, he is real genius. He told the Queen his great-grandfather hailed from Aberdeen and was called Greig. His wife sang, very funny to look at and her voice 'passée', but interesting all the same.[6]

Two days after the concert Grieg was still glowing with pride at the evening's success. In a letter to another friend, Frants Beyer, he recalled:

The other day we visited Queen Victoria at Windsor ... It was *very* interesting, compared to other court affairs. She's a *woman*, and one who is interested and interesting to talk with. She speaks German superbly. Nina sang at her best, I played at my ditto – and Johannes Wolff his. She gave me her Jubilee Medal and Nina received a brooch inscribed with her [the Queen's] name.[7]

The royal command performance proved to be a useful marketing tool. With seats still available for the following Saturday's concert at the Brighton Dome, the local newspaper trumpeted:

Edvard Grieg, fresh from a brilliantly successful appearance before the Queen and court at Windsor, where he played a selection of his delightful compositions, and was presented with the Diamond Jubilee Medal by Her Majesty, will give his eagerly anticipated Recital at the Dome tomorrow ...[8]

Although the Queen never met the composer again, she remained a fan of his work. Twelve days after the concert she wrote in her journal at

Osborne, 'Only the Ladies to dinner, including Minnie Cochrane, who has come for 2 days. She & Beatrice played lovely things by Grieg in the Drawingroom afterwards.'[9] Three days after Christmas 1897 she noted, '20 members of my Band, who have come for some days, played a very pretty selection of music, by Grieg.'[10]

Three months before her death, the Queen invited Johannes Wolff for a final performance, once again assisted by Princess Beatrice on the piano: 'Afterwards we had some charming music. Wolff played beautifully, pieces by Grieg, Beethoven, Wieniawski & Thomé, Beatrice accompanying him. My Band also played in between.'[11]

The Windsor Castle concert wasn't the composer's first brush with the British Royal Family. On 22 March 1889 the Prince and Princess of Wales with three of their children – Prince Albert Victor, and Princesses Victoria and Maud – heard him play at a private concert at the French Embassy near Hyde Park. (The Griegs would become close to Maud when the latter became Queen Consort of Norway in 1905.) Alexandra invited Grieg and his wife to visit her at their London residence, Marlborough House. At this subsequent meeting Grieg was flattered to see a selection of clearly much-used copies of his works lying on the piano. The Princess gave him a diamond breast pin and Nina a diamond brooch.

On 28 May 1906, during his last visit to England, Grieg visited Edward and Alexandra, by now King and Queen, at Buckingham Palace. Afterwards Grieg noted in his diary that Edward, '(who is said to be the most unmusical Englishman of all), told me that he was very fond of my music, which he often heard when it was played outside the Palace by the military band.' The King persuaded the Norwegian to play for them and so 'I let loose on the Bechstein, and, remembering the Queen's deafness, pounded away at the Menuetto from the Piano Sonata'. His host proved he was 'unmusical' by talking animatedly to another guest. Grieg paused and looked 'questioningly' at the King, who responded with a broad smile. The pianist continued and minutes later Edward started chatting again. 'Now I got angry and made a longer pause … It's pretty rude to request music and act like that.' Another eyewitness noted the monarch maintained a 'pained but absolute silence' for the rest of the recital.[12]

The composer was still seething about the incident when he returned to Norway and mentioned it to King Haakon, Edward's son-in-law. Haakon loyally explained that Edward was one of those rare people who can listen to a concert and carry on a conversation at the same time.

Grieg was having none of it: 'Well, whether he is a King of England or an ordinary man, it's wrong and I do not accept it. There are some things that out of regard for my art I absolutely cannot do.' He added for good measure, 'It's all very well for him to want to defend his father-in-law, but there's a limit to everything.'[13]

Grieg was en route to England the following year when he collapsed and died of heart failure on 4 September 1907, aged 64. By chance Queen Alexandra was holidaying in Norway with her daughter Victoria and her sister, the Dowager Empress of Russia. Together with Queen Maud they attended a special mourning performance of *Peer Gynt* at the National Theatre that same evening – a clear indication of the effect the news of Grieg's death had on the royal families and the country of his birth.

Notes

1 Ramm, Agatha (ed.): *Beloved and Darling Child*: Alan Sutton: 1990: p.209
2 RA VIC/MAIN/QVJ (W) Monday 6 December 1897 (Princess Beatrice's copies). Retrieved 26 March 2018
3 RA VIC/MAIN/QVJ (W) Monday 23 September 1888 (Princess Beatrice's copies). Retrieved 5 April 2018
4 RA VIC/MAIN/QVJ (W) Thursday 3 October 1889 (Princess Beatrice's copies). Retrieved 5 April 2018
5 Carley, Lionel: *Edvard Grieg in England*: Boydell: 2006: p.280
6 Mallet, Victor: *Life With Queen Victoria*: John Murray: 1968: p.120
7 Carley: Op. Cit.: p.281
8 Carley: Ibid.: p.289
9 RA VIC/MAIN/QVJ (W) Saturday 18 December 1897 (Princess Beatrice's copies). Retrieved 26 March 2018
10 RA VIC/MAIN/QVJ (W) Tuesday 28 December 1897 (Princess Beatrice's copies). Retrieved 26 March 2018
11 RA VIC/MAIN/QVJ (W) Saturday 20 October 1900 (Princess Beatrice's copies). Retrieved 26 March 2018
12 Carley: Op. Cit.: pp.388–9
13 Carley: Op. Cit.: p.397

13

'THESE HORRIBLE CRIMES'
VICTORIA AND 'JACK THE RIPPER'

Victoria had her own ideas of how to catch Jack the Ripper. (*Illustrated London News*)

VICTORIA'S JOURNALS contain a single reference to the Whitechapel murders. At Balmoral on 4 October 1888 she wrote, 'Dreadful murders of unfortunate women of a bad class, in London. There were 6, with horrible mutilations.'[1]

It is interesting that she refers to six murders. The generally accepted number of women murdered – known as the 'Canonical victims' – is five, and all date from 1888. They are Mary Anne Nichols (31 August), Annie Chapman (8 September), Elizabeth Stride (30 September), Catherine Eddowes (also 30 September) and Mary Jane Kelly (9 November). Clearly Kelly's murder occurred after the Queen's journal entry, which leads one to believe she had included two of the dozen or more alleged victims. It is an interesting point, since she would have been privy to the information supplied by the police to her government.

In early October, Victoria received a petition signed by 400–500 'women of East London' highlighting 'the lives of those of our sisters who have lost a firm hold on goodness, and who are living sad and degraded lives'. They urged the Queen to direct her 'servants in authority' to 'close bad houses within whose walls such wickedness is done, and men and women ruined in body and soul'.

Victoria passed on their letter to the Home Office and Godfrey Lushington, the Under-Secretary of State, replied on the Queen's behalf. He told the women that the Home Secretary was in communication with the police commissioners 'with a view to taking such action as may be desirable in order to assist the efforts of the petitioners, and to mitigate the evil of which they complain'.[2]

The day after Kelly's murder, the Queen sent a blunt message to the Prime Minister, Lord Salisbury:

> This new most ghastly murder shows the absolute necessity for some very decided action.
>
> All these courts must be lit, and our detectives improved. They are not what they should be. You promised, when the first murder took place, to consult with your colleagues about it.[3]

Three days later the Home Secretary, Henry Matthews, received an even more exasperated missive from Balmoral:

> The Queen fears that the detective department is not so efficient as it might be. No doubt the recent murders in Whitechapel were committed in circumstances which made detection very difficult; still, the Queen thinks that, in the small area where these horrible crimes have been perpetrated, a great number of detectives might

be employed, and that every possible suggestion might be carefully examined and, if practicable, followed.

Have the cattle boats and passenger boats been examined?
Has any investigation been made as to the number of single men occupying rooms themselves?
The murderer's clothes must be saturated with blood and must be kept somewhere.
Is there sufficient surveillance at night?
These are some of the questions that occur to the Queen on reading the accounts of this horrible crime.[4]

From this letter it was clear the Queen – operating as a one woman CSI from Deeside – was aware of rumours that the Ripper might be a crewman of a sea vessel or a lodger in a London boarding house.

Over the following century or more, the Ripper has been linked with a 'Who's Who' of late nineteenth-century manhood, with everyone from the artist Walter Sickert to Winston Churchill's father Randolph in the frame. It was even suggested that Victoria's grandson, Prince Albert Victor, was a possible contender. The Prince was the eldest son of the Prince of Wales and therefore set to be the future king until his untimely death from influenza in 1892.

In 1970 Dr Thomas Stowell, in an article in the *Criminologist*, wrote that an unnamed 'heir to power and wealth' had committed the murders. His theory was that the 'heir' (although it was not long before it emerged whom he was referring to), in the final stages of syphilis of the brain, contracted from prostitutes, had sought revenge on 'ladies of the night' and that the Queen's physician-in-waiting, Sir William Gull, had helped cover up the scandal. This argument was discredited two years later when a trawl through the Court Circulars for 1888 proved that the Prince had alibis on the dates the atrocities were committed. For instance on 30 September he was in Scotland and he had lunch with the Queen on the day two of the women were butchered.[5]

Interestingly, the Albert Victor link surfaced again in February 2016, when two confidential letters from the Prince to his doctor were put up for auction. In them he describes the sufferings he was going through from 'glete' – a term used to describe the discharge caused by gonorrhoea – most likely caught from a prostitute, as it was known he visited brothels.

'Ripperologists' however still refute the possibility of his involvement, citing the argument, mentioned above, about his well-documented engagements.

Notes

1 RA VIC/MAIN/QVJ (W) 4 October 1888 (Princess Beatrice's copies). Retrieved 24 November 2016

2 *East London Observer:* Saturday 27 October 1888

3 Queen Victoria to the Marquess of Salisbury (Cypher Telegram) Balmoral Castle, 10 November 1888

4 Hibbert, Christopher: *Queen Victoria in her Letters and Journals:* John Murray: 1984: p.314

5 Rappaport, Helen: *Queen Victoria – A Biographical Companion:* ABC-Clio: 2003: pp.209–12

14

THE CHURCHILLS
WINSTON CHURCHILL'S MOTHER AND FATHER IMPRESS THE QUEEN

Lord and Lady Randolph Churchill.

LORD RANDOLPH Churchill (1849–95), the third son of the 7th Duke of Marlborough and his wife Lady Frances Vane, was a Tory radical whose disloyalty to the Prime Minister, Lord Salisbury, infuriated Queen Victoria and prematurely ended his promising political career. His American-born wife, Jennie Jerome (1854–1921), was a legendary beauty whom the Queen thought 'so handsome' and the Prince of Wales added to his long list of amoureuses.

The parents of the wartime leader Winston Churchill met at Cowes Regatta on the Isle of Wight in the summer of 1873. They were introduced by the Prince of Wales, known to his family as 'Bertie'. Randolph was one of the Prince's Marlborough House set, named after Bertie's official London residence, whose 'members' shared a fondness for racing, card games and parties. The Prince was already friends with Randolph's elder brother, the Marquess of Blandford. He took an immediate shine to the stunning, erudite Jennie and his Private Secretary Francis Knollys was best man at their wedding in April 1874.

Three weeks into her marriage, Jennie was presented to the Queen at a Drawing Room held on 5 May by her mother-in-law, the Duchess of Marlborough, who was a friend of Victoria's. In a letter to her mother, Clara Jerome, Jennie recounts that the Duchess 'was very kind and lent me some rubies and diamonds, which I wore in my hair, and my pearls on my neck, I also had a bouquet of gardenias'. The Queen was, inevitably, dressed in black silk with a matching train trimmed with black ostrich feathers, a white tulle veil and an emerald and diamond diadem.

In the same letter Jennie tells how nerves got the better of her, causing her to break with protocol, much to Victoria's surprise. As she was making her curtsey to the Queen, 'I reached to kiss her hand ... she pulled me towards her and kissed me, which proceeding so bewildered me that I kissed her in return and made several little bobs to the other royalties instead of curtseys'.[1]

On 30 November 1874, Jennie gave birth to a son, Winston Leonard Spencer Churchill, at Blenheim Palace. The young parents were still socially in the ascendancy, but a clumsy action on the part of Randolph just over a year later incensed the Prince of Wales and then his mother.

In October 1875, Bertie embarked on an extensive tour of the Indian subcontinent. He would visit twenty-one towns and cities before returning to England in May 1876. Accompanying the Prince was 'Sporting Joe', the 7th Earl of Aylesford, another of the Marlborough House set. While the royal party was in Nepal a letter to the Earl from his wife Edith Aylesford informed him that she had been unfaithful with the Marquess of Blandford. She wondered if Joe would like her to leave him now or to wait until his return, as 'she was willing to live as his wife before the world but no more'.[2]

Bertie, who himself was having an intermittent affair with Lady Aylesford, declared Blandford had openly compromised Edith and that he should leave his own wife, Albertha, and marry Edith.

At this point Randolph recklessly wrote to the Prince and demanded he should withdraw his total support for Sporting Joe or he, Churchill, would publish compromising love letters written by Bertie to Lady A. Hearing about this, Victoria insisted the Prince of Wales should forward Randolph's letter to her. 'What a dreadful, disgraceful business,' she wrote to her eldest son. 'Poor Lord Aylesbury should not have left her.' Then, as if to prove that when it came to society gossip she still had her finger on the pulse, she added, 'I *knew* last summer that this was going on.'[3]

Society now turned its collective back on the Randolph Churchills who, after an extended tour of Canada and the USA, moved to Dublin with the Duke of Marlborough, who had been appointed Viceroy of Ireland. The Duke managed to convince his younger son to pen a full apology to Bertie. The Queen prepared an even more contrite one and had him sign that too.

The final reconciliation was marked with a dinner party hosted by the Churchills for the Prince and Princess of Wales and other VIPs including William Gladstone. Benjamin Disraeli, who had died two years earlier, had predicted that once Randolph's political career had started to take off, the Prince would be unable to resist resuming the friendship, as '[he] is always taken by success'.[4]

Jennie too was firmly back in favour. Four days before her dinner party she attended another of Victoria's Drawing Rooms at Buckingham Palace and was making occasional visits, with and without Randolph, to Sandringham.

In 1885 Randolph was made Secretary of State for India in Lord Salisbury's first ministry. The Queen said she had 'no insuperable objection' to the appointment, although she certainly objected two months later when he threatened to resign after she made her favourite son, the Duke of Connaught, Commander-in-Chief of the Bombay Army without consulting Churchill. Recurrent bouts of ill-health, traditionally said to have been caused by tertiary syphilis contracted in his university days (although multiple sclerosis or a brain tumour have also been suggested), account for his often near-hysterical reactions. These were frequent but never lasted long. Over the Connaught appointment, a weary Salisbury was able to reassure Victoria, 'he has returned to reason "having taken calomel" and is not going to resign.' The Queen urged the Prime Minister to 'restrain Lord Randolph as much as he can'.[5] He didn't have long to restrain him since Salisbury's caretaker government was dissolved on 1 February 1886 and the Churchills were obliged to head home.

It was during this tenure that Jennie received a personal honour from the Queen. On 30 November 1885, Victoria's Private Secretary, Henry Ponsonby, wrote to Randolph, 'The Queen wishes to personally confer the Insignia of the Order of the Crown of India on Lady Randolph Churchill on Friday next, the 4th of December at three o'clock. Will she come back here to luncheon?' Jennie was delighted to accept and received a brief note from a Lady-in-Waiting about what to wear: 'Lady Randolph Churchill – Bonnet and morning dress, gray gloves.'

She recounted the meeting in her memoirs, written shortly after Victoria's death: 'The Queen, with one of the princesses and a Lady-in-Waiting received me in a small room. She stood with her back to the window, wearing a long white veil which made an aureole round her against the light.' Then, after a 'few kind words to me', the Queen pinned the order on to Jennie's left shoulder, quite literally, as it turned out. 'I remember that my black velvet dress was thickly embroidered with jet, so much so that the pin could find no hold, and unwittingly the Queen struck it straight into me.' Jennie gave a start 'and the Queen realizing what she had done was most concerned'.

As the recipient curtsied her way out of the room, Victoria 'suddenly stepped forward saying with a smile, "Oh! You have forgotten the case," holding it out to me at the same time'. It was a nice little natural touch that Jennie always remembered.[6] A few days later, Lady-in-Waiting Jane Ely wrote to Jennie to let her know, 'the Queen told me she thought you so handsome, and that it had all gone off so well.'

Shortly after the ceremony, the Churchills were asked to a 'dine and sleep' at Windsor. Jennie recalled:

we dined in [a] small room, the walls of which were hung with family portraits by Winterhalter. Conversation was carried on in whispers, which I thought exceedingly oppressive and conducive to shyness. When the Queen spoke, even the whispers ceased. If she addressed a remark to you, the answer was given while the whole company listened.

Nevertheless she was pleased that 'the Queen was most amiable ... and talked to me for some time'.

While they were there 'the household seemed slightly agitated, and the Queen retired earlier than usual'. It transpired that Princess Beatrice had given birth to a son, Prince Alexander of Battenberg.[7] Following the 200-year-old tradition, a government minister had to be present to witness the arrival of the royal child. The Home Secretary, Henry Matthews, was rushed across from London. Jennie was put out by this snub to her husband. Apparently Victoria thought Randolph 'too young', though he was married, a father, and actually on site.

The Queen's account of the dinner was cryptic: 'Talking in the corridor till ½ p. 10. Ly Randolph (an American) is very handsome, & very dark. He said some strange things to me, which I will refer to later.' Apparently this concerned the government's conduct in India. Victoria noted, 'Lord Randolph was looking very ill.'[8]

By then Randolph was part of Lord Salisbury's second ministry. The Queen had noted in her journal in July that Salisbury had 'feared Lord Randolph Churchill must be Chancellor of the Exchequer and Leader, which I did not like. He is so mad and odd, and also in bad health.'[9]

Her opinion changed as the ministry progressed, as one of her letters to him testifies:

> Now that the session is just over the Queen wishes to write and thank Lord Randolph Churchill for his regular and full and interesting reports of the debates in the House of Commons, which must have been most trying. Lord Randolph has shown much skill and judgement in his leadership during this exceptional session of parliament.[10]

She was even amused when she discovered that the grey substance in the government boxes turned out to be ash from the highly strung, cigarette-smoking minister.

She was less amused when she heard that Churchill had decided to step down from his post while staying with her at another Windsor 'dine and sleep'. Not only had he failed to tell her of his intentions during his stay – although she did note he looked 'gloomy' and 'tired' – but he tendered his resignation to Salisbury on Windsor Castle notepaper. While the Queen fumed at Windsor, the Prince of Wales wrote to his mother accusing her of being, 'if you will allow me to say so, rather hard on Lord R. Churchill', whom he felt 'has at any rate the courage of his opinions'.[11] The two men enjoyed each other's company and often corresponded. When the Prince forwarded one of Churchill's letters to his mother, the

Queen, more furious than ever, 'blasted this most objectionable and even dangerous correspondence' and ordered Bertie to 'break off all communication with Lord Randolph'.[12]

It has been alleged that Bertie and Jennie were having a physical relationship by the late 1880s. The evidence is circumstantial, though the bulk of his many friendly notes and letters to her date from 1886 to 1890. Jennie's letters to the Prince remain under lock and key at Windsor and were never released to her several biographers.[13]

It was Jennie's close relationship with the Prince, rather than her marriage to an aristocratic MP, that gave her a prime position in Westminster Abbey at the Queen's Golden Jubilee thanksgiving service in June 1887. She described to her sister the gorgeous uniforms and dresses warmly illuminated by the 'dim religious light pierced here and there by the rays of the summer sun as it streamed through the ancient stained glass windows'. She also noted the effect the service had on Victoria, 'as silent tears were seen to be dropping one by one upon the Queen's folded hands'.[14] On a lighter note she had the Prince of Wales in hysterics at dinner parties by pretending she had a jubilee bustle that played 'God Save the Queen' when she sat down. In actual fact it was a small servant hidden under the table with a music box, but the ruse worked well.

The following December the Churchills paid a private visit to Russia. Alexandra, Princess of Wales had given them a letter of introduction so they could meet her sister the Empress Marie and brother-in-law Tsar Alexander III. Jennie was already a close friend of the Emperor's sister, another Marie, who was married to Victoria's second son, Prince Alfred. When news of the visit reached the Queen's ears it once again pitched her into conflict with the Prince of Wales. Bertie told his mother, 'my impression is that he [Randolph] will be careful.'

The Queen sent a strongly worded letter to her heir, telling him she couldn't understand '*your* high opinion of a man who is clever, undoubtedly, but who is devoid of all principle … who is very impulsive and utterly unreliable'. Once again she urged the Prince to have nothing to do with the former minister.

On his return to Britain, Lord Randolph forwarded details of his meeting with the Tsar and the latter's insistence that the United Kingdom should not involve itself in the Black Sea and the Dardanelles, as Russia would only countenance Turkey or itself dominating the area. Rather than treating the account with respect, Lord Salisbury forwarded it to the Queen with the curt note, 'It seems odd that so clever a man should attach the slightest value to such a promise on the part of Russia.'[15]

By 1894, the onset of general paralysis was affecting Randolph's ability to speak, and his last address to the House of Commons was in June of that year. He and Jennie went on an extensive tour that took them to the United States, China, Japan and finally India, where his worsening condition forced them to return home. He died on 24 January 1895 in London. By coincidence his eldest son, Sir Winston, died in the capital on the same day exactly seventy years later.

Despite having once been thrown out of the Churchill home by Randolph for openly flirting with Jennie, the Prince of Wales penned a touching note to the young widow:

My dear Lady Randolph, the sad news reached me this morning that all is over … & I felt that for his and your sakes it was best so … There was a cloud in our friendship but I am glad to think that it is long been forgotten by both of us.

Jennie's last meeting with Queen Victoria was at another 'dine and sleep' at Windsor in November 1899. She and several other rich American ladies based in Britain, including the Duchess of Marlborough (the former Consuelo Vanderbilt, who was married to Randolph's nephew, the 9th Duke) and Mrs Joseph Chamberlain, who funded an American hospital ship for the relief of the wounded troops in the Boer War. Concerts, entertainments and private donations raised £45,000 in two months. The steamship *Maine* was adapted into a floating hospital and Jennie and her committee managed to get retail companies involved. Quaker Oats donated several hundred packages of porridge, the American Tobacco Company gave 10,000 cigarettes and the California Wine Company donated crates of their finest.

When the American staff arrived from New York they were taken to Windsor to meet the Queen. Jennie, who had not seen Victoria since the death of Randolph, introduced them on the morning of 6 November, having dined with the Queen the previous evening. After greeting the assembled crew, Her Majesty's only comment was, 'I think the surgeons look very young.'[16]

At the time of the Queen's death in January 1901, Winston was on the Winnipeg leg of a lecture tour of the USA and Canada. Like his mother he wondered what life would be like for her in the reign of King Edward VII. 'So the Queen is dead,' he wrote rather irreverently to Jennie. 'A great and solemn event and I am curious to know about the King … Will he become desperately serious? Will he continue to be friendly to you? Will the Keppel [Bertie's *maîtresse en titre* and the great-grandmother of the current Duchess of Cornwall] be appointed 1st Lady of the Bedchamber? Write to tell me all about this to Queenstown.'[17]

As it turned out, Bertie the King remained as loyal to Jennie as Bertie the Prince. At his Coronation in August 1902 she shared a special VIP seating area with Alice Keppel and other paramours past and present – an area which was waggishly referred to as 'the King's Loose Box'. He remained on close terms with Jennie until his death, aged 68, in the spring of 1910.

He also kept an avuncular eye on the fatherless Winston. In one lengthy letter he asked the future PM to come to see him to discuss his plans. In an effort to dissuade the young Churchill from pursuing 'the monotony of a military life', Bertie wrote, 'I can well understand that it must be very difficult for you to make up your mind what to do, but I cannot help feeling that Parliamentary & literary life is what would suit you best.'[18] The rest, as they say, is history.

Notes

1   Sebba, Anne: *Jennie Churchill*: John Murray: 2007: p.67
2   Ridley, Jane: *Bertie – A life of Edward VII*: Chatto and Windus: 2012: p.183
3   Martin, Ralph: *Lady Randolph Churchill*: Cassell: 1969: p.100
4   Ibid.: p.138
5   Ibid.: p.168
6   Cornwallis-West, Mrs George: *The Reminiscences of Lady Randolph Churchill*: The Century Co.: 1908: p.177ff
7   Ibid.: p.180ff
8   Martin: Op. Cit.: p.173
9   RA VIC/MAIN/QVJ (W) Sunday 25 July 1886 (Princess Beatrice's copies). Retrieved 16 May 2018
10 Martin: Op. Cit.: p.185
11 Sebba: Op. Cit.: p.153
12 Leslie, Anita: *Jennie*: Hutchinson: 1969: p.124
13 Sebba: Op. Cit.: p.153
14 Martin: Op. Cit.: p.196
15 Ibid.: p.208
16 Leslie: Op. Cit.: p.234
17 Sebba: Op. Cit.: p.252
18 Leslie: Op. Cit.: p.224

ANIMAL MAGNETISM
QUEEN VICTORIA AND LANDSEER

Edwin Landseer. (Wellcome Collection)

FAMED FOR his iconic painting *Monarch of the Glen* and for sculpting the Trafalgar Square lions, Edwin Landseer (1802–73) was quite literally artist in residence to Queen Victoria. With photography in its earliest blurred infancy, painting was still the only viable way for the young monarch to accurately document her growing family and innumerable pets. Along the way Landseer taught Victoria and Albert how to sketch and etch, and became a friend and artistic adviser, staying with them at Balmoral, Osborne and Windsor. His maddening dilatoriness in completing the royal commissions led to a ten-year break in the friendship until the newly widowed Victoria once again sought him out to help console her.

Landseer came to Victoria's notice in 1836 when her mother, the Duchess of Kent, commissioned him to paint the Princess's beloved King Charles spaniel Dash as a surprise seventeenth birthday present. 'After my lesson,' Victoria noted in her journal, 'Mamma gave me a portrait of dear Dash's head, the size of life, most beautifully painted by Edwin Landseer. It is extremely like.'[1]

The success of the portrait led to commissions from Victoria herself the following year, shortly after her accession. The first was to paint her dogs and her pet parrot Lory. In January 1838 she called the ongoing work 'a most splendid picture exquisitely painted of Dash, Hector and Nero'. On 9 April the artist presented the finished work, which the Queen felt was 'the most *beautiful* thing imaginable'.[2] She was however more critical of a small sketch of her first Prime Minister, Lord Melbourne, at a time when the young monarch was besotted with him. She felt it was 'like, but too fat, and though flattering is not in my opinion half pleasing enough'. She did, however, concede in the same journal entry that 'He certainly is the cleverest artist there is'.[3]

Landseer would go on to paint a total of twelve portraits of the royal dogs, including a critically acclaimed portrait of Eos, an Italian greyhound bitch that belonged to Prince Albert and accompanied him to England in 1840.

As with the Dash portrait mentioned above, some of these works were clandestine 'surprise' portraits commissioned by one member of the Royal Family, usually either the Queen or Prince Albert, for another. The go-between for these presents as well as the more above board commissions was Marianne Skerrett, dresser to the Queen from 1837 to 1862 and a name familiar to viewers of the ITV series *Victoria*. Miss Skerrett kept up a regular correspondence with Landseer and from her flirtatious but motherly missives it is easy to deduce that she was more than a little in love with him. Besides conveying the Queen's demands about the works she had ordered, Skerrett, in her letters, worries over the artist's health, urges him to have holidays and coquettishly admonishes him whenever he delays in replying to her. Landseer was amused by the short, thin and rather plain dresser. He called her 'the dearest and most wonderful little woman I ever knew. If anything goes wrong in Buckingham Palace, Balmoral or Windsor, whether a Crowned head or scullery maid is concerned, Miss Skerrett is always sent for to put it right.' Unfortunately her crush wasn't reciprocated and Landseer was known to amuse guests with stories about the Queen and her right-hand servant, and occasionally referred to the latter disparagingly as 'old Skerrett'.[4]

Among the 'surprise' portraits was a full-length side view of Victoria which she commissioned at the time of her betrothal to Albert and which he placed in his Writing Room at Windsor. The Queen wrote that she had 'sat for some little time to Landseer, who has made in three days the likest little sketch in oils of me, that was ever done; en profile, the back seen, in my morning dress … and with my blue [Garter] ribbon'.

Already references to Landseer's tendency to procrastination appear in the Queen's journals. In February 1839 she records a discussion with 'Lord M' on 'Landseer being lazy'. The 'surprise' anniversary presents, with their usually short notice and a deadline, were a particular worry. For Albert's twenty-second birthday on 26 August 1841 the Queen commissioned a portrait of the baby Princess Royal with Eos and a dove. With the big day looming and still no sign of the finished work, Victoria resorted to desperate measures. At 11 p.m. on the 25th a servant was despatched from Windsor to the artist's studio to seize the painting 'done or not done'. He arrived at two in the morning and was back at the castle at six with the work wrapped in a tablecloth but at least ready for the big day.[5]

During the 1840s Landseer worked on several conversation pieces which highlighted the couple's domestic life in a naturalistic way, and which were a world away from the formal, static royal portraits of previous generations. One of the most majestic, *Windsor Castle in Modern Times*, shows Victoria and Albert in the castle's Green Drawing Room. The central figure of the Prince, legs apart, hand on thigh, leather-booted and immaculately suited, seems to fill the silk and gold sofa. He is the hunter-gatherer surrounded by the day's kill. A display of lifeless ducks and pheasants are strewn across the priceless stools and rugs to show what he-man Albert has fetched home for the family, while the baby Princess Royal totters around holding a similarly blasted woodpecker. Meanwhile the Queen, looking demure in a cream silk gown, is femininity personified, holding a small posy and staring lovingly into her husband's eyes. Only the fact that she is standing, and therefore the highest of the three humans on the canvas, testifies to her elevated position as monarch. Although it was 12 June 1841 when Victoria wrote 'We saw Landseer, & settled about his picture of us', it took another four years before its completion. Despite the delay the Queen seems to have been delighted with it:

Landseer's Game Picture, (begun in 1840!!) with us 2, Vicky, & the
dear dogs Eos, old Islay, Cairnach & Dandie, is at last hung up in our
sitting room here, & is [a] very beautiful picture, & altogether very
cheerful & pleasing.[6]

A more unusual commission was Prince Albert's invitation in 1842 for
Landseer to join seven other distinguished Academicians in painting frescoes for the octagonal room of the Buckingham Palace summer house.
The instruction was to paint scenes from Milton's *Comus*, which the
Prince had seen at Covent Garden that March. The end result was lacklustre, with three of the demotivated artists repeating the same scene, and
two of them duplicating another. Sadly this peculiar work of art was not
cherished by Victoria's successors. A shortage of manpower in the Great
War left it unloved and untended. Damp and decay rendered the frescoes
past the point of a possible restoration and the summer house itself was
pulled down in 1928 on the orders of George V.[7]

By the 1840s Landseer could consider himself a privileged friend of
the royal couple. He stayed with them at the various royal residences
and walked with the Queen, helping her over stiles and advising her on
painting landscapes. He corrected her sketches, shared some of his own
with her, and taught her how to etch, with some of her earlier work
taken from his own drawings. The Queen has left an account of copying
Landseer's work while she was staying at Ardverikie House in Scotland's
Western Isles in 1847. She records how she 'amused myself by trying to
copy Landseer's fine drawings on the wall, & succeeded fairly well with
the stag'. Ardverikie House was destroyed by fire in October 1873. Queen
Victoria's drawings, still in the Royal Collection, along with one set of
photographs, are now the only records of the appearance of Landseer's
wall paintings.

On one occasion Victoria even surprised him by arriving unan-
nounced at his St John's Wood studio on horseback, to help him with
an equestrian portrait of her. She waited patiently by his gate while he
changed into a suitable outfit before he mounted a groom's horse and
then accompanied him. He kept the resulting sketch of her on prominent
display in his studio for the rest of his life.

The Queen also found his never-ending supply of weak and rather
obvious jokes appealing, although the humourless Prince disliked them,
such as the one about the Highlander who had trained his collie to search

out a hidden 5-pound note. 'And did he?' exclaimed Victoria eagerly. 'Well, Your Majesty, not the note,' replied Landseer, 'but he brought back the five sovereigns in change.' Later Albert, rather unnecessarily, sent a servant to tell the artist the Queen *hadn't* believed his story about the 5-pound note.[8]

Landseer was also a frequent guest at royal receptions. He enjoyed recounting how, in 1854, during the state visit of the teenaged King Pedro V of Portugal, the guest of honour collared him to say, in limited English, 'I am so happy to make your acquaintance. I am so very fond of beasts!'[9]

Friendship with the Royal Family had its drawbacks. Victoria and Albert were used to their peremptory requests, often issued at short notice, to attend them at one of the royal homes being respectfully agreed to. Landseer once ruefully commented to a friend about 'the good little Q' who 'is a very *inconvenient* treasure'.

The artist himself could also be maddening and Victoria's writings refer to his 'idleness and laziness', his 'never sending in bills' and his 'not coming to Windsor when I said he might paint me'. As for his seeming inability to complete works on time, that would be his eventual royal undoing.

The beginning of the end for Landseer came in 1850, the year he was knighted by the Queen. That summer he stayed with the Royal Family at the newly built Balmoral Castle, to which he would return briefly over the next three summers. Part of the reason for the visits was to paint a large portrait of Victoria and her family at Loch Muick. Known as *Royal Sports on Hill and Loch*, it was more familiarly known as the 'boat picture' since it showed the Queen stepping ashore from a small vessel after a fishing expedition and being greeted by Albert, the young Prince of Wales and several ghillies. There, also greeting her, was a recently killed stag which is inconveniently laid across a tartan-covered gangplank. Victoria, her family and her staff gave numerous sittings for the painting but eventually both they and Landseer grew tired of the project and a deflated monarch noted in her journal in April 1854 that she had sat for Landseer 'for the last time'.

The artist worked on the painting off and on until near his death. His constant reworkings in order to achieve a likeness of the Queen, which seems to have defeated him, ended with the surface of the canvas being ruined. It eventually entered the Royal Collection shortly after his death in 1873, though, like the Buckingham Palace summer house, it was allowed to deteriorate while in storage at Windsor Castle until

George V, the summer house bulldozer, ordered it to be destroyed. Today only an engraving survives. (Landseer himself experienced the cavalier attitude of the court to works of art when, early in the reign of Victoria, he witnessed an 'inspector of palaces' called Saunders cutting down a Gainsborough painting of George III's three eldest daughters so it would fit a space as an overdoor. Despite being topped and tailed, the cropped classic is still part of the Royal Collection, along with an engraving of how it was meant to look.)

After the 'boat picture' debacle it would be another ten years before Queen and artist met again. Several years into her deep and introspective widowhood, Victoria constantly reflected on her two decades of blissful union with the Prince Consort and their domestic happiness, especially in Scotland. Landseer had been on hand to document those years and in her grief the Queen reached out to him as a familiar figure from the past. Their meeting at Windsor was an emotional one for the artist, as Victoria revealed in a letter to Vicky: 'I saw Sir E. Landseer for the first time on Wednesday, and he cried dreadfully.'[10]

The Queen immediately commissioned a contrasting pair of paintings. *Prince Albert at Balmoral in 1860*, also known as *Sunshine*, shows the Prince looking handsome and undeniably masculine, with his gun nonchalantly balanced on his shoulder and yet another dead stag at his feet. This is in stark contrast to *Her Majesty at Osborne in 1866*, known as *Sorrow*. This shows the Queen in heavy mourning, side-saddle on her horse and diligently working on some of the never-ending official documents that are central to the life of a British monarch. Behind her sit two of her fatherless daughters, another focus of concern for Victoria who now had to be both parents to her children. It might well have been sympathetically received by critics and the public had it not been for the prominence of John Brown, the faithful ghillie, who accompanied the Queen everywhere. The painting helped spread the rumours that it wasn't only the Queen's reins he grasped tightly in his hands, and Victoria would soon be dubbed 'Mrs Brown' by the chattering classes.

During his last few years Landseer declined into a confusing world of mental instability, though he still managed to work. The Queen last saw him in 1871 'at Bertie's garden party', where she thought he was 'hardly fit to be about and looked quite dreadful'. For old time's sake she sent him a posy of flowers, telling him she was glad to hear 'you are gaining health so steadily'.[11]

In fact the artist was in a terminal decline and died on 1 October 1873. Victoria's tribute in her journal is surprisingly detailed and emotional:

After luncheon heard that the great artist & kind old friend had died peacefully at 11. A merciful release, as for the last 3 years he had been in a most distressing state, half out of his mind, yet not entirely so. … He was a great genius in his day, & one of the most popular of English artists. It is strange that both he & Winterhalter, our personal attached friends of more than 30 years standing, should have gone without 3 or 4 months of each other! I cannot at all realise it. How many an incident do I remember, connected with Landseer! He kindly had shown me how to draw stags' heads & how to draw in chalks, but I never could manage that well. I possess 39 oil paintings of his, 16 chalk drawings (framed), 2 Frescos & many sketches.[12]

A few days after his funeral procession through the streets of London, culminating with a service at St Paul's Cathedral, Victoria wrote to Vicky, 'You will have seen in the papers the account of dear old Sir Edwin Landseer's funeral and the great feeling shown at it by all classes and especially by the people.'[13]

Among the many tributes was a message that would have touched Landseer deeply. Attached to a wreath that was given pride of place was the message, 'A tribute of Friendship and Admiration for Great Talents. From Queen Victoria.'[14]

Notes

1 RA VIC/MAIN/QVJ (W) Monday 23 May 1836 (Lord Esher's typescripts). Retrieved 16 May 2018
2 Ormond, Richard: *Sir Edwin Landseer*. Thames and Hudson: 1981: p.144
3 RA VIC/MAIN/QVJ (W) Thursday 7 December 1837 (Lord Esher's typescripts). Retrieved 16 May 2018
4 Ormond: Op. Cit.: p.15
5 Lennie, Campbell: *Landseer – The Victorian Paragon*: Hamish Hamilton: 1976: p.121
6 RA VIC/MAIN/QVJ (W) Thursday 2 October 1845 (Princess Beatrice's copies). Retrieved 16 May 2018
7 Lennie: Op. Cit.: p.119
8 Ibid.: p.121
9 Weintraub, Stanley: *Victorian Yankees at Queen Victoria's Court*: University of Delaware Press: 2011: p.76
10 Lennie: Op. Cit.: p.217
11 Ibid.: p.233

12 RA VIC/MAIN/QVJ (W) Wednesday 1 October 1873 (Princess Beatrice's copies). Retrieved 16 May 2018

13 Fulford, Roger (ed.): *Darling Child*: Evans Brothers: 1976: p.112

14 Ormond: Op. Cit.: p.22

16

'SO TERRIBLE A CALAMITY'
VICTORIA MOURNS ABRAHAM LINCOLN

The assassination of Abraham Lincoln. (Library of Congress)

ON 29 APRIL 1865, and after a blustery walk with Princess Louise along the private beach in front of Osborne House, the Queen returned to her study and penned a highly emotional letter to Mary Todd Lincoln, widow of the recently murdered President of the United States:

Dear Madam,

Though a Stranger to you I cannot remain silent when so terrible a calamity has fallen upon you & your Country & must personally express my deep & heartfelt sympathy with you under the shocking circumstances of your present dreadful misfortune –

No one can better appreciate than I can, who am myself utterly broken-hearted by the loss of my own beloved Husband, who was the Light of my Life, – my Stay – my all, – what your sufferings must be; and I earnestly pray that you may be supported by Him to whom Alone the sorely stricken can look for comfort, in this hour of heavy affliction.

With the renewed Expression of true sympathy, I remain,

dear Madam,

Your Sincere friend

Victoria R.

The Queen's journal entry for the same day suggests the letter was perhaps meant for a wider audience:

> Wrote to Mrs Lincoln (widow of President Lincoln), which was much wished, & was quite touched by a letter from Mr Goldwin Smith (a great Democrat) who was so anxious I should write, saying it would do more good than anything else, as I was so much respected in the U. States.[1]

Mrs Lincoln was touched by the message from someone whose grief at the loss of a husband was still unassuaged more than three years after his death. 'Madam,' the former First Lady wrote from Washington on 21 May 1865:

> I have received the letter which Your Majesty has had the kindness to write. I am deeply grateful for this expression of tender sympathy,

coming as they do, from a heart which from its own sorrow, can appreciate the intense grief I now endure. Accept, Madam, the assurances of my heartfelt thanks and believe me in the deepest sorrow,
Your Majesty's Sincere and grateful friend.
Mary Lincoln.

Abraham Lincoln's letters to Queen Victoria are scrupulously deferential to the British monarch and occasionally excessive in sympathising or celebrating key moments in the Queen's life. After the death of Victoria's mother on 16 March 1861, Lincoln wrote:

Great and Good Friend: I have received the letter in which you have made known to me the affliction you have sustained in the death of your justly lamented parent, the Duchess of Kent. I tender to you my sincere condolence, with that of the whole American people, in this great bereavement, and pray God to have Your Majesty and your whole Royal Family constantly under his gracious protection and care. Written at Washington, this twenty-sixth day of June, in the year of our Lord one thousand eight hundred and sixty-one.
Your Good Friend,
ABRAHAM LINCOLN.[2]

The death of the Prince Consort the following December led to a volcanic eruption of sentiment from the White House. 'Great and Good Friend,' he wrote on 1 February 1862:

By a letter from your son, His Royal Highness, the Prince of Wales, which has just been received, I am informed of the overwhelming affliction which has fallen upon Your Majesty, by the untimely death of His Royal Highness the late Prince Consort, Prince Albert, of Saxe Coburg. The offer of condolence in such cases is a customary ceremony, which has its good uses, though it is conventional, and may sometimes be even insincere. But I would fain have Your Majesty apprehend, on this occasion, that real sympathy can exist, as real truthfulness can be practised, in the intercourse of Nations … The late Prince Consort was with sufficient evidence regarded as your counsellor in the same friendly relation. The American People, therefore, deplore his death and sympathize in Your Majesty's irreparable bereavement with an unaffected sorrow … And so, commending Your Majesty and the Prince Royal, the Heir Apparent, and all your afflicted family to the tender mercies of God, I remain Your Good Friend, ABRAHAM LINCOLN.[3]

Apart from the exchange of letters between the two widows, the other Lincoln letters were in fact official communications emanating from the State Department and were the voice of William H. Seward, Secretary of State, who had met Victoria and Albert in 1859. As far as we know, rather than interrupting his Civil War focus to write to a monarch across the ocean whom he'd never met, Lincoln is unlikely to have personally written a single word and simply signed them as required.[4] (Clearly neither man had any idea the Queen privately referred to Lincoln's North in the Civil War as 'that remnant of the United States'.)[5]

Nevertheless the letters are today still highly prized by the Royal Archives and in May 2011 they were displayed at Buckingham Palace and shown to President and First Lady Obama by Elizabeth II during the former's state visit. The Queen also presented her guests with a leather-bound facsimile of the US presidential letters held in the Royal Collection, as well as an antique gold-and-red coral brooch for the First Lady.[6]

More Lincoln/Seward collaborations were sent to the Queen and her 'August Family' on the occasions of the marriage of her second daughter Princess Alice to Prince Louis of Hesse in 1862, and the protection of the Almighty was invoked when the Prince of Wales married Alexandra of Denmark in 1863 and again the following spring after the Waleses welcomed an heir – Prince Albert Victor – on 8 January 1864.

A little-known memento in the Abraham Lincoln Presidential Library and Museum collection is a white swan's feather sent by the Queen in 1876 to Lincoln's Tomb (2 miles north of the museum), for display there shortly after its formal dedication in 1874. It is thought the feather came from St James's Park, or perhaps Windsor Great Park. It was displayed in the Museum in 2015 at the 150th anniversary of Lincoln's death.

While the Queen never met Abraham Lincoln face to face, she met his surviving son Robert Lincoln, who was US Minister to the Court of St James's from 1889 to 1893. The statuesque (6ft 4in) Lincoln must have towered over the diminutive monarch when he shook hands with her at Windsor at the start of his tenure. Victoria gave the occasion the briefest of mentions in her journal: 'Saw Ld Cross after luncheon, who introduced Mr Lincoln, son of the murdered President of that name.'[7]

In July 1889 Lincoln Jnr and his wife dined with the Queen at Windsor and after another Windsor dinner in 1893 she recorded that 'Mr Lincoln is very pleasant and sensible'.[8] A few weeks later Lincoln was the second minister of the morning to hand the Queen his letters of recall at the end of his term of office. Victoria noted 'he too is a loss'.

Notes

1 RA VIC/MAIN/QVJ (W) Saturday 29 April 1865 (Princess Beatrice's copies). Retrieved 11 April 2018

2 Basler, Roy (ed.): *Collected Works of Abraham Lincoln, Vol. 4*: Rutgers University Press: 1953

3 Basler, Roy (ed.): *Collected Works of Abraham Lincoln, Vol. 5*: Rutgers University Press: 1953

4 Email to the author from James Cornelius, Curator of the Lincoln Collection at the Lincoln Presidential Library, 10 April 2018

5 Weintraub, Stanley: *Victorian Yankees at Queen Victoria's Court*: University of Delaware Press: 2011: p.99

6 www.theguardian.com/world/2011/may/24/obama-palace-lunch-art-collection

7 RA VIC/MAIN/QVJ (W) Saturday 25 May 1889 (Princess Beatrice's copies). Retrieved 11 April 2018

8 RA VIC/MAIN/QVJ (W) Saturday 11 March 1893 (Princess Beatrice's copies). Retrieved 11 April 2018

17

LISZTOMANIA
QUEEN VICTORIA AND FRANZ LISZT

Franz Liszt.

FRANZ LISZT (1811–86) – Hungarian composer, virtuoso pianist and
conductor – met Queen Victoria three times and on one of these
occasions thought her so ill-mannered he refused to play. Their final
meeting occurred in April 1886, three months before his death, and
the Queen thought 'he played beautifully'.

Sixty-two years before he played for Victoria at Windsor, Liszt played for her uncle George IV at the same royal residence.

As a child prodigy he visited England three times in the 1820s. Accompanied by his father, Adam, he arrived in London in May 1824 and stayed in lodgings at 18 Great Marlborough Street. His debut took place at the Argyll Rooms on 5 June but the climax of the visit was his command performance for the King. Master Liszt played the royal piano for two hours and particularly impressed George with his improvisation on the Minuet from *Don Giovanni*. Turning to Adam, George exclaimed, 'This is quite unlike anything I have every heard. The boy surpasses Moscheles, Cramer, Kalkbrenner and all the other players, not only in the actual playing but in the wealth and development of his ideas too.'[1] The King even invited Liszt and his father to stay overnight at the castle, and when the two returned to Britain the following year, Liszt junior was again invited to play at the court. It was during this second visit that the future composer toured St Paul's Cathedral and was overwhelmed to hear a massed choir of several thousand children from the Free Schools. The memory of this impressive spectacle stayed with him for life and is said to have inspired the rousing climaxes of his oratorio *Christus*.

During the 1840s, when his career as a virtuoso pianist was firmly in the ascendant, Liszt twice played for Queen Victoria, first at Buckingham Palace in 1840 and five years later in Germany.

Their first meeting on 25 May 1840 was the day after Victoria's twenty-first birthday. It was only fifteen weeks since her marriage to Prince Albert at the Chapel Royal, St James's Palace on 10 February and she was almost as many weeks pregnant with her first child, also called Victoria, who was born on 22 November.

Three days before his visit to the palace, Liszt wrote from London to his mistress, the Countess Marie d'Agoult (1805–76):

> Next Monday, I am playing for the Queen, which everyone regards as being a big step as she never commands soloists to perform before her. It was d'Orsay* who arranged this by going around saying that the Queen was rather silly by bothering herself with Italian singers while there were artists such as Bull** and myself in London.[2]

---

* Alfred Guillaume Gabriel, Comte d'Orsay (1801–52), was a French aristocrat who lived in London with Marguerite Gardiner, Countess of Blessington (1789–1849).

** Ole Bull (1810–80) was a Norwegian violinist who also played at the palace concert.

Two days after the concert, Liszt again wrote to the Countess:

> The Queen was almost alone with Prince Albert the other evening.
> I think that I entertained her. She laughed a lot (which she is subject
> to do) when I said to her 'that my pride was not at all wounded that
> she did not remember me' (her mother had just asked me whether
> I hadn't played for her 14 years ago).[3]

In August 1845 Victoria and Albert travelled to attend a three-day festival marking the seventy-fifth anniversary of the birth of Beethoven, the
highlight of which was the unveiling of a large bronze statue of the composer on the Münsterplatz in Bonn, the city of his birth. The event took
place on 12 August and Liszt composed a special work to mark the event:
Festival Cantata for the Inauguration of the Beethoven Monument in Bonn.

Queen Victoria and Prince Albert were present as well as their hosts,
King Frederick William IV of Prussia and his consort, Queen Elisabeth.
A parchment signed by them was sealed inside a lead casket and placed
inside the monument. Guests from the world of music included the com-
posers Hector Berlioz and Giacomo Meyerbeer, the conductor Charles
Hallé, the soprano Jenny Lind and dancer Lola Montez.

The ceremony was witnessed by the royal guests from the balcony
of Prince Fürstenberg's palace. Due to an oversight the committee had
failed to provide places for the royal visitors in the square itself. Owing to
the positioning of the statue in relation to the palace, the viewing royalty
was presented with a view from the rear![4]

The event was followed by the signing of the Foundation Charter, now
in the Beethovenhaus, Bonn, with the signatures, inter alia, of Queen
Victoria and Liszt.[5]

The following day there was a four-hour concert, during which Liszt's
Festival Cantata was once again performed (or twice to be accurate, since
it was played once before the royal arrivals and a second time after they
had arrived). In honour of Beethoven his *Egmont* overture was given as
well as Leonora's aria from *Fidelio.*

Later that evening Victoria noted in her journal, from her suite at
Brühl Castle, near Cologne:

> At 9, we Queens, Kings & Princes & Princesses assembled &
> went into the Salon, which was full of people, & there was a fine

Concert. Meyerbeer accompanied, & fine Cantata composed by him, in my honour was sung by Standigl, Pischek, &c& Chorus. Mme Lind sang charmingly a piece out of Meyerbeer's new Opera 'das Nachtlager in Schlesien', & Mme Viardot, very well. Then Liszt played on the Piano.[6]

The reason the Queen clearly chose not to wax lyrical about the much-feted musician may lie in a series of events described by Liszt's friend and fellow Hungarian, Janka Wohl, in her memoirs. Wohl recounts that among the various dignitaries was the Archduke Friedrich of Austria. The Prussian court, with its rigid and inflexible attitude to ceremonial, gave him precedence over Victoria's beloved Albert:

This irritated the young woman to such an extent that it spoilt the whole entertainment for her. She abused the Ladies-in-Waiting, she got an 'attack of nerves', and took a gloomy view of everything.

The evening came, and the concert began. Queen Victoria arrived rather late, and did not appear to be herself at all, Liszt was to play an 'Introduction' but he had scarcely seated himself at the piano before the Queen complained of the heat, at which a chamberlain ran to open a window. In two minutes the Queen found the draught insupportable. Then the chamberlain hurried off again and shut the window. This produced a bustle and a going to and fro capable of ruining the effect of the finest performance in the world.

When the 'Introduction' was finished, the master, instead of playing the piece itself, got up, made a bow, and went out into the park to smoke a cigar. When, half an hour afterwards, he came back to the hall, King Frederick William got up from his place and said to him: ' You ran away just now; what was the matter?'

'I was afraid,' replied Liszt, 'of disturbing her Majesty Queen Victoria, while she was giving her orders.' The king laughed heartily, and begged him to continue his programme, which he did in the midst of respectful silence, Queen Victoria having left the hall shortly after his disappearance.[7]

Victoria wasn't the only head of state who irritated the maestro during a performance. Tsar Nicholas I of Russia clattered his way into the room during one of Liszt's concerts and then began to talk loudly throughout what remained of the recital. Liszt abruptly stopped playing and, when the Tsar asked why, the pianist stood up, bowed stiffly and said, 'Music herself should be silent when Nicholas speaks.' As the twentieth-century writer Sacheverell Sitwell noted, it was the first time that 'music herself' had answered back. (Perhaps Liszt's biting comment might have something to do with a gift presented by the Tsar. Whilst the rulers of Belgium, Turkey and Spain all bestowed orders of chivalry on the composer, the Emperor of Russia instead gave him two performing bears.)

When the Queen and Liszt met for the final time neither of them mentioned the Bonn debacle, only their earlier encounter at Buckingham Palace. The maestro had not been in Britain for over four decades and when news of his visit scheduled for the spring of 1886 was released he was inundated with requests to perform. He wrote to his friend Walter Bache, who had begged him to come to England one last time:

> They seem determined in London to push me to the piano. I cannot allow this to happen in public, as my 75 year old fingers are no longer suited to it, and Bülow, Saint-Saëns, Rubinstein, and you, dear Bache, play my compositions much better than what is left of my humble self.

Liszt spent three weeks in Britain in April 1886. On the 6th he received a standing ovation when he attended a performance of his oratorio *St Elisabeth* at St James's Hall in the presence of the Prince and Princess of Wales. They invited him to dine with them at Marlborough House on the 11th and afterwards he played for them.

The next day he journeyed to Windsor to meet the Queen. She had sent her Master of the Queen's Musick, Sir William Cusins, to ask Liszt to attend; which he did, although it prevented him from seeing another performance of *St Elisabeth* by pupils of the London Academy of Music.[8]

In a more glowing journal entry than her last one about the composer she wrote:

> After luncheon, we went to the Red Drawingroom, where we saw the celebrated Abbé Liszt, whom I had not seen for 43 years, &

who, from having then been a very wild fantastic looking man, was now a quiet benevolent looking old Priest, with long white hair, & scarcely any teeth. We asked him to play, which he did, several of his own compositions. He played beautifully. He is 76, & before leaving England in a few days, is going to sit to Boehm for his bust.[9]

Liszt began with an improvisation on themes from *St Elisabeth* and then at Victoria's request played *The Miracle of the Roses*. This was followed by a *Hungarian Rhapsody* before the performance ended with Chopin's *Nocturne in B-flat minor*, Op.9.

There is a rare and fascinating eyewitness account of the performance in a letter written by Princess Marie of Battenberg (1852–1923), whose brother Henry was married to Victoria's daughter Princess Beatrice, while another brother, Louis, was married to Princess Victoria of Hesse (the grandparents of the current Duke of Edinburgh). She writes:

Today the Abbé Liszt came to luncheon at Windsor. He was enter-tained at the table of the Master of the Household, and the Queen did not see him until later. As he was to play, he had brought his own grand piano from London,* and when we came into the drawing-room the famous artist, in his clerical costume, was stand-ing beside his instrument. The Queen greeted him very kindly, and I much appreciated the sight of the two figures as they stood facing one another. Both little, both white haired, both in black, both dignified and amiable, both a little embarrassed. She the ruler of the great British Empire, he ruler in the realm of music. Franz Liszt played for about half an hour, the notes falling from his fingers like pearls, while sounds as from another world floated through the room. The intellectual head and the soutane would have suited an organ well, although, with the Abbé Franz Liszt, the man of the world showed everywhere through the priestly garment. The Princess and I had armed ourselves with our birthday-books, in order to obtain Liszt's autograph, but when he was about to take leave of the Queen none of us could make up our minds to proffer

---

* A recent biographer, Michael Short, writes, 'This is highly unlikely. The piano may well have been furnished by the manufacturer and delivered to Windsor Castle for the occasion.'

our request; we all felt too bashful. In the end, I was pushed forward, crossed the room, and boldly laid my book on the piano before the great man.

He bowed smilingly and wrote his name in it, and also in those of the shy Princesses, who were hanging back, and finally in that of Her Majesty herself. The Queen sent me later, as a remembrance, a little bust of Franz Liszt by the sculptor Boehm, and often teased me about the bold attack I had made on the great man ...[10]

The music critic Hermann Klein was given an account of the meeting from the Abbé's own lips. He said that it had given him greater pleasure than any similar incident in his eventful career:

Your Queen showed me by her observations and questions that she is a true musician, a veritable amateur and lover of good music. She also expressed belief that the English people were only just beginning to perceive the beauty of my compositions, which had so far been too 'advanced' for them.[11]

Before Liszt left Windsor the Queen presented him with a marble bust of herself sculpted by Edgar Boehm. On it was the inscription 'Presented to Dr. Fr. Liszt by Queen Victoria, in remembrance of his visit to Windsor, April 7, 1886.'[12]

Later she acquired a photograph of the composer taken by James Ganz during his stay in London. Still part of the Royal Collection, it shows him in a three-quarter-length portrait wearing a lapelled jacket, his arm casually leaning on a wooden stand with books on it.

Immediately after the visit she wrote to Vicky: 'We have just heard Liszt who is such a fine old man. He came down here and played four pieces beautifully. What an exquisite touch.'[13]

On 12 August she again wrote to her eldest daughter: 'I also forgot in each letter saying how grieved we were at old Liszt's death. Such a distinguished man and so sad that he should be taken after all his successes.' She ended with a typical no-nonsense diagnosis: 'I fear his visit here and all the parties he was asked to killed him.'[14]

Notes

1 Christian, Ian: *Discovering Classical Music: Liszt – His Life, The Person, His Music*: Pen and Sword Books: 1991

2 Short, Michael (ed. and translator): *Correspondence of Franz Liszt and the Comtesse Marie d'Agoult*: Pendragon Press: 2013 (Letter 218 dated 22 May 1840)

3 Ibid. (Letter 221)

4 From an unpublished biography of Liszt by Michael Short

5 Ibid.

6 RA VIC/MAIN/QVJ (W) Wednesday 13 August 1845 (Princess Beatrice's copies). Retrieved 13 December 2017

7 Wohl, Janka: *Francois Liszt – Recollections of a Compatriot*: Ward and Downey: 1887: p.109ff

8 Klein, Hermann: 'The Most Eminent Victorian', reprinted in *The Musical Standard*, 29 December 1928: pp.220–1

9 RA VIC/MAIN/QVJ (W) Wednesday 7 April 1886 (Princess Beatrice's copies). Retrieved 13 December 2017

10 Williams, Adrian: Princess Marie of Battenberg letter dated 7 April 1886: cited in *Liszt Society Journal, Vol. 5:* 1980: p.21

11 Klein: Op. Cit.

12 Walker, Alan: *Franz Liszt, Vol. 3 – The Final Years, 1861–1886*: Faber and Faber: 1997: p.486

13 Ramm, Agatha (ed.): *Beloved and Darling Child – Last Letters Between Queen Victoria and Her Eldest Daughter 1886–1901*: Alan Sutton: 1990: p.32

14 Ibid.: p.38

18

'MY SINGING TEACHER'
QUEEN VICTORIA AND MENDELSSOHN

Felix Mendelssohn. (Library of Congress)

FELIX MENDELSSOHN (1809–47) dominated German music in the 1830s and '40s as a conductor, pianist, organist and most famously as a composer. Queen Victoria described him as 'the greatest musical genius since Mozart'. She met him four times at Buckingham Palace and her journal entries convey her clear admiration of the man and his talent. In her later years, more than once, she said, 'I was taught singing by Mendelssohn!'

It was the German-born Prince Albert who introduced Victoria to the work of his countryman Mendelssohn. From the time of their marriage in February 1840, the Queen frequently recorded in her journal the many evenings they played duets of the composer's works or the occasions when one of them sang, accompanied by the other on the piano. This entry for 6 November 1840 is typical: 'We played an Overture by Mendelssohn full of power & feeling, – a Marche Funèbre by Beethoven, & the Overture to "Zaide" by Mozart. Both, were fine. Am so happy to be able to amuse my dear Albert.'[1]

Mendelssohn visited Prince Albert at the palace on 14 June 1842 when he hand-delivered a message from his mentor, King Frederick William IV of Prussia, a distant cousin of Albert and godfather to the infant Prince of Wales. He was invited to return to the palace two days later to meet the Queen. Afterwards the composer wrote to his mother:

> Yesterday evening I was sent for by the Queen, who was almost alone with Prince Albert, and who seated herself near the piano and made me play to her; first seven of the 'songs without words', then the serenade, two impromptus on 'Rule Britannia', Lützow's 'Wilde Jagd', and 'Gaudeamus igitur'. The latter was somewhat difficult, but remonstrance was out of the question, and as they gave the themes, of course it was my duty to play them.

The royal couple then took Mendelssohn to have tea in the Picture Gallery, 'where two boars* by Paul Potter are hanging, and a good many other pictures which pleased me well'.

The Queen, he reported, 'looks so youthful, and is so gently courteous and gracious', 'speaks such good German' and, most flattering of all, 'knows all my music so well; the four books of songs without words and those with words, and the symphony, and the "Hymn of Praise"'.[2]

Victoria's account of the evening began with her usual forensic description of a guest:

> After dinner came Mendelssohn Bartholdy, whose acquaintance I was so anxious to make. Albert had already seen him the other

---

* Acquired by George IV, *Two Pigs* – a gruesome depiction of two pig carcasses – was thought to be the work of Paulus Potter but was later identified as a 1657 work by Cornelius Saftleven.

morning. He is short, dark, & Jewish looking. – delicate, – with a fine intellectual forehead. I should say he must be about 35 or 6. He is very pleasing & modest, & is greatly protected by the King of Prussia.

He impressed her by asking the royal couple to name two popular tunes he could improvise into one melody:

We gave him 2, 'Rule Britannia', & the Austrian National Anthem. He began immediately, & really I have never heard anything so beautiful; the way in which he blended them both together & changed over from one to the other, was quite wonderful as well as the exquisite harmony & feeling he puts into the variations, & the powerful rich chords, & modulations, which reminded one of all his beautiful compositions. At one moment he played the Austrian Anthem with the right hand he played 'Rule Britannia', as the boss, with his left! He made some further improvisations on well-known tunes & songs. We were all filled with the greatest admiration.

Unsurprisingly she ends, 'Poor Mendelssohn was quite exhausted, when he had done playing.'[3]

Keen to meet the composer again before his return to Germany, Prince Albert invited Mendelssohn to the palace on 9 July. It was clear from another detailed account to his mother that the royal couple were not just being social, but that they had a genuine interest in music:

Prince Albert sent for me on the Saturday at half past one so that I could also try his organ before I left England … I begged the Prince to begin playing me something, so that I could boast of it in Germany. He played a chorale by heart, with the pedals – and so charmingly, precisely and accurately that it would have done credit to a professional.

Meanwhile:

in came the Queen dressed quite informally. She was just saying that she had to leave for Claremont in an hour's time, when she looked round and exclaimed, 'Heavens, how untidy!' – for the wind had scattered some sheets of music from a large portfolio all over the room and even among the organ pedals. Down she got on hands and knees and started picking them up ...

Then it was the turn of Mendelssohn to play, with the royals in accompaniment:

> I began with the chorus from St. Paul, 'How lovely are the messengers'. Before I had come to the end of the first verse they both began singing the chorus, and Prince Albert managed the stops so cleverly for me ... that I was quite enchanted.

Then:

> The Queen asked me whether I had written any new songs, because she was very fond of singing my published ones. 'You ought to sing one to him,' said Prince Albert; and after a moment's hesitation she said she would try the 'Spring Song' in B flat.

Having been ambushed into performing, Victoria, who admitted to being nervous, resorted to delaying tactics before finally singing. First of all she remembered she'd packed the sheet music away to take with her on a weekend visit to Claremont. Undeterred Mendelssohn persisted, 'Couldn't it possibly be unpacked?' Albert offered to go and locate it, but to no avail and so the Queen went herself. A few minutes later she returned to announce the Lady-in-Waiting had 'taken all my things with her; it's really most annoying'. (Mendelssohn reported to his mother, 'You can imagine how that amused me!')

Next, after a quick discussion with the Prince, Victoria announced she would sing something by Gluck. By now the group had grown to include Albert's brother Ernest and his wife Alexandrine and the Duchess of Kent. They all headed across the palace to the Queen's boudoir. Mendelssohn recalled:

> While they were all talking I rummaged about among the music on the piano and soon discovered my first set of songs; so of course I asked the Queen to sing one of these instead of the Gluck, and she agreed.

Then there was another pause when the Queen announced, 'But first we must get rid of the parrot, or he will scream louder than I can sing.' Prince Albert rang the bell and the Prince of Gotha said 'I'll take him out;' so I came forward and said, 'Please allow me!' and lifted up the big cage and carried it out to the astonished servants.

Finally Victoria sang. 'And which of my songs did she choose?' Mendelssohn rhetorically queried in his letter to his mother:

'Schöner und schöner schmückt sich' – and sang it quite charmingly, strictly in time and in tune, and very nicely enunciated. Only when it came to the line 'Der Prosa Last und Müh', where it goes down to D and then rises again chromatically, each time she sang D sharp; and since I gave her the note the first two times, in the third verse she sang D where it ought to have been D sharp! But except for this little mistake it was really charming, and I've never heard an amateur sing the last sustained G better, more purely or more naturally.

The composer had to admit to the Queen that this was one of his sister Fanny's compositions and asked if she would sing one of his own:

She said she would gladly try, so long as I gave her plenty of help, and then she sang 'Lass dich nur nichts dauern' really quite faultlessly and with much feeling and expression. I thought that this wasn't the moment to indulge in extravagant compliments, so I merely thanked her several times. But when she said 'Oh, if only I hadn't been so frightened! I generally have a pretty long breath,' then – and with the clearest conscience – I praised her warmly, because it was precisely that particular passage at the close, with the long-sustained C, that she had managed so well.

Finally Albert sang a song, before Mendelssohn took over the piano and multitasked two tunes the couple suggested plus the songs Victoria had sung. 'Everything conspired to make it perfect,' he wrote in the same letter to his mother, 'for I never improvised better.' As he took leave the Queen said several times, 'I hope you will come back to England again soon and pay us another visit.'[4]

Victoria's own account of the meeting suggests her nerves at performing for her idol:

> With some trepidation, I sang, accompanied by him, 1rst, a song which I thought was his composition, but which he said was his sister's, & then one of his beautiful ones, after which he played to us a little. We thanked him very much, & I gave him a handsome ring as a remembrance.[5]

During the visit Mendelssohn asked permission to dedicate his *Scottish Symphony* to the Queen. Still on an emotional high from the encounter, the composer told his mother, 'the only really nice, comfortable house in England ... where one feels completely at home, is Buckingham Palace.'

Two years later Mendelssohn met the royal couple again at Buckingham Palace. The Queen, once again full of flattery, noted:

> We went over to the Drawingroom to see Mendelssohn, & talked to him for some time, then, he played to us beautifully, some of the fine compositions, he has written lately, amongst them music for the 'Midsummer Night's Dream', 2 of his 'Lieder ohne Worte', & improvised wonderfully on Gluck's beautiful Chorus: 'Que de grâces, que de Majéste', bringing in besides a song by his sister, which we often sing. He is such an agreeable clever man & his countenance beams with intelligence & genius.[6]

Victoria and Albert saw Mendelssohn twice during his final visit to Britain in the spring of 1847. On 23 April they visited Exeter Hall on the Strand to hear the composer's new oratorio *Elija*, which Victoria thought 'is extremely fine. He conducted himself, & the whole went off very well.' Though she thought 'the recitatives might be shortened,' overall 'the whole is a splendid work'.[7]

The following day, Prince Albert sent a copy of the concert programme to Mendelssohn, inscribed in his own hand with the message, written in German:

> To the noble artist who, surrounded by the Baal-worship [referring to the story of *Elijah*] of debased art, has been able, by his genius and science, to preserve faithfully, like another Elijah, the worship

of true art, and once more to accustom our ear, amid the whirl of empty, frivolous sounds, to the pure tones of sympathetic feeling and legitimate harmony: to the Great Master, who makes us conscious of the unity of his conception, through the whole maze of his creation, from the soft whispering to the mighty raging of the elements. Inscribed in grateful remembrance by Albert. Buckingham Palace, 24 April 1847

A few days later they had their final meeting. The Queen recorded:

We had the great treat of hearing Mendelssohn play, & he stayed an hour with us, playing some new Compositions, with that indescribably beautiful touch of his. I also sang 3 of his songs, which seemed to please him. He is so amiable & clever. For some time he has been engaged in composing an Opera & an Oratorio, but has lost courage about them. The subject for his Opera is a Rhine Legend & that for the Oratorio, a very beautiful one, depicting Earth, Hell, & Heaven, & he played one of the Choruses out of this to us, which was very fine.[8]

After the performance the Queen asked whether, as he'd given them so much pleasure, there was anything they could do for him. The composer said he'd like to see the royal nursery, so he was duly taken to see the youngest members of the Royal Family.

Exhausted by his visit to Britain, Mendelssohn was ill-prepared for a family tragedy on his return to Germany. On 14 May his sister Fanny, to whom he was particularly close, suffered a stroke while rehearsing one of her brother's oratorios with her choir. Felix collapsed when he was told, and he himself died of the same cause on 4 November 1847, aged only 38.

On hearing the news, Victoria wrote:

We were horrified, astounded & distressed to read in the papers of the death of Mendelssohn, the greatest musical genius since Mozart, & the most amiable Man. He was quite worshipped by those who knew him intimately, & we have so much appreciated & admired his wonderfully beautiful compositions. We liked & esteemed the excellent man & looked up to & revered, the wonderful genius, & the great mind, which I fear were too much for the frail delicate body. With it all, he was so modest & simple.[9]

A few days later Victoria's pianist, Lucy Anderson, who taught the Queen as well as her eldest children over a number of years, gave her an account of Mendelssohn's death sent to her by the composer's friends, Ignaz and Charlotte Moscheles. 'It was a succession of fits of apoplexy, which killed him,' recorded the Queen in her journal, continuing:

> At 1rst the physicians hoped, as consciousness was returning, that he might do well, provided there were no further attacks. But alas! they returned & from that hour all consciousness vanished. The great soul passed peacefully away, without a struggle, after 9 o'clock. Moscheles & his wife were there the whole time with poor Mme Mendelssohn & his brother Paul. — After luncheon … we read & played that beautiful 'Lied ohne Worte' which poor Mendelssohn arranged & wrote out himself for us this year. To feel, when one is playing his beautiful music, that he is no more, seems in comprehensible![10]

Notes

1 RA VIC/MAIN/QVJ (W) Friday 6 November 1840 (Princess Beatrice's copies). Retrieved 14 February 2018
2 Bartholdy, Paul Mendelssohn (ed.): *Letters of Felix Mendelssohn Bartholdy*: Longman: 1863
3 RA VIC/MAIN/QVJ (W) Thursday 16 June 1842: (Princess Beatrice's copies). Retrieved 14 February 2018
4 Bartholdy: Op. Cit..
5 RA VIC/MAIN/QVJ (W) Saturday 9 July 1842 (Princess Beatrice's copies). Retrieved 14 February 2018
6 RA VIC/MAIN/QVJ (W) Thursday 30 May 1844 (Princess Beatrice's copies). Retrieved 14 February 2018
7 RA VIC/MAIN/QVJ (W) Friday 23 April 1847 (Princess Beatrice's copies). Retrieved 14 February 2018
8 RA VIC/MAIN/QVJ (W) Saturday 1 May 1847 (Princess Beatrice's copies). Retrieved 14 February 2018
9 RA VIC/MAIN/QVJ (W) Saturday 1 May 1847 (Princess Beatrice's copies). Retrieved 14 February 2018
10 RA VIC/MAIN/QVJ (W) Saturday 13 November 1847 (Princess Beatrice's copies). Retrieved 14 February 2018

19

DARLING GRANDMAMA
QUEEN VICTORIA, NICHOLAS AND
ALEXANDRA

Nicholas II and Alexandra Feodorovna, with their children, Marie, Anastasia, Alexei, Olga
and Tatiana. (Library of Congress)

PRINCESS ALIX of Hesse (1874–1918) was, most historians agree, the
Queen's favourite granddaughter. With the sudden death of the
Princess's mother, Princess Alice, Victoria took over in loco parentis.
Mercifully she didn't live to see Alexandra's last tragic years.

Despite giving birth nine times, Victoria was no fan of babies. 'An ugly baby is a very nasty object,' she protested; 'the prettiest are frightful when undressed' and their habit of jerking their little limbs around she found 'a terrible frog-like action'. The news that the fourteenth of her forty grandchildren, 'a mere little red lump', had safely arrived in the world she thought 'a very uninteresting thing for it seems to me to go on like the rabbits in Windsor Park!'[1]

An exception to her sweeping rule was her favourite granddaughter, Princess Alix of Hesse, born to Victoria's second daughter Princess Alice, on 6 June 1872. Known to her family as Alix, Alicky or Sunny – the latter thanks to her ever-smiling disposition – she is best remembered today as the ill-fated Alexandra Feodorovna, the last Empress of Russia.

Victoria was besotted with her. In her journal entry for 16 July 1878 the Queen wrote, 'Alicky is a glorious child, handsomer than ever, a great darling, with brilliant colouring, splendid eyes, & a sweet smile.'[2] A month later she enthused to her eldest daughter, 'Alicky the handsomest child I ever saw.'[3] Most of the granddaughters fared far worse. The parents of Princess Marie Louise, born two months after Alix, received the abrupt telegram from the baby-sitting Queen: 'Children very well, but poor little Louise very ugly.' When the latter remonstrated years later about the brutal assessment, she was told by an unrepentant Victoria, 'My dear child, it was only the truth!'[4]

In the autumn of 1878 Alicky's young world was devastated by an outbreak of diphtheria at the Hessian court. News reached Victoria on 12 November that the 6-year-old princess had been taken ill. Over the next few days, while she rallied, her sisters Irene and May developed high fevers. Their father Louis and brother Ernest both contracted it as well. The family was nursed by Princess Alice until she too fell victim, supposedly after kissing her son on the cheek. Four-year-old May, who shared her birthday, 24 May, with Victoria, died on 16 November and was buried with her mother, Princess Alice, who died aged 35 on 14 December, the seventeenth anniversary of the death of her father, Prince Albert.

The Queen took the five motherless Hesse children under her wing. She made occasional visits to see them in Darmstadt where they had been born and each year the children stayed with their grandmother at Balmoral or Osborne. Their father, the easy-going Grand Duke Louis of Hesse, was devoted to his mother-in-law and allowed her to adopt a role 'in loco parentis'.

The Hesse family's English nanny, Mrs Orchard, and their governesses, Miss Jackson and Miss Pryde, sent regular reports to the Queen on the children's behaviour and education. Even the girls' dress patterns were sent to Victoria for approval.

On their many visits to see their grandmother it was Alicky who always received the most glowing accounts in Victoria's journal:

> Took a short drive with Beatrice, Louis & Alicky, who looked very sweet in her long cloak. I feel a constant returning pang, in looking at this lovely little child, thinking that her darling mother, who so doted on her, was no longer here on earth to watch over her.[5]

Aged 15, Alicky joined the entire Royal Family at events to mark the Queen's Golden Jubilee. She was allowed to attend the luncheon at Buckingham Palace on 20 June 1887, fifty years to the day since Victoria's accession. During the festivities she drove with the Queen through Windsor, where they reviewed a detachment of firemen sent from all four corners of the UK, before driving through Home Park where 6,000 local schoolchildren were enjoying a party.

Two years later Alicky was with the Queen during a rare visit to North Wales. They stayed at Palé Hall, home of the prolific railway builder Henry Robertson and, according to the royal journal, enjoyed watching sheep trials. 'When the sheep neared the pen,' recorded the Queen:

> the shepherd came down & assisted his dog, but is never allowed to touch the sheep. Each dog had different sheep, who were all 4 years old & strange both to the dogs & the ground, having been brought down from the hills for the purpose. 'Bob' a white Lancashire dog worked beautifully.

Afterwards they headed for Wrexham: 'a great place for coal'.[6]

The sudden death of Grand Duke Louis from a stroke, aged only 54, left Alicky parentless at the age of 19 and increased Queen Victoria's concern for this special grandchild and her siblings, especially 'Ernie' who, at 23, succeeded his father as Grand Duke Ernest Louis. 'Orphans!! It is awful,' the Queen wrote to Princess Victoria, the eldest of the Hesse sisters. 'But I am <u>still there & while</u> I live Alicky, till she has married, will be <u>more</u> than <u>ever my own child</u>.'[7]

Marriage was also on the mind of the British press which, the same year, was speculating on a romance between Alexandra and her first cousin, George, Duke of York, later George V. As early as 1887 Victoria had said with all her 'heart and mind' that she was 'bent on securing dear Alicky for either Eddie or Georgie'.[8] Eddie was the feckless Prince Albert Victor, Duke of Clarence. Second in line to the throne, he was an unpromising future monarch, and the Queen felt her calm, dignified and regal granddaughter was an ideal choice for a supportive consort. Much to Victoria's surprise, Alicky refused point blank to consider the union. 'I fear all hope of Alicky's marrying Eddie is at an end,' lamented a defeated Victoria to her eldest daughter in May 1890:

> She has written to tell him how much it grieves her to pain him, but that she cannot marry him, much as she likes him as a cousin … It is a real sorrow to us … but she says that if she is forced she will do it but that she would be unhappy and he too.

Grudgingly the Queen admired her granddaughter's strong conviction: 'She shows great strength of character as all her family and all of us wish it and she refuses the greatest position there is.'[9]

The real reason behind Alicky's reluctance to marry the future British king was that she had fallen in love with the heir to the Russian throne, the Tsarevich Nicholas. The two had met in St Petersburg in June 1884 when Nicholas's uncle, the Grand Duke Serge, married Alicky's sister Elizabeth of Hesse, known to the family as Ella. At the time the Tsarevich was only 16 and Alexandra just 12.

Love blossomed five years later when Alicky paid a lengthy visit to Russia to stay with her sister. Nicholas recorded his attraction to the Princess in his diary in 1892:

> My dream is some day to marry Alix H. I have loved her a long while and still deeper and stronger since 1889 when she spent six weeks in Petersburg during the winter! For a long time I resisted my feelings, and tried to deceive myself about the impossibility of achieving my most cherished wish! But now that Eddy has withdrawn or been rejected, the only obstacle between us is the question

of religion. It is the one and only barrier; I am almost certain that our feelings are mutual!'[10]

Alexandra was certainly besotted after their second meeting but by then 'the one and only barrier' was in place. The Princess had been confirmed into the Lutheran faith. Profoundly religious, there was no way she would ever contemplate converting to the Russian Orthodox Church and so marriage to Nicky could never be an option. She did however agree to correspond with him privately, using Ella as a go-between.

There were two other stumbling blocks to the love match. Firstly Nicholas's parents opposed the union. Tsar Alexander III and the Empress Marie (the younger sister of Alexandra, Princess of Wales) were both anti-German and felt that the fourth daughter of a Grand Duke was not really important enough to be a future Tsarina. Moreover Alexandra's shy, reserved personality and unsmiling countenance did nothing to impress.

The second problem was Queen Victoria, whose dislike of Russia unsurprisingly dated from the Crimean War and who firmly believed in the low moral standing of Russian society, despite the fact her second son Prince Alfred was married to Tsar Alexander's sister Marie.

In December 1890 the Queen heard that the Tsarevich was in love with her granddaughter and that Ella was actively encouraging the match. Victoria was incensed and, all guns blazing, wrote a strongly worded letter to Victoria of Hesse: 'For the youngest Sister to marry the son of the Er. [Emperor] would ... lead to no happiness.' The Queen went further and with a flurry of underlinings instructed: 'This must not be allowed to go on. Papa [i.e. Grand Duke Louis of Hesse] must put his foot down, & there must be no more visits of Alicky to Russia – & he must & you & Ernie must insist on a stop being put on the whole affair.' Victoria concluded with some anti-Russian vitriol for good measure: 'The state of Russia is so bad, so rotten that at any moment something dreadful might happen ... the wife of the Thronfolger [heir to the throne] is in a most difficult & precarious position.'[11]

The Queen resumed her matchmaking and the following September wrote once again to Princess Victoria, outlining her latest machinations:

You know how much dear Papa and I wish dear Alicky shld some day marry Max of Baden, whom I formerly wished for Maud ... If (as I anticipate) nothing comes of this [i.e. a Max and Maud union] I hope dear Papa will <u>lose no time</u> in inviting him.[12]

The Queen appears to have been losing her touch. Maud married her cousin, Prince Carl of Denmark, and ended up as Queen of Norway, while Alicky quietly and determinedly bided her time and Nicholas wrote in his diary in April 1892, 'I never stop thinking of Alix!'

Meanwhile Ella was determinedly encouraging her sister's romance and wrote to their brother Ernie to brief him on how to deal with the Queen should the need arise. 'Alix is sure to speak to you about a certain person & tell you all I wrote to her,' Ella began in her long, ungrammatical and virtually unpunctuated letter:

> Give her courage & be yourself very careful what you say in conversation with Grandmama it would be much better not to speak about Pelly [the Hesse family name for Nicholas] or if she does tell her their [sic] had been nothing between [them] … but that if she wishes to know frankly your opinion about Pelly say what a perfect creature in every way & that he is adored by all & deserves this loving being … Give an idea of the happy family life so that Grandmama's prejudices may be lessened …

Ella went on to write, 'Through all the idiotic trash in the newspapers she [the Queen] gets impossible untrue views and founds all her arguments on facts which probably never existed.'[13] (Though the Grand Duchess was well aware of Victoria's anti-Russian stance, she clearly had no idea their grandmother had a virtual hotline to the Imperial court via the Princess of Wales.)

The Queen had a golden opportunity to assess Nicky's character for herself when the Tsarevich came to London at the end of June 1893 for the wedding of his cousin Prince George to Princess May of Teck a few days later. (She had actually met him once before in July 1873 when, as a 5-year-old, he visited her at Osborne with his five Wales cousins and the Queen recorded 'they were in tremendous high spirits'.) Alix declined her grandmother's invitation to the celebrations on the grounds of expense, having recently visited Italy and Berlin. Nicholas had no such concerns and, after the opulence of the Winter Palace, described his single room at the Prince of Wales's residence, Marlborough House, as 'cosy'. He was amused at having to take turns to bathe in the one bathroom he was sharing with his uncle, Prince Valdemar of Denmark, and the bridegroom.

On 1 July Nicholas changed into full uniform and set out for Windsor Castle by train. The Queen noted in her journal:

> Just before two, the young Cesarewitch arrived, and I received him at the top of the staircase. All were in uniform to do him honour, and to show him every possible civility. He is charming and wonderfully like Georgie [his cousin]. He always speaks English, and almost without a fault.

Before his departure she invested him with the Order of the Garter, to his surprise. Her verdict afterwards was 'he is very simple and unaffected'. (Simple, meaning unpretentious and straightforward, was one of the Queen's favourite accolades.)[14]

Had Victoria read Nicholas's diary entry for the same day, in which he breezily dubbed Windsor Castle 'a typical old building – the best of its kind' and the Queen herself as 'a round ball on unsteady legs', she might well have revised her opinion of him.

The Queen and Nicky met again four days later, when she hosted an eve-of-wedding dinner in the Supper-room at Buckingham Palace. 'I sat between the King of Denmark and the Cesarewitch, who is charming,' noted Victoria. 'His great likeness to Georgie leads to no end of funny mistakes, the one being taken for the other!'[15]

In November 1893 Alicky broke off her romance with Nicky on the grounds of her faith. 'I think it is a sin to change my belief,' she wrote from Darmstadt. 'I should be miserable all the days of my life, knowing that I had done a wrongful thing.'[16] The Tsarevich was bereft. 'All my hopes are shattered by this implacable obstacle,' he confided in this journal. '… my best dreams and my most cherished wishes for the future … All day I went about in a daze.'[17]

It was the wedding of two more of the Queen's grandchildren that proved the catalyst to Nicholas and Alexandra's own betrothal. In April 1894 Alexandra's brother Ernest married Victoria Melita of Saxe-Coburg and Gotha, daughter of Victoria's second son, Prince Alfred and his wife, Marie of Russia. The nuptials, held in Coburg, were witnessed by the largest gathering of the Queen's extended family since the Golden Jubilee of 1887 and were headed by the royal matriarch herself.

Nicholas, undeterred by Alexandra's previous refusals to marry, begged her to reconsider. This time he was aided by a trio of royal religious converts including Ella, his aunt the Grand Duchess Vladimir, and, via a letter, his mother the Empress Marie Feodorovna, all of whom had changed from Lutheranism to Russian Orthodoxy. The ever forceful Kaiser Wilhelm II, another of Alix's cousins, waded in to urge her to marry. Finally, tearful and overwrought, she agreed.

There was more emotion later in the morning when the news was broken to the Queen. 'Breakfasted alone with Beatrice,' Victoria noted in her journal on 19 April:

> Soon after Ella came in, much agitated, to say that Alicky & Nicky were engaged, & begging they might come in. I was quite thunder-struck, as though I knew, Nicky much wished it, I thought Alicky was not sure of her mind. Saw them both. Alicky had tears in her eyes, but looked very bright & I kissed them both. Nicky said 'she is much too good for me'. I told him he must make the religious difficulties as easy as he could for her, which he promised to do.

The Queen added, 'People generally seem pleased at the engagement', though Ernest and Victoria Melita could have been forgiven for being a tad annoyed at having their nuptials completely overshadowed.[18] The interest was global, and Victoria received 'many kind congratulatory telegrams' and noted, 'many satisfactory articles have appeared about it in the newspapers, one especially in the "Standard" was excellent.'[19]

The Queen was quite taken with Nicky. She had made a memorable entrance into Coburg, accompanied by a detachment of Dragoon Guards. The day after the engagement she instructed them to play a whole programme of music under the Prince's bedroom window which he found 'very touching!' She instructed him to call her 'Granny', asked him to breakfast with her for the remainder of her stay, and sent for the Munshi, her Indian manservant, to offer his congratulations on the royal engagement. Usually the Queen had an aversion to engaged couples walking or driving on their own – a practice she labelled 'very American'. By 1894 she had clearly relaxed and Nicholas was able to report to his mother, 'Granny has been very friendly and even allowed us *to go out for drives* without a chaperone. I confess I didn't expect that!'[20]

The Queen also added Nicholas to her lengthy list of regular cor-respondents. Shortly after returning to Windsor the Queen wrote to the Tsarevich firmly emphasising her 'in loco parentis' role in Alix's life:

> As she has no Parents, I feel I am the only person who can really be answerable to her … Now poor dear Alicky is an Orphan and has no one but me at all in that position. Anything you wish, I hope you will tell me direct.

She signed herself 'your devoted (future) Grandmama, Victoria RI'.[21]

Admitting to his brother that he found it difficult to read the Queen's virtually indecipherable handwriting and even more prob-lematic to concoct a suitably 'grand and old-fashioned like style' in his replies, nevertheless 'Your most affectionate and devoted (future) grandson, Nicky' soon became the model progeny in his very defer-ential letters. 'I am already looking forward with such a pleasure and impatience for the day when I will be able to come and see you and my darling Alix at Windsor,' he wrote in May. After thanking her for her 'precious help' he concludes, 'I really don't know how to thank you enough for having taken the trouble of writing to me such a charming letter.'[22] Once again the Queen may have been less than impressed to hear that, two days later, Nicholas was rather brazenly informing his brother Georgy, 'The old Queen (belly woman) often writes to me – that's nice, isn't it?'[23]

After a brief stay in Darmstadt, Alix journeyed to Britain to spend most of the summer with her grandmother. She decorated her room at Windsor with several framed photos of Nicky 'with their beautiful big eyes', started to learn Russian, resumed her sewing, played Grieg on the piano to her grandmother, and took daily carriage drives with the Queen, who interrogated her on every detail of the engagement.

Also of concern to Victoria was her granddaughter's sciatica, which had plagued her since childhood. The Queen blamed the Hessian royal physi-cian – 'stupid doctor' – for not prescribing 'a strict regime of life as well as diet'. The previous autumn Alix had found Balmoral too bracing and so her grandmother packed her off to the spa town of Harrogate to take the waters. The Princess stayed at Cathcart House, travelling incognito as 'Baroness Starkenburg'. The alias fooled none of the locals, who lined the route to the Victoria Bathing House, some glued to opera glasses, to see the royal guest pass by in a bath chair, less than discreetly followed by a detective on a bicycle.[24]

During her stay the hotelier, Mrs Allen, gave birth to twins. Alix thought this a good omen for her forthcoming marriage and asked if they could be called Nicholas and Alix. She became godmother to her namesake and sent yearly birthday gifts to the children. In March 2017 a jewelled cutlery set sent from the Empress to baby Alix on her first birthday sold for £20,000 at auction in Harrogate.[25]

Nicholas decided to spend the summer of 1894 in England with his fiancée and her family. 'You don't know, dearest Grandmama,' he wrote, with his usual deference, to the Queen shortly before he left, 'how *happy* I am to come and spend some time with you and my beloved little bride.'[26]

Nicky arrived in mid-June and spent three idyllic days by the River Thames at Walton with Alix's older sister Victoria and her husband Prince Louis of Battenberg, before they were obliged to join the Queen at Windsor and then Osborne. He brought with him a magnificent *sautoir* necklace of pearls, the most expensive item ordered by the Imperial family from the renowned jeweller Fabergé.[27] 'Now Alix, do not get too proud,' admonished the Queen.

Despite his occasional misgivings about the Queen, the Tsarevich was made to feel at home at Windsor. 'It feels funny to me,' he wrote to Georgy:

> the extent I have become part of the English family. I have become almost as indispensable to [the Queen] as her Indians and her Scotsmen; I am, as it were, attached to her and the best thing is that she does not like me to leave her side … She exudes such enormous charm.[28]

The days were spent breakfasting, luncheoning, having tea and dinner with the Queen as well as taking daily carriage drives. Even the latter proved hazardous to Nicky. 'She was so kind and amiable and in good spirits,' he wrote to his mother, 'but from time to time poked me in the eye with her parasol, which was less pleasant.'[29]

During their stay the future Edward VIII was born at White Lodge, Richmond Park. Nicky and Alix journeyed with the Queen from Windsor in the late afternoon of 14 June. The Tsarevich very nearly didn't make it since he managed to get locked in one of the Windsor Castle lavatories:

There was no way I could get out for over half an hour. Alix at last managed to open the door from the outside, although I shouted long and loud, and tried to open the door myself as the key was on my side.[30]

Out in time to make it to Richmond with Grandmama, Nicky was rewarded by being asked to be godfather to the infant prince and was able to attend the christening on 4 July, when the Tsarevich was interested to see the baby was not totally immersed in holy water as it would be in an Orthodox ceremony, but merely sprinkled with it.

An unexpected family tragedy affected Nicholas and Alexandra's wedding plans. The Tsarevich's father Alexander III developed terminal kidney disease (nephritis) and died on 1 November 1894 at the age of only 49. One of his last acts was to dress in full military uniform to greet Alexandra, who had hurried to Russia to be with her fiancé, and to give the young couple his blessing.

'What a horrible tragedy this is,' wrote the Queen to her eldest daughter on the 5th, reflecting that Alix would become wife and Empress at the same moment:

And what a position for these dear young people. God help them! And now I hear that poor little Alicky goes with them to St Petersburg and that the wedding is to take place soon after the funeral. I am quite miserable not to see my darling child again, before, here. <u>Where</u> shall I <u>ever</u> see her again?[31]

Victoria's fears were justified. Alexandra's pregnancies and the lengthy journey from Russia to Britain meant grandmother and granddaughter would only meet one more time during the remaining six and a half years of the Queen's life.

Nicholas and Alexandra married a week after Alexander's funeral, the bride swapping a constant stream of black mourning gowns for a rich silver brocade dress covered in a trailing mantle of cloth of gold, lined with ermine. Alexandra, Princess of Wales was in raptures about her appearance and the groom's lookalike cousin, George, Duke of York, assured his grandmother that 'Nicky is a very lucky man to have got such a lovely and charming wife and I must say I never saw two people more in love with each other and happier than they are'.

Meanwhile, back at Windsor Castle, Victoria hosted a large dinner party to celebrate her granddaughter's wedding. She proposed the imperial couple's health and stood to attention for the playing of the Russian national anthem. She was heard to exclaim, 'Oh! How I do wish I had been there!'[32]

For a wedding present Victoria made Nicky Colonel-in-Chief of the Royal Scots Greys regiment. In her accompanying letter she apologised that her other gift 'is unfortunately not finished as I am having something purposely made for you'. One wedding present was ready to despatch: 'I send you also the humble offering of my Munshi Abdul Karim for the wedding. It is some very beautiful Indian embroidery.'[33] (Nicky and Alix apparently didn't share the almost unanimous dislike of the Munshi at the British court, and the new Empress wrote to tell her grandmother that 'it was really most kind of the Munshi sending those pretty stuffs'.)

Alexandra also thanked the Queen for her gifts of jewellery and materials: 'The pendant with Your dear portrait is *too* beautiful and I shall prize it very much – the lovely ring I wore for the Wedding and ever since … The stuffs, shawls and capes are charming and will be most useful.'[34]

Just over a year later, on 15 November 1895, Victoria was travelling from Balmoral to Windsor on the royal train when she heard that Alexandra had given birth to a daughter: 'At Carlisle got a telegram from Nicky saying: "darling Alix has just given birth to a lovely enormous [the baby weighed 10lb (4.5kg)] little daughter, Olga. My joy is beyond words. Mother & child doing well. Am so thankful."'[35]

Victoria, still taking her 'in loco parentis' role seriously, set about recruiting a sound British nanny to bring up her latest great-grandchild. The Queen was delighted to have been asked to be godmother to Olga, but horrified to hear that Alexandra was planning to breastfeed her baby. Despite it being fashionable at the time, the Queen said she had a 'totally insurmountable disgust for the process'. She tried to ban her daughters from doing so when they had their own children. Much to her annoyance they ignored her advice, prompting another regal outburst: 'It makes my hair stand on end that my daughters have turned into cows.'[36] She was no doubt surprised when Nicholas himself brought up the subject in a letter shortly after the birth: 'She [Alexandra] finds such a pleasure in nursing our sweet baby herself. For my part I consider it the most natural thing a mother can do and I think the example an excellent one.'[37]

The following summer the Queen was distressed to hear about a major catastrophe following Nicholas and Alexandra's coronation. Food and souvenirs were to be handed out to the poor at a huge fete on the outskirts of Moscow. A rumour spread that there weren't enough refreshments to go round. The crowd swarmed over the vast field, which had been cut up by unseen trenches. Some 1,389 people were trampled to death or suffocated and another 1,300 were injured. The Imperial couple were widely criticised not only for failing to cancel a celebratory ball scheduled for the same day, but also for attending it. Afterwards they sent a touching telegram to Queen Victoria voicing their distress, but their detractors said it showed callousness on the part of the Emperor and Empress, and in a pattern that would frequently recur over the next twenty years, most of the blame fell upon Alexandra.

Three months later grandmother and granddaughter were reunited at Balmoral Castle. The Queen pulled out all the stops to give this very personal state visit the dignity she felt it deserved. The Imperial couple arrived at the port of Leith near Edinburgh on board their yacht, the *Shtandart*. Here they took the train to Ballater, the nearest village to the royal estate. Bonfires on all the hillsides adjacent to the rail track illuminated the night sky. A five-carriage procession battled through torrential rain and as they arrived at Balmoral the bells of nearby Crathie Kirk rang out. Victoria's kilted retainers, carrying burning torches, escorted the guests on the last part of their journey before the Queen herself greeted them in the doorway of the castle.

'Dear Nicky and Alicky are quite unspoilt and unchanged and as dear and simple as ever and as kind as ever,' the Queen reported to Vicky, adding, 'He is looking rather thin and pale and careworn, but sweet Alicky is in great beauty and very blooming. The baby is magnificent, bigger than she or Ella ever were, and a lovely lively [great] grandchild.'[38] In fact so enamoured was the Queen with Olga that she even went to see her having her daily bath.

Not all the Royal Household was enjoying the family reunion. Victoria's Private Secretary, Sir Arthur Bigge, referred to it as the 'Russian occupation', as the British courtiers were obliged to squash together so that the footmen's quarters was likened to a slave ship. All was forgotten when, as Nicholas prepared to leave, he generously handed the Master of the Household £1,000 (£126,000 / $173,600 at today's rates) to distribute to the servants.

Nicholas didn't thrive in the arctic wastes of Royal Deeside. He complained to his mother that his uncles insisted on taking him 'shooting all day long' and that he couldn't manage to hit anything. Also the temperatures in the castle were lower than Siberia, thanks to the Queen's imperviousness to the cold. Over the years other guests agreed. The 4th Earl of Clarendon claimed he'd got frostbite in his toes over dinner and Mary Ponsonby, wife of Private Secretary Henry Ponsonby, claimed she was only warm on the estate when she was in bed. Nicholas developed toothache as a result of the cold, and a problem with a decayed molar. Victoria's personal physician, Sir James Reid, managed to cure the pain and the grateful Tsar gave him a gold cigarette case with his Imperial arms in gold and diamonds.

Two landmark events occurred during the Russian visit. On 23 September 1896, the day after Nicky and Alix arrived, the Queen became the longest reigning British monarch, beating the record set by her grandfather George III. 'People wished to make all sorts of demonstrations,' she wrote, 'which I asked them not to do until I had completed the sixty years next June.'[39]

The second major event was on 3 October when the Queen and her visitors, on the last day of their stay, took part in an early film. 'At 12 went down to below the Terrace, near the Ball Room,' wrote Victoria in her journal, '& were all photographed by Downey by the new cinematograph process, which makes moving pictures by winding off a reel of films. We were walking up & down & the children jumping about.'[40] It would be another seven weeks before Victoria was able to see the results of Downey's efforts for herself at a special screening at Windsor Castle: 'After tea went to the Red Drawingroom where so called "animated pictures" were shown off, including the groups taken in September at Balmoral. It is a very wonderful process, representing people, their movements & actions, as if they were alive.'[41]

Before leaving Scotland the Imperial couple planted a tree on the Balmoral estate. Alexandra was upset at leaving and wrote to her old governess, Madge Jackson, 'It has been such a very short stay and I leave dear Grandmama with a heavy heart. Who knows when we may meet again and where.'[42]

The following summer Alix again gave birth. Queen Victoria sent a note to her youngest daughter Beatrice: 'Alicky has got a 2nd daughter which I fully expected.'[43] When two years later the Grand Duchess

Maria was born, Victoria shared the disappointment of Russian society at the lack of a male heir. 'I am so thankful that dear Alicky has recovered so well,' the Queen wrote to Nicky, adding pointedly, 'I regret the 3rd girl for the country. I know that an Heir would be more welcome than a daughter.'[44]

Victoria would not live to see the birth of a son to her beloved Alix. When the Queen died at Osborne on 22 January 1901, Alexandra was four months pregnant with another daughter, Anastasia, and forbidden by her doctors from travelling to England for the funeral. Instead she attended a special memorial service in Moscow's English Church where she was seen to weep openly at the loss of this second mother.

Nicky wrote to his uncle, Edward VII:

It is difficult to realize that beloved Grandmama has been taken away from this world. She was so remarkably kind and touching towards me since the first time I ever saw her, when I came to England for George's and May's wedding. I felt quite like at home when I lived at Windsor and later in Scotland near her and I need not say that I shall forever cherish he memory.[45]

Sixteen years later, Nicholas was forced to abdicate following the 1917 revolution, and the provisional government led by Alexander Kerensky prepared to evacuate the Romanov family to Tobolsk in the Urals. Alexandra decided to burn her family papers to avoid them falling into the wrong hands or incriminating the family in any way. Among them were the many she had received from her beloved grandmama, which were cast into the flames and so lost to history.

Notes

1   Fulford, Roger (ed.): *Your Dear Letter.* Evans Brothers: 1971: p.200
2   RA VIC/MAIN/QVJ (W) Tuesday 16 July 1878 (Princess Beatrice's copies). Retrieved 13 December 2017
3   Fulford, Roger (ed.): *Beloved Mama*: Evans Brothers: 1981: pp.23–4
4   Marie Louise, Princess: *My Memories of Six Reigns*: Penguin: 1959: p.19
5   RA VIC/MAIN/QVJ (W) Tuesday 21 January 1879 (Princess Beatrice's copies). Retrieved 14 December 2017
6   RA VIC/MAIN/QVJ (W) Saturday 24 August 1889 (Princess Beatrice's copies). Retrieved 14 December 2017
7   Hough, Richard: *Advice to a Grand-Daughter.* Heinemann: 1975: p.1167
8   St Aubyn, Giles: *Queen Victoria*: Sinclair-Stevenson: 1991: p.565
9   Ramm, Agatha (ed.): *Beloved and Darling Child*: Alan Sutton: 1990: p.108

10 Maylunas, Andrei: *A Lifelong Passion:* Weidenfeld & Nicolson: 1996: p.20
11 Hough: Op. Cit.: p.110
12 Ibid.: p.111
13 Warwick, Christopher: *Ella, Princess Saint and Martyr.* Wiley: 2006: p.149
14 RA VIC/MAIN/QVJ (W) Saturday 1 July 1893 (Princess Beatrice's copies). Retrieved 14 December 2017
15 RA VIC/MAIN/QVJ (W) Wednesday 5 July 1893 (Princess Beatrice's copies). Retrieved 14 December 2017
16 Maylunas: Op. Cit.: p.32
17 Ibid.: p.33
18 RA VIC/MAIN/QVJ (W) Friday 20 April 1894 (Princess Beatrice's copies). Retrieved 5 February 2018
19 RA VIC/MAIN/QVJ (W) Monday 23 April 1894 (Princess Beatrice's copies). Retrieved 5 February 2018
20 Hardy, Alan: *Queen Victoria Was Amused*: John Murray: 1976: p.140
21 Maylunas: Op. Cit.: p.59
22 Ibid.: p.66
23 Ibid.: p.67
24 Rappaport, Helen: *Four Sisters*: Macmillan: 2014: p.20
25 www.bbc.co.uk/news/uk-england-york-north-yorkshire-39130981
26 Maylunas: Op. Cit.: p.71ff
27 Aronson, Theo: *Grandmama of Europe*: John Murray: 1973: p.86
28 Hibbert, Christopher: *Queen Victoria*: HarperCollins: 2000: p.456
29 Hardy: Op. Cit.: p.184
30 Maylunas: Op. Cit.: p.75
31 Ramm: Op. Cit.: p.172
32 Aronson: Op. Cit.: p.89
33 Maylunas: Op. Cit.: p.107
34 Ibid.: p.112ff
35 RA VIC/MAIN/QVJ (W) Friday 15 November 1895 (Princess Beatrice's copies). Retrieved 27 April 2018
36 www.express.co.uk/news/uk/365836/Mean-Victoria-Queen-revealed-to-loath-her-ugly-frog-like-children
37 Maylunas: Op. Cit.: p.131
38 Ramm: Op. Cit.: p.195
39 Hibbert: Op. Cit.: p.456
40 RA VIC/MAIN/QVJ (W) Saturday 3 October 1896 (Princess Beatrice's copies). Retrieved 27 April 2018
41 RA VIC/MAIN/QVJ (W) Monday 23 November 1896 (Princess Beatrice's copies). Retrieved 27 April 2018
42 Rappaport: Op. Cit.: p.41
43 Ibid.: p.44
44 Ibid.: p.51
45 Maylunas: Op. Cit.: p.204

20

'WE ARE MUCH PLEASED WITH HER'
FLORENCE NIGHTINGALE IMPRESSES THE QUEEN

Florence Nightingale. (Library of Congress)

BORN JUST twelve months apart they were two, some would say the two, towering female figures in a male-dominated nineteenth-century Britain. After becoming a household name following the Crimean War, Nightingale was invited to meet the Queen and Prince Albert, and was never shy in using her royal contacts to further her aims of reforming the nursing services.

Queen Victoria first mentions Florence Nightingale in her journals at the start of the Crimean War. By the end of that two-year conflict Nightingale had been fast tracked in the public consciousness as 'the Lady with the Lamp', and Victoria was one of the first to honour her. The Queen had been frustrated that her own role during the conflict was, necessarily, a symbolic one, whereas Nightingale's was very much a practical one: 'I envy her being able to do so much good and look after the noble brave heroes.'[1]

After the war the Queen would prove to be an essential ally in Nightingale's driving mission to reform the Army Medical Services as well as improving nursing organisation.

Initially it was young Florence who hero-worshipped the Queen rather than the other way round. Although she had felt no willingness to pray for King George IV or his successor William IV, 'when Victoria came to the throne, I prayed for her in a rapture of feeling, and my thoughts never wandered'.[2]

The two women came face to face at a Drawing Room – the forerunner of debutante presentation parties that were abolished by Elizabeth II in 1958 – held on 23 May 1839 to mark Victoria's twentieth birthday the following day. Nineteen-year-old Florence wore a white dress she'd bought in Paris earlier that spring. She joined a throng of 2,000 guests in the state apartments of St James's Palace and admitted that she 'was not nearly so frightened as I expected … The Queen looked flushed and tired, but the whole sight was very pretty.'[3]

Later in the year she passed on some juicy royal tittle-tattle to her sister about Victoria, her first Prime Minister and her beloved King Charles spaniel, Dash:

> We had a pleasant journey up to town the next day with Colonel Buckley full of the Queen's virtues and Lord Melbourne's easy and good term with her. He calls her dog a frightful little beast and sometimes contradicts her flat, all which she takes in good part. She reads all the newspapers and knows all that the Tories say of her and makes up her mind to it, but hates 'em cordial …[4]

The following year as she left chapel with her uncle, Florence saw the newly married Victoria with Prince Albert. She wrote to her sister Parthenope, 'I saw the Queen, a capital view, she a careworn, flabby countenance, poor soul, I thought, he a remarkably agreeable look-ing youth.'[5]

She also shared gossipy royal stories in letters to Selma Benedicks, a young Swedish woman she had met in Italy the previous year. In May 1839 Victoria had behaved unconstitutionally by refusing to give up her Whig Ladies-in-Waiting, which was a necessary prerequisite for Robert Peel's Tory party to take over power. In the face of the wilful monarch's intransigence, Peel was unable to form an administration and Lord Melbourne returned as Whig Prime Minister. Writing a few months after this crisis, Florence noted, 'Our little Queen looks pale and worn but is now perfectly idolized among our party for her firmness and spirit', and was 'enthusiastically cheered' at the opera.[6]

Thanks to family contacts, the young Florence happened to brush shoulders with the monarch and her consort before she was formally welcomed by them as a war hero. In 1825 the Nightingales had moved to the Hampshire country estate of Embley Park, now a private school. Their near neighbour was Lord Palmerston, Foreign Secretary for two lengthy periods between 1830 and 1851, then Home Secretary and Prime Minister in 1855 and again in 1859. Florence's father, William, himself a Whig, rapidly became friends with 'Pam' and was frequently asked to join shooting parties at his lordship's mansion, Broadlands, best known today as the home of Earl Mountbatten of Burma. Besides being Florence's father, William has another footnote in history, since on 11 May 1812 he was in the lobby of the House of Commons when a shot fired out and a man near him fell to the ground. Nightingale raised him in his arms and discovered it to be the Prime Minister, Spencer Percival, who was mortally wounded by an assassin.[7]

Florence was also invited to the weekend house parties. 'I should get quite fond of him, if he were not Lord Palmerston,' she said of her host after one visit. She also witnessed Prince Albert being taught billiards and was amused at the typically overgenerous sportsmanship that the royal presence engendered. When the Prince missed, 'which he did every time, they said oh that does not count, you play again'.[8]

Another family friend of the Nightingales was Sir James Clark, personal physician to Victoria from her accession to 1860. In 1852 Florence's sister Parthenope was staying as a guest of Sir James's at Birkhall in Aberdeenshire, a mile or so from Balmoral Castle along the South Deeside Road. During the visit she suffered from some form of breakdown and urged the Clarks to summon Florence as soon as they could. The younger sister arrived on 13 September and shortly afterwards encountered Victoria while out walking. Florence was an eyewitness after the Queen's niece, Victoria of Hohenlohe, had been thrown from her horse and Sir James had been summoned to help, watched over by the anxious monarch.

Florence also met the Queen's two oldest sons, Bertie, Prince of Wales, aged 8 and his 6-year-old brother Alfred, who came to lunch at Birkhall. She thought the future Edward VII was 'as nice a little boy as I ever saw – so simple, so unaffected; but Prince Alfred was more high-spirited in comparison'. She also made the astute assumption that the heir looked 'a little cowed', perhaps due to being 'over taught'. Perhaps she had heard from Sir James how Prince Albert had devised a rigorous educational programme for the future king, who failed to rise to the challenge.[9]

It was another useful contact that encouraged Florence's interest in nursing. She had been holidaying in Rome in the winter of 1847–48 and met Sidney Herbert – a statesman who had served in Robert Peel's second ministry – and his wife Elizabeth. They shared her social concerns and they rapidly became friends. On their return to Britain, Herbert suggested Florence took on the role of unpaid superintendent to the Establishment for Gentlewomen during Illness, in Harley Street. She soon made an impression, thanks to her nursing skills and organisational abilities. In August 1854 there was a severe outbreak of cholera in Soho and Nightingale went to help with the influx of patients at the Middlesex Hospital. Once again she proved she had 'a remarkable flair for imposing her will on institutions'.[10]

The Crimean War broke out in March 1854 and British and French troops arrived for the invasion of Crimea in September. Within weeks William Howard Russell, legendary war correspondent for *The Times*, wrote a series of features highlighting the lack of medical care and basic supplies. Sidney Herbert, by now Secretary of War for the second time, was criticised by press and public alike. Urgent action was needed and on 15 October he wrote to Florence asking her to lead a party of nurses to Scutari, at the government's expense.

Elizabeth Herbert and Lady Charlotte Canning, Chairwoman of the Establishment for Gentlewomen, where Florence had worked, managed to bring together a unit of thirty-eight nurses within five days and by 4 November they had arrived in Scutari. Victoria was as concerned as her subjects about the vast number of casualties already and she mentioned the decision to send Nightingale in her journals before the latter had even set sail. 'The sickness amongst the troops, alas! very great,' she wrote on 18 October at Windsor. '6,000 in Hospital. Reinforcements must be hurried out.' The same day she had a meeting with the Duke of Newcastle, the new Secretary of State for War – a separate position to that of Herbert's. He told her, 'he had settled to send out 30 Nurses for the Hospitals at Scutari & Varna, under a Miss Nightingale, who is a remarkable person, having studied both Medicine & Surgery & having practised in Hospitals at Paris & in Germany.'[11] Victoria would almost certainly have heard about Florence from Lady Canning, the Chairwoman of the Establishment for Gentlewomen, who also happened to be one of the Queen's most trusted Ladies-in-Waiting.

In December 1854 Queen Victoria wrote a moving letter to her children's governess, Miss Hildyard, who was in touch with Florence Nightingale via Elizabeth Herbert. In her letter the Queen expressed her admiration for the wounded soldiers:

> Let Mrs Herbert also know that I wish Miss Nightingale and the ladies would tell these poor wounded and sick men that *no-one* takes a warmer interest or feels *more* for their sufferings or admires their courage and heroism *more* than their Queen. Day and night she thinks of her beloved troops. So does the Prince. Beg Mrs Herbert to communicate these my words to those ladies, as I know that *our* sympathy is valued by these fellows.[12]

Florence took the royal order to heart and asked army chaplains to read Victoria's words aloud. She also posted copies all over the hospital walls and Parthenope, realising the significance of such a message, asked her sister, 'May we spread the Queen's letter a little?'[13] Unfortunately it was spread to the British press, much to the Queen's annoyance, as she noted in her journal on 6 January 1855: 'We have been somewhat startled by the appearance in the papers of a letter of mine, in fact a note of mine to Miss Hildyard asking her to give Mrs S. Herbert a message for Miss Nightingale.'[14] She was however mollified to realise, 'Startled as I was at first, it has called forth such very kind observations in the different papers, that I feel it may be the means of my *real* sentiments getting known by the Army. Therefore I can no longer regret it.' Not only did she 'no longer regret it' but she acquired a colour lithograph that sentimentally depicted the moment her letter was read by candlelight to a group of overwhelmed patients. It is still in the Royal Collection, entitled *Reading the Queen's letter, Scutari Hospital.*[15]

The royal message was a morale-booster for the men, as Nightingale communicated in a letter which Victoria copied into her journal:

> The men were touched to the heart by the Queen's message, saying that it was a very feeling letter, & with tears, that she was thinking of them, – that each man ought to have a copy, which they would keep to their dying day, &c. I will tell you many more things, by next post.

'What has gratified me, & amply rewarded me,' Victoria added, 'is that my wishes have been fulfilled, in that these poor noble men for, & with them – know that we feel.'[16]

By December 1854 Victoria was writing to Florence directly and praised her 'goodness and self devotion in giving yourself up to the soothing attendance upon these wounded and sick soldiers'. The grateful monarch also asked Nightingale if there was something she herself could do 'to testify her sense of the courage and endurance so abundantly shown by her sick soldiers'.[17]

If Victoria was expecting the typical 'I could not presume to ask someone as busy as Your Majesty to help ...', she was mistaken. Florence was never one to resist bending the ear of an influential contact to get what she wanted. Now with a direct line to the ultimate authority figure – and her husband – she mustn't have been able to believe her luck.

A letter shot from Scutari to Windsor within days. Nightingale pointed out that sick soldiers had their pay docked by 9d a day, while wounded soldiers had 4½d deducted. She suggested both should be on the lower rate, provided the sickness was incurred while on active service. She also asked that the Sultan should decree that military cemeteries at Scutari should be given over to the British. Victoria agreed and both changes were made during February 1855.[18]

Along with hundreds of other well-meaning friends and families back in Britain, Victoria sent a steady stream of gifts to Scutari for her sick and wounded troops. Florence called the free gifts 'these frightful contributions'. They became more of a curse than a blessing to the overworked

'Lady with the Lamp' since they, and the Queen's in particular, had to be carefully administered, distributed, and diligently thanked for. In September 1855 Florence explained the process to Lady Canning:

> The Queen's Gifts ... were immediately divided into proportionate quantities among *all* the Hospitals – a double portion only having been given to the Palace Hospital, where most *Officers*, who would prize most such Articles as the Queen sent. Of the distribution of these, I also kept a record.[19]

Some of the royal gifts were well received, such as water beds to prevent bed sores in patients; some less so, such as Victoria's offer of a shipment of eau de cologne – Florence privately thought someone should tell her a little gin would go down better.[20] Some were thoughtful, such as games for the wounded soldiers, and some, such as £200 sent to Florence 'to lay out for the Queen in any comfort which it might seem well for her to give', were a headache as she had to work out what was 'well for her to give'. As she explained to Lady Canning, 'tobacco is above all the luxury which the soldier most enjoys' but she felt it was 'not exactly a *Queen's* present' and the only thing she could come up with was 'a tent for the Convalescents to air themselves under, which cost £21'.[21]

In December 1854 the Queen wrote to Sidney Herbert asking if it were possible for Nightingale's letters to his wife to be forwarded on to her, 'as I hear *no details of the wounded* though I see so many from officers etc., about the battlefield and naturally the former must interest *me* more than anyone'.[22] Once again, Florence didn't shy away from the truth, knowing the value of keeping the Queen totally aware of the horrors of the war.

After Victoria invited a group of thirty-eight wounded soldiers to meet her at Buckingham Palace she recorded in her journal:

> one of these is a sadly dreadful object, though recovered, & is I think the man described by Miss Nightingale, in one of her 1rst letters as 'one poor fellow has a shot through the nose & behind one eye the bullet coming out through the side of the head. He says he cannot see, but his head did not ache, & really he seemed little the worse'. Poor fellow, he is an awful sight, the face being quite distorted, & a deep hole in one cheek! It quite haunts me.[23]

In May 1855 Victoria was alarmed to hear that Florence had collapsed and become seriously ill with Crimean fever. According to the Chief Medical Officer, Dr Anderson, it was 'as bad an attack of fever as I have ever seen'. Her illness took its toll and her recovery was slow. Three months later she was described as being 'white-faced, extremely weak and looking much older than her age'. A more recent analysis of her symptoms suggests she was suffering from brucellosis, which spreads through the bloodstream, causing rigors and debility. This ties in with her later acute relapses every few years, which left her bedridden for lengthy periods.[24]

On 24 May Florence was visited by Lord Raglan, the commander of the British army, the man responsible for the ill-fated Charge of the Light Brigade the year before, who himself would die from dysentery just a month after visiting her. He was able to telegraph home that evening that she was out of danger. Four days later Victoria wrote how she was 'truly thankful to learn that that excellent and valuable person Miss Nightingale is safe'.[25]

A month later Victoria recorded that she had lately seen a letter sent by Florence:

> before she was taken ill, which is very affecting. The soldiers so adored her, that they brought her fruit & flowers & she was much touched at being cheered by the 39th Regt, which amply repaid her noble devoted heart for all! I envy her![26]

Parthenope Nightingale realised her sister's main strength lay in her administrative skills rather than her nursing ones. 'When she nursed me,' the elder sister noted before the Crimean War, 'everything which intellect and kind intention could do was done but she was a shocking nurse.'[27] The men on the front line, the public at home, and their Queen would beg to differ. When her illness was made apparent at Scutari the men 'turned their faces to the wall and cried. All their trust was in her,' one sergeant wrote home.[28]

Back home the legend of the 'Lady with the Lamp' was well and truly flourishing, boosted by the accounts of returning soldiers. 'The people love you,' wrote Parthenope, 'with a kind of passionate tenderness which goes to my heart.'[29] Mawkishly sentimental songs from 'God Bless Miss Nightingale' to 'The Soldier's Cheer' flooded the popular press. They kept being penned even after the war ended and in 1857 Parthenope thanked one correspondent for sending copies of 'six pretty new ones'. Before she had even returned to British shores, a brief biography of her was circulating at 1d a copy, Staffordshire pottery firms depicted her in ceramic and Madame Tussauds produced a waxen Florence tending to the sick. Her name was bestowed on merchant ships, a lifeboat and even a racehorse.[30] The only thing not in circulation was a portrait of the heroine, as she flatly refused to allow one to be produced. Ever the realist, Florence knew, in her own words, 'there is not an official who would not burn me like Joan of Arc if he could, but they know the War Office cannot turn me out because the country is with me'.[31] More importantly the Queen herself was with her.

A committee was formed to honour Florence's service in the east, chaired by Victoria's cousin the Duke of Cambridge. The idea, according to Parthenope, was to come up with an inscribed gift, 'something of the teapot and bracelet variety'. In the end so much was raised that it was decided a Nightingale Fund would be a better solution. Soldiers fighting in the east pledged a day's pay and raised £9,000 between them.

Victoria opted to send an inscribed gift and asked Albert to design a gold enamelled brooch made up of the St George's Cross encircled with the words 'Crimea' and 'Blessed are the merciful'. On the reverse were the words, 'To Miss Florence Nightingale, as a mark of esteem and gratitude for her devotion towards the Queen's brave soldiers from Victoria R. 1855.' Made by Garrard & Co., the royal jewellers, it is now kept in the National Army Museum. In an accompanying note, the Queen added that she would like to make Nightingale's acquaintance on her return.

By now it was clear the alliance of monarch and medical reformer was one that couldn't be ignored by the British Government. Nightingale used the opportunity of thanking the Queen for her brooch to highlight two pressing issues that the army top brass in the Crimea were ignoring: drunkenness in the troops and the problems the men had in remitting money to their families back home due to fraud. Victoria forwarded the letter and it was discussed at a Cabinet meeting on 21 December. Lord Palmerston, the Prime Minister, thought it excellent and ordered four offices to be set up near to where the troops were stationed so that money orders could be obtained. Some £71,000 was sent home in the first six months, and another outcome was that less money was spent in the drink shops.[32]

The Crimean War officially ended on 30 March 1856, as Victoria noted in her journal:

> On coming home, received the telegraphic news, that Peace had been signed at 2 today! It was 2 years ago, yesterday, that War had been declared! As matters stand, with the great sickness prevalent in the French Army & the unwillingness of the Emperor & his people to proceed any further with the war, it is better it should be so, for I am sure Pélissier would have done nothing & we could not have hoped to gain any successes. This has reconciled me to the Peace, which, otherwise, I consider, came too suddenly, & is not a very favourable one, for *us*.[33]

Florence's work in the east wasn't finished until 16 July, when the last patient left the Barrack Hospital and she was finally able to return to Britain.

While she was still out of the country, her hero-worshipping compatriots had to make do with the other members of Florence's family. Her mother Fanny was invited by Queen Victoria to have a VIP position in the palace forecourt to watch the return of a detachment of guards. 'The Queen was on her balcony just above us, with all the children,' Mrs Nightingale wrote later, 'and the fine fellows, care worn and weary, in thin old Crimean clothes before us within a few feet. It was most touching to be in such close contact with some of those for whom she had been toiling.'[34]

Cecil Woodham-Smith writes, 'After Miss Nightingale's return from the Crimea she never made a public appearance, never attended a public function, never issued a public statement. Within a year or two most people assumed she was dead. She destroyed her fame deliberately as a matter of policy.'[35] She did however make one exception. In early September 1856, just a month after Florence's return, Sir James Clark invited her to stay with him again at Birkhall. He wrote at the request of the Queen, who was staying at nearby Balmoral. She wanted very much to have an official meeting with the legendary nurse but also several private ones at Birkhall. Nightingale realised it was a golden opportunity to bend the royal ear on army reform and hopefully generate a Royal Commission to look into it. En route to Aberdeenshire she stopped off in Edinburgh for a four-day brainstorming session with

Sir John McNeill and Colonel Alex Tulloch, whom she had met in the Crimea when they were researching their own report on front-line army conditions.

Florence arrived at Birkhall on 19 September, accompanied by her father. Two days later she had her first meeting at Balmoral with the Queen and Prince Albert. 'She put before us,' wrote Albert in his journal, 'all the defects of our present military hospital system and the reforms that are needed. We are much pleased with her. She is extremely modest.' 'I wish we had her at the War Office,' wrote Victoria, in a typically forthright manner, to the Duke of Cambridge.[36]

In her journal that night, the Queen gave a detailed account of their meeting:

At 3 we received Miss Nightingale, the celebrated Florence Nightingale whom Sir J. Clark brought into the Drawing Room, leaving her with us for nearly an hour. It is impossible to say how much pleased we were with her. I had expected a rather cold, stiff, reserved person, instead of which, she is gentle, pleasing & engaging, most ladylike, & so clever, clear & comprehensive in her views of everything. Her mind is solely & entirely taken up with the *one* object, to which she has sacrificed her health, & devoted herself like a saint. But she is entirely free of absurd enthusiasm, without a grain of 'exaltation', which so often leads to over strained religious views, – truly simple, quite pious in her action, & her views, yet without the slightest display of religion or a particle of humbug. And together with this, an earnest wish never to appear herself, – travelling under a feigned name, so as not to be known, & refusing all public demonstrations. Such a character, & one so singularly forgiving, is in a woman most rare & extraordinary! She talked principally of the want of system & organisation which had existed, & been the cause of so much suffering & misery, – the necessity for this being improved.

Albert stated in his usual clear, comprehensive way, where, in his opinion, the root of the evil lay, & how instead of improving this, all that had been done, had made matters even worse, being a step backwards instead of forwards. Miss Nightingale spoke of the nurses, how some had answered so well, & others not, – both Roman Catholic & Protestant, – of the men, their conduct, patience, forbearance, & self denial, for which she had the greatest admiration. She thanked me for my support & sympathy saying, that to a man, the soldiers had all deeply felt & appreciated my sympathy & interest. She is tall, & slight, with fine dark eyes, & must have been very pretty, but now she looks very thin & care worn. Albert saw her again afterwards.[37]

Florence's impression of the royal couple is insightful. Victoria she thought 'the least self-reliant person she had ever known', relying on Albert to conduct the conversation.[38] She repeated this in a conversation recalled by another friend years later: 'She says the Queen is a remarkably conscientious person, but so mistrustful of herself, so afraid of not doing her best, that her spirits are lowered by it.'[39] Albert she thought was oppressed by his situation in life and 'was like a person who wanted to die'.[40] It was prescient comment. Albert died five years later and some biographers have referred to him having a death wish. In the last months of his life he confessed to Victoria, 'I do not cling to life; you cling, but I set no store by it ...'[41]

Victoria paid a series of private visits to Birkhall, twice driving herself alone in a pony carriage. She noted in her journal on the 26th:

> I drove to Birkhall with the little girls & the Dss Wellington. It was fine, clear & bright. At the commencement of the approach, we met Sir J. Clark & Miss Nightingale, so we got out & walked with them to the house, & I had much conversation with her. She is so simple, pleasant, & agreeable. In speaking of the poor men, she said that those suffering from disease were much the saddest to see, — that my gifts had been so immensely valued. She, herself had always attended to the night work. We took tea, & then drove back.[42]

Florence dined with the royal couple at the castle and joined them at nearby Crathie Kirk for Sunday worship. There were more lengthy discussions about the war, during which Florence was able to satiate the Queen's hunger for graphic detail. 'Had some long conversation with excellent Miss Nightingale,' she noted on 4 October:

whose affection for my poor good soldiers, is really most touching, & whose philanthropy & truly Christ-like spirit of *true* charity are beautiful. She spoke with much interest of Corporal Country of the 44th, whom we were much interested in at Chatham, last year. He had had 3 bullets in his head & Miss Nightingale discovered him under a stair case, where he had been overlooked, getting the surgeon to remove the bullet out of his eye. For 5 months the poor man's life was in danger & she told him that if he drank he would be a dead man. She has since heard from him & says that *my* notice & kindness has not been thrown away upon him, indeed she is sure that it will generally keep these poor men straight.[43]

During her three-week stay on Royal Deeside, Florence attended several court balls at the castle. After one of them Victoria wrote:

At 1rst people were shy, but afterwards the dancing became very animated. There were Quadrilles, Reels, Country Dances, Jigs, & a pretty Sir Roger de Coverley. Refreshments were served in the Dining Room. Miss Nightingale came, dressed in black with a simple little cap, tied under her chin, her hair having been cut off (actually on account of the insects with which the poor men were covered in the Hospitals!) All was over by 1[44]

Nightingale was less fulsome in her praise for the entertainment on offer. 'Flo says the balls are dull affairs,' reported Blanche Clough, Florence's cousin, '& the Queen ought not to dance. When she is quiet her manner is just what it ought to be ... but she looks very undignified ... [dancing a] Sir Roger de Coverley.'[45]

Victoria was anxious to help Nightingale's cause and she insisted the latter should stay on at Birkhall until Lord Panmure, the Secretary of State for War, came to attend on the Queen in early October. Before the visit she wrote to the minister, 'Lord Panmure will be much gratified and struck with Miss Nightingale – her powerful, clear head and simple modest manner.' The Queen also sent him a copy of Florence's outline for army reform.[46]

Having colluded with Florence to win Panmure over to their viewpoint, the Queen was delighted to note in her journal on 5 October, 'Ld Panmure had much conversation with Miss Nightingale, which I hope will be of use.'[47] It certainly proved to be. A Royal Commission was set up, along the lines drawn up by Florence, and she was asked to submit a 'Confidential Report'. She paid to have her contribution published anonymously and sent the Queen one of the 2,000 copies in October 1858.[48]

Shortly after the heroine's return from the Crimean, Victoria asked for a photograph of Miss Nightingale for the Royal Collection. Florence had previously refused sittings for paintings or photographs. In her Bible she annotated the passage in Ecclesiastes 12, 'Vanity of vanities ... all is vanity', with the words 'and the vanity of vanities – the idolatry of our fellow mortals'. The royal request was one of only two sittings she gave during these years.[49] Earlier images reproduced in the press or as *carte de visites* were idealised ones that often had no bearing on reality, such as the one acquired by Victoria in 1854 and still in the Royal Collection showing Florence reading a book.[50] The Queen also acquired several photos of the military hospital at Scutari.

In the autumn of 1856 Florence moved into the Burlington Hotel in London's West End between Cork Street and Old Burlington Street, where she remained a virtual recluse, rarely venturing out but still keen to see visitors who could contribute to her plans for medical reform of the army. (Five years later Victoria offered her a Grace and Favour apartment at Kensington Palace, which she declined as it was easier to hold meetings and transact business from Mayfair.) Both the Duke of Cambridge and the Queen's eldest daughter, Victoria, Princess Royal, who was married to the Prussian heir, visited her at the hotel. 'I have a fresh acolyte,' Florence wrote to Sir John McNeill in 1868:

> in the person of the Crown Princess of Prussia, quick intelligence and is cultivating herself in knowledge of sanitary (and female) administration for her future career. She comes along like a girl, pulls off her hat and jacket like a five year old, drags about a great portfolio of plans and kneels by my bedside correcting them.[51]

Vicky and Miss Nightingale corresponded about the former's ambition to build a hospital in Berlin, and at the outbreak of the Franco-Prussian War in 1870 Florence sent over a Nightingale-trained matron, Miss Lees, to organise the nursing at the capital's three large war hospitals.

Other requests from liberal-minded royals arrived for Florence's attention. The King of Portugal wanted to build a hospital in Lisbon, and plans and a design were sent by the Burlington's most famous resident. The Queen of Holland submitted her hospital plans in person, and was another frequent visitor until she was graciously but firmly blocked by the visitee: 'I really feel it is a great honour, she is a Queen of Queens. But it is quite quite impossible,' wrote Florence in June 1865.[52]

She felt no such reluctance in keeping contact with the British Royal Family. Victoria was sent a copy of Nightingale's new book, *Notes on Nursing: what it is and what it is not*, inscribing it, 'To Her Majesty the Queen offered with the humble duty of Her Majesty's devoted and faithful subject Florence Nightingale, July 1860.'[53] The previous December she lobbied Prince Albert about the fate of St Thomas's Hospital, which was then situated in Borough and which lay in the path of the proposed rail link between London Bridge and Charing Cross. A deadlock was reached in negotiations and, having studied the case, Florence thought the site should be sold and a new hospital built elsewhere. She wrote to the Prince Consort, who was a governor of the hospital, and his Private Secretary, Colonel Phipps, sent her a gushing acknowledgement for her memorandum, 'which has received the immediate attention any communication from you would be sure to command'. Albert incorporated her suggestions and even quoted her verbatim in a letter to the other governors, and according to Mr Whitfield, the hospital's Resident Medical Officer, it 'wrought wonders'.[54]

Albert was as driven as Florence in his attention to detail and public duty. Exhausted and overworked, the Prince died at Windsor Castle on 14 December 1861 from, it is usually assumed, typhoid fever, though historian Helen Rappaport has recently put forward a convincing argument that he died from Crohn's disease.[55]

Four days after Albert's death Florence wrote to her father:

The loss of the prince is incalculable. The Prince of Wales is nobody. Albert was the only *man* about the Queen, the only influence to which she deferred. On Sunday ministers were quite appalled. It was thought she might turn out a Joanna of Spain [Juana the Mad of Castile, the sister of Catherine of Aragon]. But she rallied and is actually doing business. (My news comes from Lord de Grey.*)[56]

---

* George Robinson 1827–1909, Earl de Grey and Ripon, and Under-Secretary of State for War at this time.

Nightingale's lack of respect for Victoria's heir was made clear another four days later when she wrote, 'One of the causes which brought on Albert's illness and about which he talked when delirious was the shortcomings of the Prince of Wales.'[57] Neither would she have much time for the Prince's wife – 'that silly little girl, Alexandra' – whom he married in 1863.[58]

Florence had been devastated four months earlier by the loss of her friend and mentor Sidney Herbert, and compared her own grief with that of the Queen's. 'The Queen has really behaved like a hero,' she wrote to her cousin Mary Clarke:

> That nervous, fidgety woman, whose love for him was quite abject in its devotion, has buckled to business at once … She is the only woman in these realms, except perhaps myself, who has a *must* in her life – who must set aside private griefs and attend to the respublica.[59]

By the following spring both women were in physical and emotional turmoil. Florence developed a sudden illness on Christmas Eve 1861 which left her with severe spinal pain, and a feeling that her death was imminent. Victoria, as Florence noted to her mother:

> is never able to see but one person at a time … She told Lord Palmerston that she should not live long. But I hear there is no reason for fearing this. L'd P says she is half the size she was.[60]

Ironically, despite their presentiments of death, Victoria would live for another four decades and Florence for five.

Both women felt Albert's death was a national disaster. 'He was really a minister,' Florence wrote to Mary Clarke. 'This very few knew. He neither liked nor was liked but what he has done for this country no one knows.'[61] Victoria's loss was ever-present in the back of Florence's mind. 'She always reminds me of the woman in the Greek chorus,' she wrote in 1863, 'with her hands clasped above her head, wailing out her inexpressible despair.'[62] Concern for the clasping and wailing didn't however stop Florence from sending her latest volume on nursing, concerning the dire sanitary conditions facing the army in India. An inscribed copy of *Observations by Miss Nightingale* landed on the royal desk with Florence keeping fingers crossed 'she may look at it because it has pictures'.[63]

Victoria would send Florence two books hugely prized by both women. Four weeks after Albert's death the Queen sent a copy of *The Principal Speeches and Addresses of His Royal Highness, the Prince Consort*. She inscribed it 'To Miss Florence Nightingale in recollection of the greatest and best of Princes from the beloved Prince's broken-hearted widow, Victoria R, Osborne 13 January 1862.' In later years she would also send a similarly autographed copy of the *Life of the Prince Consort*.[64]

Florence responded with another of her books – a third edition of *Notes on Hospitals* – which she sent to the Queen on 14 December 1863, the second anniversary of Albert's death, despite the fact she'd sent a first edition in 1860. In the letter accompanying this presentation copy of one of her books, she refers to the part played by 'our beloved Prince' in the design of a hospital in Lisbon.[65] Whether it was meant to help assuage Victoria's grief or merely a cynical attempt to prolong their friendship, it was a futile hope, as the Widow of Windsor spent the day making two visits to Albert's tomb in the Royal Mausoleum and held a prayer service there and another outside the room where he died. As always she bemoaned her loss in her journal: 'It seems impossible that this dreadful day should have come round again. How every moment of that day is engraved on my mind & how sick my heart is within me!'[66]

Henceforth their worlds crossed only occasionally. In December 1867 five Nightingale nurses set sail for Australia following a request from the Colonial Secretary to New South Wales. They were accompanied by Florence's distant cousin, Lucy Osburn. Just a week after their arrival in Sydney, Victoria's second son, Prince Alfred, whom Nightingale had met at Birkhall all those years before, was shot at while on a visit to the city. The bullet was safely extracted and the Prince was nursed back to health by two of the nurses and Osburn. A reassured Victoria sent them a note of thanks in which she praised their skills as 'fair sisters of charity'.[67]

Victoria's journals make no reference to meeting Florence at the opening of St Thomas's Hospital in 1871. She was however aware of her attendance at the royal review of troops returning from the Egyptian Campaign on 18 November 1882. The Queen then invited Florence to attend the opening of the Law Courts the following month, where she spoke to her and afterwards sent her a note to say how pleased she was to see her there 'looking well'.[68] This final face-to-face encounter was recorded flatly in the journal: 'Not far from the dais, I recognised

Florence Nightingale, whom I had not seen for years, but who had come out on purpose.'[69]

The two continued to correspond, with Florence, as ever, using the opportunity of contact with the Queen to highlight causes close to her heart. For example, when old Mrs Nightingale died at the age of 92 in 1880, Victoria sent her condolences. Florence responded with a detailed account of her mother's final hours and her funeral, knowing that the Queen, like many of her contemporaries, relished a graphic death-bed account. 'When it came to the last,' Florence wrote:

> she closed her eyes, folded her hands, and went home without a sigh, like a child falling asleep … Her people, even the children, liked to stay by the coffin, and give one holy kiss, as long as the dear old face was there.

In the final paragraph there is a sense of back to business, when the mourning daughter adds, 'I have been humbly desiring to address Your Majesty upon one of the India matters which interests me greatly,' adding a quote from Corinthians to flatter the monarch, '"I speak as a fool" but Your Majesty is wise.'[70] Similarly in 1883, Nightingale used the opportunity of thanking Her Majesty for awarding her with the Royal Red Cross to highlight her concerns about War Office organisation. The award, instituted by the Queen on 23 April 1883, honoured exceptional service in military nursing and was the first example of a British military order solely for women. Eleven days later, another letter from Florence arrived on the Queen's desk. This time she raised the subject of the contentious 'Ilbert Bill' which proposed to allow native Indian magistrates and judges the right to try European criminal cases at the District level. Victoria, no doubt wary of replying herself to such politically sensitive issues, asked her Private Secretary, Sir Henry Ponsonby, to respond to 'the two very interesting communications' on her behalf. On the Ilbert Bill, Ponsonby wrote, 'The Queen is unwilling to express any opinion upon the measure at present.' Her reaction to Nightingale's concerns about the War Office was equally disappointing. With typical courtier-like diplomacy, Ponsonby does however add that Victoria was 'extremely sorry to have missed you at Windsor', when Nightingale was too ill to collect her Royal Red Cross and had to decline the offer to stay overnight at the castle. With even more diplomacy, he ended that the Queen would 'always be glad to receive any communications from you'.[71]

Florence was perhaps pushing her luck with her next communication, a request in December 1883 that the Queen might dine with the visiting Prince Prisdang of Siam. She received the frosty reply from an official: the 'approaching anniversary of the Prince Consort's death makes this a bad time'.[72]

Victoria celebrated her Diamond Jubilee in June 1897 and like many loyal subjects Florence wanted to decorate her home with something suitably patriotic. She asked her friend Henry Bonham Carter, Secretary of the Nightingale Fund from 1862 to 1914, 'would a V.R. Hanging to the Drawing Room … balcony do?' He thought it 'quite enough' but to 'add some red calico to the balcony' and that 'lighting should be carefully done'. Florence also marked the occasion by spending £27 6d – 'an awful sum' – on tickets for some nurses and maids to watch the procession, at the same time feeling sorry for the 'poor Queen'.[73]

Concern to do the right thing was Florence's reaction in January 1901 when Victoria died in her eighty-second year. She asked Henry's wife, Sibella Bonham Carter, whether or not her maids should wear mourning:'I should like to do something to show that one cares, and this is the only thing that it seems one can do (it would of course be only a simple black gown, not expensive.)'[74]

Florence would outlive the Queen by almost a decade. Increasing ill health made her more reclusive than ever but, as a living legend, she remained very much in the thoughts of Victoria's successors. Queen Alexandra sent her birthday greetings in May 1901 and a rather shaky draft reply in Nightingale's own hand still exists. The new King Edward VII conferred on her the title of a Lady of Grace of the Order of St John of Jerusalem in 1904. Three years later he awarded her the Order of Merit. At first he resisted; his Private Secretary, Lord Knollys, wrote to the Prime Minister, Henry Campbell-Bannerman, 'He has always been opposed to women being given the order,' though further representations on Florence's behalf persuaded him to give way. By now Nightingale was too frail to attend a ceremony and the Order was left at her London home in South Street by Edward's representative. It is not even certain she understood the honour she was receiving, but she was heard to murmur, 'too kind, too kind'.[75]

In the same year that she received the OM, Victoria's eldest grandson, Kaiser Wilhelm II of Germany, asked his ambassador to London, Count Metternich, to send a bouquet of lily of the valley and pink carnations, with yards of pink ribbon to match, to Miss Nightingale's home. The accompanying letter was 'expressing his Majesty's esteem and appreciation of her great services to nursing, and conveying his best wishes'. A message written on her behalf was the last of 14,000 letters we have in her name that have survived.[76]

Unknowingly the invalid Florence, now permanently bed-fast in her Mayfair home, outlived Victoria's heir and became a subject of George V. The new King acceded to the throne on 6 May 1910 and one of his first acts was to send to send a telegram of congratulations to Florence on her ninetieth birthday six days later: 'On the occasion of your 90th birthday I offer you my heartfelt congratulation; and trust that you are in good health – GEORGE R & I.'

The Lady with the Lamp died peacefully in her sleep on 13 August 1910. The King sent a telegram to her relatives on the same day:

> The Queen and I have received with regret the sad news of the death of Miss Florence Nightingale, whose untiring and devoted service to the British soldiers in the Crimea will never be forgotten, and to whose striking example we practically owe our present splendid organization of trained nurses. Please accept the expression of our sincere sympathy. GEORGE R & I

The offer of a national funeral and a service at Westminster Abbey was declined, and instead Florence was buried privately near the family home at Embley Park, Hampshire. As her body left London, the procession passed Buckingham Palace, 'where the sentries presented arms and the guards turned out'.[77]

At the foot of the coffin was a cross of flowers made up of mauve orchids fringed with white lilies and roses. Attached to it was a handwritten note from the Queen Mother: 'To Miss Florence Nightingale. In grateful memory of the greatest benefactor to human suffering, by founding the Military Nursing Service in the year 1853 by her own individual exertions and heroism. – August 20 1910. – From ALEXANDRA.'[78]

Notes

1   RA VIC/MAIN/QVJ (W) 8 December 1854 (Princess Beatrice's copies). Retrieved 25 August 2016

2   Housman, Laurence: 'Florence Nightingale': in H.J. Massingham and Hugh Massingham (eds): *The Great Victorians*: Nicholson and Watson: 1932

3   Bostridge, Mark: *Florence Nightingale*: Penguin Books: 2009: p.66

4   Letter to Parthenope Nightingale, October 1839, Wellcome (Claydon copy) Ms 8991/106

5   Letter to Parthenope Nightingale, postmarked 10 March 1840: Wellcome (Claydon copy) Ms 8992/8

6   Bostridge: Op. Cit.: p.66

7   Ibid.: p.15

8   Ibid.: p.83

9   Ibid.: p.176

10 Baly, Monica E. and Matthew, H.C.G.: 'Nightingale, Florence (1820–1910)': *Oxford Dictionary of National Biography*: Oxford University Press: 2004; online edn, January 2011 www.oxforddnb.com/view/article/35241, accessed 25 August 2016

11 RA VIC/MAIN/QVJ (W) 18 October 1854 (Princess Beatrice's copies). Retrieved 13 September 2016

12 Woodham-Smith, Cecil: *Florence Nightingale*: Constable: 1950: p.196

13 Bostridge: Op. Cit.: p.260

14 RA VIC/MAIN/QVJ (W) 6 January 1855 (Princess Beatrice's copies). Retrieved 13 September 2016

15 Royal Collection – RCIN 751018 – Reading the Queen's letter, Scutari Hospital lithograph.

16 RA VIC/MAIN/QVJ (W) 6 January 1855 (Princess Beatrice's copies). Retrieved 13 September 2016

17 Woodham-Smith: Op. Cit.: p.196

18 Ibid.: p.197

19 Vicinus, Martha and Nergaard, Bea: *Ever yours, Florence Nightingale – Selected Letters*: Virago: 1989: p.130

20 Woodham-Smith: Op. Cit.: p.238

21 Vicinus: Op. Cit.: p.122

22 Woodham-Smith: Op. Cit.: p.196

23 RA VIC/MAIN/QVJ (W) 23 February 1855 (Princess Beatrice's copies). Retrieved 14 September 2016

24 *The Sunday Telegraph*, 19 May 1996. 'What bugged Florence Nightingale?'

25 Woodham-Smith: Op. Cit.: p.221

26 RA VIC/MAIN/QVJ (W) 13 June 1855 (Princess Beatrice's copies). Retrieved 14 September 2016

27 Woodham-Smith: Op. Cit.: p.107

28 Ibid.: p.220

29 Ibid.: p.234

30 Ibid.: p.235

31 Ibid.: p.232

32 Ibid.: p.240

33 RA VIC/MAIN/QVJ (W) 30 March 1856 (Princess Beatrice's copies). Retrieved 17 September 2016

34 Bostridge: Op. Cit.: p.258

35 Woodham-Smith: Op. Cit.: p.262
36 Ibid.: p.265
37 RAVIC/MAIN/QVJ (W) 21 September 1856 (Princess Beatrice's copies). Retrieved 30 September 2016
38 Bostridge: Op. Cit.: p.308
39 Woodham-Smith: Op. Cit.: p.270
40 Bostridge: Op. Cit.: p.308
41 Lamont-Brown, Raymond: *Royal Poxes and Potions*: The History Press: 2009
42 RAVIC/MAIN/QVJ (W) 26 September 1856 (Princess Beatrice's copies). Retrieved 30 September 2016
43 RAVIC/MAIN/QVJ (W) 4 October 1856 (Princess Beatrice's copies). Retrieved 30 September 2016
44 RAVIC/MAIN/QVJ (W) 22 September 1856 (Princess Beatrice's copies). Retrieved 30 September 2016
45 Bostridge: Op. Cit.: p.307
46 Woodham-Smith: Op. Cit.: p.268
47 RAVIC/MAIN/QVJ (W) 5 October 1856 (Princess Beatrice's copies). Retrieved 30 September 2016
48 Royal Collection – RCIN 1075240 – Notes on Matters Affecting the Health, Efficiency and Hospital Administration of the British Army 1858
49 Woodham-Smith: Op. Cit.: p.361
50 Royal Collection – RCIN 659458 – Unknown Person: Miss Florence Nightingale published 28 November 1854 – Lithograph.
51 Woodham-Smith: Op. Cit.: p.507
52 Ibid.: p.430
53 Royal Collection – RCIN 1075238 – *Notes on nursing: what it is and what it is not* by Florence Nightingale, 1860
54 Woodham-Smith: Op. Cit.: pp.336–67
55 Rappaport, Helen: *Magnificent Obsession*: Windmill Books: 2012
56 Florence Nightingale: Letter to W.E. Nightingale, 18 December 1861, Wellcome (Claydon copy) Ms 8999/46
57 Florence Nightingale: Letter to W.E. Nightingale, 22 December 1861, Wellcome (Claydon copy) Ms 8999/48
58 McDonald, Lynn (ed.): *The Collected Works of Florence Nightingale, Vol. 5: Florence Nightingale on Society and Politics, Philosophy, Science, Education and Literature*: Wilfred Laurier University Press: 2003: p.420
59 Woodham-Smith: Op. Cit.: p.383
60 Bostridge: Op. Cit.: pp.388–9
61 Woodham-Smith: Op. Cit.: p.383
62 Ibid.: p.377
63 Ibid.: p.408
64 McDonald: Op. Cit.: p.418
65 Royal Collection – RCIN 1075237 – Florence Nightingale (1820–1910) – *Notes On Hospitals 1863*
66 RAVIC/MAIN/QVJ (W) 14 December 1863 (Princess Beatrice's copies). Retrieved 10 November 2016
67 Bostridge: Op. Cit.: p.450
68 McDonald: Op. Cit.: p.422
69 RAVIC/MAIN/QVJ (W) 4 December 1882 (Princess Beatrice's copies). Retrieved 15 November 2016

70 Letter from Florence Nightingale to Queen Victoria dated 27 February 1880. Royal Collection, Windsor Castle, RA VIC/W 86/417

71 McDonald: Op. Cit.: p.424

72 Ibid.: p.426

73 Ibid.: p.427

74 Bostridge: Op. Cit.: pp.518–9

75 Woodham-Smith: Op. Cit.: p.592

76 'The German Emperor in London', *The Times*: Issue 38513: Wednesday 11 December 1907: p.11

77 McDonald: Op. Cit. p.275. Letter of Louis Hilary Shore Nightingale to Margarate Verney, 23 August 1910

78 *The Times*: Monday 22 August 1910

21

LAMB ON A PERSIAN RUG
QUEEN VICTORIA RECEIVES THE SHAH

Naser al-Din Shah Qajar

NASER AL-DIN Shah Qajar, born in 1831, was the King of Persia (now Iran) from 1848 to 1896, making him one of the longest-reigning monarchs in Iranian history. He was also the first Persian monarch in modern times to visit Europe. In 1873 he toured Russia, Germany, France and Belgium, and in Britain he was the guest of Queen Victoria. They formed an unlikely friendship and he made a return visit to see her in 1889. To the Queen's great sadness, he was assassinated on 1 May 1896.

In the summer of 1873, at the suggestion of her Prime Minister, William Gladstone, the Queen agreed to receive the Shah of Persia since, the Prime Minister maintained, a friendship with his country would help improve Britain's relationship with the Middle East.

After leaving Tehran in the late spring, the Shah spent fourteen days in Russia, followed by twenty days in Germany and Belgium before his arrival in London. As he progressed westwards across the continent, an increasingly agitated Victoria digested tales of Naser's rumoured behaviour. He was said to wipe his wet hands on the coat tails of whichever gentleman happened to be seated next to him, was clumsy using a knife and fork, preferring to put his fingers into dishes instead, would occasionally pull chewed food out of his mouth to examine it, had been known to drink out of the spout of a teapot and was in the habit of sacrificing a cock to the rising sun.

Victoria was also worried that he might make improper suggestions to her ladies, and might well be rude to them. The latter proved true when he met the philanthropist Baroness Burdett-Coutts at court. He looked her directly in the eye and using his schoolboy French exclaimed, 'Quelle horreur!'[1]

Gladstone was scandalised when he heard the Shah might leave three of his wives in Europe – most of his complement of two dozen had stayed in Persia – but bring some other charmers in his entourage. He threatened to withdraw government hospitality, but in the end they were kept under wraps.

Meanwhile, an increasingly irritated Victoria queried why he was termed 'Imperial' in the programme. Her Private Secretary, Henry Ponsonby, explained, 'Because he is the Shah-in-Shah.' 'Well that's no reason!' exploded the monarch, and she had the title removed from the paperwork.[2] (It would be another three years before the Royal Titles Bill promoted her to Empress of India, putting her on an equal footing with other 'imperials'.)

Vicky, who had already helped to host the Prussian leg of the Shah's tour, warned her mother, 'he is a strange guest ... His unpunctuality is something dreadful – to keep everyone waiting three quarters of an hour is nothing at all out of the way.' On a more positive note, she added, 'he talks most of England and of you'.[3]

In another letter six days later, Vicky warned her mother that the Shah 'always has a lamb roasted in his room, which he pulls to pieces with his fingers distributing it to all his ministers all sitting on the floor'. He also 'throws his pocket handkerchief across the room at his Prime Minister when he has used it, upon which this dignitary makes a profound bow and puts the handkerchief in his pocket'.[4]

Vicky's entertaining tales seem to have calmed the Queen rather than alarmed her. 'Your account of the Shah is most amusing ... and has somewhat relieved me,' wrote the Queen on 18 June, the day of his arrival in London, adding, 'But I think if these Eastern potentates wish to travel they ought not to carry their uncivilised notions and habits with them!'[5] Suitably forewarned, Victoria instructed her Household to install a movable carpet into the visitor's suite at Buckingham Palace where he was to stay for the next few weeks (although the Queen only saw him at Windsor). It was a sensible move since he did indeed regularly roast lamb over a tripod on the floor and upon his departure the carpet was found to be severely burnt.

Despite Vicky's assurance that he 'has a perfect adoration for England and everything English,' the Queen had a last minute panic: 'Felt nervous & agitated at the great event of the day, — the Shah's visit.' Later she noted:

> All great hustle & excitement. The guns were fired & bells ringing for my Accession Day, & the latter also for the Shah. The Beefeaters were taking up their places, Pages walking about, in full dress ... crowds appeared near the Gates, the Guard of Honour & Band marched into the quadrangle & then I dressed in a smart morning dress, with my large pearls, & the star & ribbon of the Garter, the Victoria & Albert order, &c.

Her two younger sons, Arthur and Leopold, went to the station to meet the VIP guest and his entourage. At the castle:

> The Band struck up the new Persian march & in another moment the carriage drove up to the door ... I stepped forward & gave him my hand, which he shook expressing to the Gd [Grand] Vizier my great satisfaction at making the Shah's acquaintance. Then took his arm & walked slowly upstairs, & along the Corridor speaking to each other in French.

As usual the Queen documented the visitor's appearance with forensic detail in her journal:

The Shah is fairly tall & not fat, has a fine countenance & is very animated. He wore a plain coat (a tunic) full in the skirt & covered with very fine jewels, enormous rubies as buttons & diamond ornaments, the sword belt & epaulettes made entirely of diamonds, with an enormous emerald in the centre of each. The sword hilt & scabbard were richly adorned with jewels, & in the high black Astrakhan cap, was on aigrette of diamonds.

After the presentations of family and household by both sides, 'I asked him to sit down, which we did on 2 chairs in the middle of the room (very absurd it must have looked, & I felt very shy), my daughters sitting on the sofa'. After she'd invested the Shah with the Order of the Garter:

he then took my hand & put it to his lips & I saluted him ... After this the Shah gave me his 2 orders, the one being his miniature, set in magnificent diamonds, the *Sovereign's* order, but has never been given to a woman before. It is worn round the neck.

Placing the second order over her shoulder, he almost dislodged her widow's cap, until the Grand Vizier came to the rescue.

Over luncheon in the Oak Room, the Shah was clearly on his best behaviour, avoiding the meat course and the unfamiliar cutlery, opting for just fruit and iced water. A band played 'the Pipers at Dessert, walking round the table, which seemed to delight the Shah'.[6]

On his return to Persia, the Shah published his diary account of his European tour. Victoria was given an English translation of it and would have been flattered to read, 'The age of the Sovereign is fifty [she was actually 54], but looks no more than forty. She is very cheerful and pleasant of countenance.' He was however intrigued to see Prince Leopold in his kilt and noted in the diary, 'This son today had come to the station to meet me. He is very young-looking and very graceful. He wore the Scotch costume. The peculiarity of the Scotch costume is this: the knees are left visible up to the thighs.'[7]

The day after the meeting at Windsor, the relieved Queen wrote to Vicky, 'The Shah's visit went off admirably and he certainly is very intelligent but I thought him very dignified. There was nothing to shock one at all in his eating or anything else.'[8]

Of course at this stage Victoria had no idea the Persians were happily barbecuing inside her London palace. It was perhaps with that in mind that the Royal Household arranged for a demonstration by the London Fire Brigade. The Shah watched on as firefighters carried out a mock rescue of burnt and half-burnt 'victims' from the top floor of the palace. Some were carried over the shoulder in a firemen's lift while others were let down on ropes. The pyromaniacal Persian wrote, 'they have invented a beautiful way of saving men.'[9]

One diversion that did reach the Queen's dismayed ears was a boxing match in the gardens of Buckingham Palace. After firefighters it was the turn of prizefighters to entertain the Shah, who wrote an explanatory account for his countrymen:

> To box is to strike one another with the fists which requires great skill and dexterity. But they wore on their hands a kind of large gloves stuffed with wool and cotton. Had they not worn these gloves, they would have killed one another. It was very ludicrous and amusing.[10]

Twenty miles west of London, Victoria was also discovering a new sport. While inspecting preparations for a military review she was hosting for the Shah in the Great Park, she 'came back to see a short game of Polo played by some of the Cavalry Officers. It is a very fast game, something like Hockey on horseback.'[11]

On the day of the review itself the Queen was as excited as a young girl on a first date. She had wanted to greet her son, Arthur, upon his arrival at the castle:

> but it was too late, as I was anxious to get home in good time ... Then came the dressing. I wore my usual sort of summer dress, a black silk mantle & bonnet with black & white feathers & flowers. Round my neck, attached to a black velvet, I wore the order of the Portrait of the Shah, which I arranged to show outside as much as I could.

Before the review started, 'the Shah & the Princes went down & mounted their horses, which I watched from the Corridor. The Shah got on very easily.' Afterwards, as he prepared to leave for London:

the Shah appeared having rested & had some refreshment. I took his arm & went down with him to the door; he pressed my hand & put each of his on my shoulders, like a sort of blessing. He really is very kind & gracious & full of dignity.[12]

When the Shah came to Windsor to take leave of the Queen on 2 July, she was very clearly enthralled by him:

After luncheon, began to dress for the Shah's last visit. I put on his portrait, & the blue ribbon that belongs to it, wearing it round my neck & the other order over my shoulder ... We all went down & I received the Shah at the door, leading him upstairs. He talked French at once, on my asking where he had been & what he had seen, & about having been to the Houses of Parliament. He always talks very loud.

The Queen gave him a guided tour of the State Apartments and at one point 'called the Shah's attention to the Koh-i-Noor, which I was wearing as a brooch, & he stooped to look at & touch it'.

When it came time to say farewell, the Queen 'joined him at the top of the staircase & gave him one of my photographs signed, & took him down to the door. He seemed quite melancholy at taking leave, & kissed my hand. I wished him a good journey & health & happiness.'[13]

In his own journal entry, the Shah recounts, 'I gave my reflexion [a photograph] to the Sovereign as a souvenir; she gave me hers and that of Prince Leopold.' When the procession was about to leave the castle's Quadrangle the Queen asked her photographer to take one last shot of the Shah in his carriage.[14]

When it came to charming Victoria, the Shah certainly pressed all the right buttons. He told her he'd read her *Leaves of a Journal of our Life in the Highlands* in a Persian translation; he asked to see Prince Albert's remains in the Royal Mausoleum, where 'I laid on the tomb a nosegay which I had in my hand. I became extremely dejected and full of sadness.' He even visited the Albert Memorial in London, 'a structure which the Sovereign has reared to the memory of her husband'.[15]

Victoria's delighted report to Vicky sounds as though she might have been in the running to be wife number 25: 'I gave him a nosegay and my photograph which he kissed (I hear) as he was leaving the station! I took him again down and he kissed my hand!'[16]

There was even good news about her singed palace. Sir John Cowell, Master of the Household, told the Queen the Shah had left a tip of £1,600 (some £170,000 at today's rate) as well as gifts for each of the gentlemen of the Household.

In the days after his departure the Shah was still very much on the Queen's mind. In her journal she wrote that Princess Beatrice was reading to her out of a pamphlet on Persia and on 8 July she was 'photographed with my Persian order for the Shah'.[17] She also commissioned the artist Nicholas Chevalier to produce a watercolour of the Shah being greeted at Windsor by the Queen and an oil painting of the military review, both of which are still in the Royal Collection.

When it came to leaving the castle on 11 July for Osborne, a wistful Victoria wrote, 'left Windsor at ¼ to 10, with regret, as it was looking so beautiful, & the mornings & evenings at Frogmore were so peaceful & lovely. Then too, the Shah's visit remains a pleasant & interesting recollection.'[18]

Gladstone's ploy of arm-twisting the Queen into hosting the state visit to improve Middle Eastern relations had worked in a way no one could ever have predicted. This includes Sir Henry Ponsonby who, a year after the visit, told his wife, 'The Shah writes to the Queen on business. A boundary question. He calls her "my auspicious sister of sublime nature to whose wishes events correspond."'[19]

Notes

1 Hibbert, Christopher: *Queen Victoria – A Personal History*: HarperCollins: 2000: p.347
2 Ibid.: p.347
3 Fulford, Roger (ed.): *Darling Child*: Evans Brothers: 1976: p.93
4 Ibid.: pp.94–5
5 Ibid.: p.95
6 RA VIC/MAIN/QVJ (W) Friday 20 June 1873 (Princess Beatrice's copies). Retrieved 19 June 2018
7 Redhouse, J.W.: *Diary of H.M. The Shah of Persia During his Tour Through Europe in AD 1873*: John Murray: 1874: p.151
8 Fulford: Op. Cit.: p.95
9 Redhouse: Op. Cit.: p.190
10 Ibid.: p.191
11 RA VIC/MAIN/QVJ (W) Monday 23 June 1873 (Princess Beatrice's copies). Retrieved 19 June 2018
12 RA VIC/MAIN/QVJ (W) Tuesday 24 June 1873 (Princess Beatrice's copies).

Retrieved 19 June 2018

13 RA VIC/MAIN/QVJ (W) Wednesday 2 July 1873 (Princess Beatrice's copies). Retrieved 19 June 2018

14 Redhouse: Op. Cit.: p.213

15 Ibid.: p.203

16 Fulford: Op. Cit.: p.100

17 RA VIC/MAIN/QVJ (W) Tuesday 8 July 1873 (Princess Beatrice's copies). Retrieved 19 June 2018

18 RA VIC/MAIN/QVJ (W) Friday 11 July 1873 (Princess Beatrice's copies). Retrieved 19 June 2018

19 Kuhn, William M.: *Henry and Mary Ponsonby*: Duckworth: 2003: p.270

22

TRAGEDY AT MAYERLING
HOW THE SUICIDE OF THE AUSTRIAN HEIR AFFECTED THE QUEEN

Crown Prince Rudolph of Austria. (Library of Congress)

VICTORIA ONLY met the Austrian Crown Prince three times, but formed a strong attachment to him. He was the only royal, apart from a head of state or a member of her own family, to receive the Order of the Garter from her, and he stayed with her twice – at Osborne and Windsor during the spring of 1878 as well as representing his father, the Emperor Franz Joseph, at the Golden Jubilee celebrations of 1887.

The suicide of Crown Prince Rudolph – heir to the Austro-Hungarian throne – and his 18-year-old mistress Mary Vetsera shocked and scandalised the courts of Europe and beyond. Clumsy attempts by the Austrian court to disguise the real facts surrounding the couple's deaths only exacerbated and prolonged the worldwide fascination with the shootings. The story has never died down and the tragedy of Mayerling – the royal hunting lodge where the lovers died – has been the subject of dozens of books, two major films and a 1978 ballet by Kenneth MacMillan.

The Crown Prince's death in January 1889 both shocked and fascinated Victoria, and references in her letters and journals to 'poor Rudolph' and 'Rudolph's dreadful death' recur on an almost daily basis throughout that spring. The association between Queen and Prince dates back to 1860 when, due to Victoria and Albert's insatiable interest in photography, they acquired two photographs of the baby Austrian heir. One shows him sitting on a chair holding a book, watched over by his older sister Gisela, and a second one shows him in a wide-sleeved dress astride a toy dog on wheels.

In January 1872 the Prince and Princess of Wales paid a private visit to Vienna, where a week-long series of balls, concerts and race meetings delighted the playboy Prince and were a marked contrast to life at Victoria's mournful court. The Queen objected to the inclusion of two minor aristocrats, one of whom she labelled 'unprincipled', in the Prince's party for a forthcoming tour of Egypt, adding, 'If you ever become king, you will find these friends *most* inconvenient, and you will have to break with them *all*.' No doubt rankled by the word 'if' in his mother's admonishment, Bertie's tit-for-tat reply referenced Victoria's reclusive behaviour, suggesting the Queen could 'go oftener and remain longer in London … as the people – not only Londoners – cannot bear seeing Buckingham Palace always unoccupied'. Then in another pointed comment he told her that Rudolph – 'a very nice young man, but not at all good-looking' – was 'treated almost like a boy by his parents'. Rudolph was only 13 at the time, whereas Bertie, aged 30, was still being treated like a boy by his mother and would be until he was nearly 60.

Rudolph and Victoria met twice during the spring of 1878. The Crown Prince had arrived in England shortly after Christmas to study political and economic conditions. The Austrian parliamentary system was barely a decade old and Emperor Franz Joseph wanted his son to see at first hand how the British Government functioned and to discover how the country had achieved its industrial might. During his visit he would collaborate on a pamphlet, *The Austrian Aristocracy and its Constitutional Task*, which was published anonymously later in the year.

Rudolph arrived with his mother, the Empress Elizabeth, an expert horsewoman who based herself in Nottinghamshire to attend the hunts. The Crown Prince stayed at a small hotel in Brook Street, London, which is now Claridge's.

On Thursday 10 January, Rudolph travelled to Osborne to meet the Queen. Victoria was preoccupied with the ongoing Russo-Turkish war and the same day had telegraphed her Prime Minister, Benjamin Disraeli, 'urging that something must be done to encourage the unfortunate distressed Turks who kept asking us for help'.[1]

Afterwards she wrote to the Prince of Wales: 'The Young C.Pce. Left today and I am much pleased with him. He, as *all* Austrians, is most easy to get on with ... He is very pleasing, but looks a little overgrown and *not* very robust.'[2]

Bertie replied, 'I am glad to hear that you were pleased with Crown Prince Rudolph. I saw him yesterday on his return from Osborne – and he seemed very pleased with his visit – I thought him very pleasing ...'[3] The Prince suggested his mother might bestow the Order of the Garter on his fellow heir, but at this stage she demurred, thinking him too young for the honour.

The Queen's fulsome praise for her young guest was repeated in a letter to her eldest daughter, Vicky, 'We liked the young Crown Prince of Austria very much. He is so simple and unaffected and yet so well informed and with such charming manners.'[4]

Victoria's delight seems to have become a family joke. Her cousin Princess Mary of Cambridge, mother of the future Queen Mary, teasingly told the Austrian Ambassador, Count Beust, 'The Queen is in love with the Crown Prince, but do not worry, she does not want to marry him.'[5]

Having already met Rudolph five years earlier, Bertie was beginning to develop a strong bond with the young man, despite their age gap of seventeen years, and this visit cemented their friendship. He hosted a dinner for the Crown Prince on 10 February, and delighted him by inviting Benjamin Disraeli as a fellow guest.[6]

Both princes had an eye for the ladies and, that spring, for the same one – Lillie Langtry. Dubbed 'The Jersey Lily' after the island of her birth and the Amaryllis belladonna – the late-blooming pink lily associated with this Channel isle – Mrs Langtry met Bertie in 1877 and they began what was to be a three-year liaison.

Rudolph met her at a ball hosted by Ferdinand de Rothschild and made his mark, quite literally, by placing an uncomfortably clammy hand on her back during a dance. Dismayed that the youthful prince was leaving sweat marks on her expensive new pale pink crêpe de Chine gown, she suggested he put his gloves on. His reply, '*C'est vous qui suez madame*' ('It's you who sweats, madam'), failed to impress her and in her autobiography she recalls that his subsequent visits to her Norfolk Street home, off Park Lane, were not met by her with any enthusiasm.

He had a more positive response from the Queen. Victoria invited Rudolph to stay with her at Windsor Castle on 22 February, two days before his return to Vienna. As before, his similar view of the ongoing crisis in Eastern Europe endeared him to the Queen, as she noted in her journal, 'After tea, received the Crown Pce of Austria, in the Audience Room, & he spoke most sensibly, & in the most strongly anti-Russian sense, hoping that Austria would act, which I told him, we had expected she would.'

The following morning he was honoured a rare accolade – a personal guided tour of the holy of holies, the tombs of Albert and the Duchess of Kent:

> Breakfasted in the Oak Room with the Crown Pce of Austria. — At 11, we 3 walked out with him to the dear Mausoleum, which we showed him, as well as Mama's. Then walked through the house to the Dairy, & from there drove home.

Rudolph left Windsor after lunch.

> He spoke terms of praise & delight of England, where everyone was so kind to him, & was full of thanks. He is very amiable, clever, & well informed, wonderfully so for a person of his age, not yet 20. Repeated earnestly my hope that Austria would came forward & act with us.[7]

In May 1881 Bertie was one of the few overseas royal guests to attend Rudolph's wedding to Princess Stephanie of Belgium, granddaughter of Victoria's beloved Uncle Leopold. Victoria, who had a soft spot for genuine love matches, was shocked that Stephanie had been dragooned into marrying, and had not even met Rudolph before their betrothal. 'Poor little Stephanie's engagement took everyone by surprise,' she wrote to Vicky:

> including the Empress [of Austria] and Leopold of B[elgium]. The poor thing has been completely shut up – never seen anyone – never been to a dance or play etc. and suddenly the C. Prince of Austria is brought, speaks to her and she is engaged and brought out!![8]

Unsurprisingly the union was ill-fated. After five years Stephanie gave birth to their only child, the Archduchess Elisabeth, known to her family as 'Erszi', a diminutive of her name in Hungarian. By now Rudolph was addicted to alcohol and drugs. He also contracted a venereal disease which according to his wife's unpublished memoirs he infected her with, causing a serious illness, officially described as 'peritonitis' and making it impossible for her to conceive again. 'From that time onwards,' recalled Stephanie, 'the Crown Prince would sometimes not return home until the early hours of the morning, and in an undesirable condition. Under these circumstances no real living together was possible any longer; my whole being rebelled against it.'[9]

Despite his sybaritic lifestyle, Rudolph behaved creditably well during his meetings with Victoria and her offspring. He came to London for the Queen's Golden Jubilee celebrations in June 1887, representing his father.

Victoria met the King of Saxony and assembled HRHs in the Picture Gallery at Buckingham Palace, before hosting her first luncheon in the large Dining Room which she hadn't used since Albert's death in 1861. She noted in her journal, 'I omitted to say that the Crown Prince of Austria came in uniform, to thank me for having given him the Garter.'[10] (Bertie had once again petitioned his mother to bestow Rudolph with the Order, and this time she'd relented.)

Besides attending the Thanksgiving Service at Westminster Abbey, the Crown Prince partook in the never-ending succession of receptions, presentations, luncheons and dinners. He complained he didn't even have time to chat to his father-in-law, Leopold II of Belgium. 'I am frightfully rushed …,' he wrote to Stephanie who had remained in Vienna. 'No one has any free time.'[11]

Rudolph was being economical with the truth, since he and Bertie had enough free time to have supper in a London restaurant with a party of friends. At about 2 a.m. the Prince of Wales decided to link arms with the beautiful Duchess of Manchester and dance Offenbach's famous can-can. As the portly prince unedifyingly high-kicked his way around the room, an embarrassed Rudolph whispered to a fellow guest, 'Tell, the waiters to go. They must not see their future King making such a clown of himself.'[12]

On the final day of the Jubilee celebrations Victoria sat next to Rudolph at the last gathering of overseas royalty before the Queen left the capital for Windsor:

> Again a big luncheon in the Dining Room. I sat between dear Fritz & the Crown prince of Austria. The latter spoke most warmly & kindly, of how anxious he was for a friendly alliance & the best understanding between Austria & England. — Gave Jubilee medals to the Kings & most of the Princes.[13]

The two heirs met again the following year when Rudolph hosted an extended jolly for his British counterpart. After attending the autumn manoeuvres of the Austrian army with Franz Joseph, the princes enjoyed a riotous few days in Vienna and Budapest. Bertie wrote to his mother that he felt 'thoroughly at home' with the Hapsburgs, emphasising the manoeuvres rather than the Viennese nightlife.

Rudolph laid on a bear-shooting expedition to Gorgeny in Transylvania, marred by the total lack of bears, as they had deserted the hot, dry foothills for the hilltops. 'It was *most* disappointing,' Edward wrote to his equally trigger-happy son, Prince George, 'and the Crown Prince was dreadfully put out ... But we were a cheery party – capital cook, Hungarian band, and splendid weather.'[14]

After a brief stopover in Vienna with the Emperor, the two men took the night train to Neuburg in the Austrian state of Styria where, in a three-hour blitzkrieg, seven rifles killed thirty chamois. Bertie had killed four and wounded two and wrote joyfully to George that it had been 'the prettiest sport I have seen for a long time'.[15]

It has never been entirely clear how Rudolph and Mary Vetsera met. She herself mentions in a letter that they were introduced by Countess Marie Larisch, the Crown Prince's first cousin, in the Prater, just outside Vienna, in the autumn of 1888. A second theory is that Bertie himself may have inadvertently set in motion the events that led to Rudolph's death at Mayerling three months later. Berthold Frischauer, the Diplomatic Correspondent for *Tagblatt*, one of the most influential Liberal newspapers for which Rudolph himself contributed occasional articles on topical government issues, claimed that the Prince of Wales introduced Mary to the Crown Prince at the Freudenau racecourse in early October 1888.

Certainly Bertie knew Mary's mother Helene as well as the latter's brother Alexander Baltazzi, who had lived in Britain for a time and like the Prince was a keen racegoer – Baltazzi's horse won the 1876 Epsom Derby. It was Alexander who identified his niece's body and accompanied her body from Mayerling.

The Prince of Wales however mentions another meeting when he wrote to his mother after Vetsera's death:

> I met the poor young lady frequently at Homburg and Vienna …
> I pointed her out to him [Rudolph] in a box at the opening of the
> new 'Burg Theatre' [14 October 1888] and said how handsome she
> was – he spoke I thought disparagingly of her …

(By speaking 'disparagingly' Rudolph of course may have been trying to discourage his equally libidinous royal friend from adding Vetsera to his list of conquests.)

Whatever the truth about how the lovers met, certainly they were seeing each other regularly by November 1888, as well as exchanging letters via Rudolph's valet and Mary's maid.

Vetsera was a useful distraction and support for the Prince, whose state of mind had reached a crisis point due to his unhappy marriage, his poor health, his frustrations in his role as Crown Prince which saw him continually at odds with his father and, most recently, his concern for the political unrest in Hungary. The Hungarian parliament had been voting on a new, controversial, Defence Bill, and this had led to unrest on the streets of the capital, Budapest.

Rudolph was so depressed that in December of that year he contacted Mizzi Kaspar, a Viennese dancer with whom he had started an affair a few years earlier, and suggested a suicide pact. He had, she said later, spoken to her several times about shooting himself, but she had never taken the threats seriously. In the weeks leading to his death he had also asked five friends and hunting companions, 'Are you afraid of death?'

The Mayerling tragedy must have been premeditated since Mary left a suicide note which Marie Larisch discovered shortly after Mary had left Vienna for the hunting lodge. A highly agitated Larisch took it to the President of Police, who told her he had no jurisdiction in Mayerling and that he feared a scandal that would damage Vetsera's name.

Meanwhile Rudolph left Vienna on the afternoon of Monday 28 January 1889, arranging with his staff that he would return to the capital the following day for dinner with his parents and Stephanie.

The following morning he breakfasted with his hunting companions Count Hoyos and Prince Philip of Saxe-Coburg and Gotha – Stephanie's brother-in-law. Over the meal he told the two men he had been feeling unwell and thought that he was developing a heavy cold, and that they should go without him.

In the afternoon Coburg had tea with Rudolph, who said that he didn't feel well enough to return to Vienna for the family meal that evening and asked Coburg, who was also invited, to apologise to his family for him. Hoyos who, like Prince Philip, at this stage had no idea Vetsera was also staying at the lodge, dined with Rudolph that evening. The Prince retired to his bedroom at 9 p.m., having arranged to breakfast with Hoyos at 8 a.m.

The small retinue of staff was fully aware of the liaison. That final evening Rudolph's coachman Josef Bratfisch came into the couple's bedroom to serenade them with some sentimental Viennese songs. Afterwards Mary wrote farewell letters to her mother and sister while Rudolph penned a brief note to his manservant Johann Loschek. At some point after this Mary lay on the bed with her tear-stained handkerchief in her hand, and the Crown Prince fired a single bullet, instantly killing the woman who had blithely agreed to accompany him on his final journey.

Rudolph delayed his suicide until the morning. At 6.30 a.m. he called Loschek and asked him to prepare breakfast and call him an hour later. Whistling softly to himself he returned to his room and locked the door. He drank a brandy, placed a flower in his lover's hand, stood in front of a mirror, pointed the gun at his head and pulled the trigger.

Loschek knocked at Rudolph's door at 7.30 a.m. as requested but there was no answer. Hoyos, who had walked across from his room in an adjacent building to join the Prince for breakfast, decided they should break the door down, until Loschek mentioned the presence of Mary.

Shortly afterwards Coburg also arrived for the hunt. Briefed of the situation he had, as a family member, the authority to order the door to be broken down. Loschek carried out the command, smashed the door panels through, climbed in through the shattered panels and returned to tell the horrified guests what he'd seen.

Rudolph was half lying across the edge of the bed, surrounded by a pool of blood. For some reason Loschek concocted the story that Rudolph's death was due to potassium cyanide poisoning, which had caused a haemorrhage. Hoyos hurried to the Imperial court, where the news was broken firstly to the Empress and then by her to Franz Joseph. The Empress also broke the news to Helene Vetsera, who had been informed by Marie Larisch that Mary had absconded with Rudolph and had come to the Hofburg Palace to entreat the Empress to find out her daughter's whereabouts. Helene, like the Imperial couple, believed at that stage that Mary had poisoned Rudolph and then herself. So fearing a scandal, Elisabeth came up with what was to be the official cover-up: 'And you will remember now,' she told Helene, 'that Rudolph died of heart failure!'[16]

Victoria heard the news the same day while staying at Osborne House, where she'd first met Rudolph in 1878. 'Shortly after luncheon,' she wrote in her journal on 30 January, 'got the startling news that poor Rudolph of Austria had died suddenly at Meyerling [sic] near Vienna this morning. We were all dreadfully shocked.'[17] She ordered the usual two weeks of full mourning followed by one week of half mourning. The same afternoon the blinds of Buckingham Palace were drawn as a mark of respect.

The following day she noted, 'The papers full of Rudolph's death, but without any details. However, something seems to have been suspected as his door was found locked, which was never the case.' *The Times* followed the misleading official Viennese reports and stated that the Crown Prince 'had died from a stroke of apoplexy'.

Sir Arthur Paget, the British Ambassador in Austria, kept Victoria informed of the rumours and developments in Vienna. 'Received a cyphered telegram from Sir A. Paget,' she wrote on the 31st:

saying that he felt it was his duty to say 'that there was a general impression' that Rudolph 'did not die a natural death but was assassinated'. He could not as yet ascertain the real truth. A white cap was drawn over poor Rudolph's head, and covered his forehead.

The Queen received a second cypher from Paget after dinner, telling her:

> that Rudolph 'had committed suicide'!! (How extraordinary!) …
> 'in a moment of aberration,' by shooting himself with a revolver
> through the head. He had been nervous and strange, it is said for
> some time, but the cause of the fatal act was not known.

She added presciently, 'We fear some scandal!' On 1 February Victoria noted,
'a telegram came from Reuters saying that it was officially announced
that Rudolph had committed suicide!', although her Prime Minister, Lord
Salisbury, continued to believe the Prince had been assassinated.

Although Rudolph committed suicide, he was declared of unsound
mind and the Pope decreed that he could have a Christian burial. Bertie
wished to attend but the only invited guests outside the immediate
family were Stephanie's parents, the King and Queen of the Belgians.
Instead the Prince of Wales and his two sons attended a service at the
Roman Catholic church in Farm Street, Mayfair, along with three
of Victoria's sons-in-law. The Queen sent a wreath of immortelles
to Vienna with the inscription she chose herself, '*Ein Zeichen innig-
ster Freundschaft*' – a token of the closest friendship. Bertie also sent a
wreath, and on his next visit to Vienna in October 1890 placed another
one on Rudolph's tomb.

Meanwhile Sir Arthur Paget kept his monarch aware of every development, although it wasn't until 6 February, two days after the Crown
Prince's funeral, that she became fully cognisant of the Mary Vetsera affair
and the suicide pact. She received 'a long and really awful account from
Sir A. Paget about this fearful tragedy at Meyerling'. In several paragraphs
of breathless prose she recorded:

> The long & short of his detailed letter was, to the effect, that the
> young lady mentioned was a Fräulein Marie Vetscera [sic], whose
> uncles were called Baltazzi, well known of the Turf here. That for
> some little time past a flirtation, which ended in a 'liaison' had
> existed, between her & Rudolph, greatly facilitated & encour-
> aged by the Empress's own niece Countess Larisch, (a daughter of
> her elder brother Duke Louis, who married a dancer) & that *she*
> arranged rendezvous, &c. How wicked! That while out driving with
> Css Larisch, Fräulein Vetsera gave her the slip, whilst the Countess

was in a shop, & that she left a paper in the carriage saying, she bid her farewell, & would be dead by next morning!!

Some facts were still unclear, as the Queen noted: 'When the door was broken open, by Philip's orders, the 2 were found both shot! Still a mystery remains as to *who* shot *her*.'[18]

That mystery was cleared up for Victoria by Bertie, who made it his business that spring to find out as much as he could about the deaths. On 12 February he wrote to his mother to tell her that 'it seems poor Rudolph had had suicide on the brain for some time past,' adding, 'He shot her first – then decked her out with flowers – and then blew his brains out – and he had only half an hour for all this.' (Bertie's account has an incorrect timescale for the two shootings.)

He spared his mother 'details I could tell you – which I cannot write – which clearly show complete aberration of the mind for some time past'. (Whether this is a reference to Rudolph's syphilitic state or his suicidal thoughts in the run-up to his death we can only conjecture.) To Bertie, 'The whole story is like a bad dream and I can think of nothing else'.[19]

Victoria also thought of little else. In a letter dated 20 February 1889 to her granddaughter Princess Victoria of Battenberg, the Queen writes that 'this unfortunate girl ' (Mary Vetsera) was 'one of the prettiest and I *fear* fastest in Vienna'.[20] That April she shared more juicy details with Vicky. 'You said B[ismarck] told you that Rudolph had a dreadful scene with his father,' the Queen wrote to her eldest daughter:

> I heard this from Lily [of Hanover] who had it from her sister who is very intimate with the imperial family … that he had promised never to see Mlle Vetsera again and that when he broke his word he felt he could never show himself before his father again and shot himself.[21]

Two years later in April 1891 the Queen's usual spring break on the Riviera was enlivened by a visit from Prince Philip of Coburg, who had of course found the bodies at Mayerling, and who was able to give Victoria an eyewitness account.

'Philip & Louise Coburg came to luncheon,' the Queen wrote at the Grand Hotel in Grasse:

Afterwards, he told me all about poor Rudolph's death, as he was the first person to have the door opened, & he said he would never forget the sight of both him & Fräulein Vetzera [sic] lying dead in that room. Philip thinks that he shot her & himself & that it was premeditated ... He said Rudolph had taken to drink & his conduct had become dreadful.[22]

During the same holiday, the Queen was also reunited with 'poor Stephanie'. Victoria thought she had 'grown very handsome. She is lively and has a sweet smile.' Her Maid of Honour Marie Mallet was less impressed and thought Rudolph's widow 'does not look the least interesting. She is only 27. She steadily refused to wear mourning for her husband (no wonder) so there is a great coolness between her and the Empress of Austria.'

Victoria was aware that Rudolph's death, like that of her son-in-law, Emperor Frederick III of Germany in 1888, who also embraced liberalism, spelt doom for the foreseeable future of a progressive Central Europe. 'The poor dear Crown Prince,' the Queen wrote shortly after his death, 'was singularly gifted and accomplished, and with large liberal views & was looked upon as one likely to withstand the 2 wicked Bismarcks' tyranny and dangerous views.'[23] She could have also added that these 'dangerous views' were also the ones espoused by her grandson, the new German Emperor, Wilhelm II.

Notes

1 Journal entry: Thursday 10 January 1878
2 Barkeley, R.: *The Road to Mayerling*: Macmillan: 1958: p.41
3 Ibid.: p.41
4 Letter dated January 16, 1878. Fulford, R.: *Darling Child*: Evans Brothers: 1976
5 Barkeley: Op. Cit.: p.41
6 Ibid.: p.41
7 Journal entry: Friday 22 February 1878
8 Fulford, Roger (ed.): *Beloved Mama*: Evans Brothers: 1981: p.68
9 Judtmann, Fritz: *Mayerling – The Facts Behind the Legend*: Harrap: 1971: pp.17–21
10 Journal entry: Monday 20 June 1887
11 Aronson, Theo: *Grandmama of Europe*: John Murray: 1973: p.4
12 Ibid.: p.28
13 RA VIC/MAIN/QVJ (W) 22 June 1887 (Princess Beatrice's copies). Retrieved 24 August 2016.
14 Magnus, Philip: *King Edward VII*: John Murray: 1964: pp.207–10
15 Ibid.: p.210
16 Judtmann: Op. Cit.: p.135

17 RAVIC/MAIN/QVJ (W) 1 February 1889 (Princess Beatrice's copies). Retrieved 23 August 2016

18 RAVIC/MAIN/QVJ (W) 7 February 1889 (Princess Beatrice's copies). Retrieved 23 August 2016

19 Ridley: Op. Cit.: p.259

20 Hough, Richard (ed.): *Advice to a Granddaughter*. Heinemann: 1975: p.98

21 Ramm, Agatha (ed.): *Beloved and Darling Child*: Alan Sutton: 1990: p.86

22 RAVIC/MAIN/QVJ (W) 5 April 1891 (Princess Beatrice's copies). Retrieved 23 August 2016

23 Barkeley: Op. Cit.: p.283: Letter to Lord Salisbury dated 3 February 1889

ONE COULD HAVE DANCED ALL NIGHT
VICTORIA WALTZES TO JOHANN STRAUSS

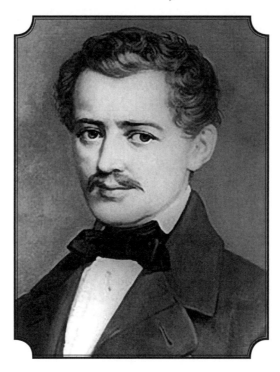

Johann Strauss.

JOHANN STRAUSS I (1804–49) and his orchestra made two hugely successful tours of Britain. The first, in the Coronation year of 1838, took them to twenty-six provincial towns and cities in England, Scotland and Ireland. More crucially for the composer's reputation was a request to play at the first ball of Queen Victoria's reign and eight more royal gatherings in two months. Strauss played for Victoria five times shortly before his death in 1849. His son Eduard was invited to play at a command performance at Windsor Castle in 1895.

One summer's morning in the late 1830s, the teenaged Queen Victoria, having danced until dawn, went out on to the roof of Buckingham Palace. Standing above the portico, in those days before the East Front was built, she was able to see the Mall, and beyond it to where the sun was rising beyond St Paul's Cathedral, which she could see distinctly. Then Westminster Abbey and the trees in Green Park began to stand out against a golden sky. Lady-in-Waiting Georgiana Liddell stood alongside the Queen and recalled in old age, 'It was one of the most beautiful sights I ever remember ... the scene remains to this day indelibly fixed on my memory.'[1]

The image of Queen Victoria as an intense, sombre widow, perpetually clad in full black mourning, has resonated down through the generations. It is easy to forget that during her early years as monarch she exuded health, vitality and a zest for life. Once court mourning for her uncle, the late King William IV, was over, the young Queen hosted a series of State Balls. She danced the waltz, the mazurka and the polka. She opened the dancing and she was the last to leave the dance floor. Her journals for the first years of her reign tell us she rarely went to bed before 5 a.m. on these occasions.

In the summer of 1838 Coronation fever was sweeping through the capital in the build-up to the ceremony on 28 June. Ambitious Austrian composer Johann Strauss decided to perform his music in the carnival atmosphere of London, where he would give seventy-nine performances from 17 April until the end of July.

The ultimate accolade was to be asked to conduct his orchestra at the first State Ball of the reign. The Queen had, loyally, asked Mr John Weippert, director of the orchestra at court balls for the past twenty years, to also officiate. Strauss and his men were set up on the south side of the Ballroom, while the Weippert orchestra held sway in the Yellow Drawing room, which was referred to in the press as a second ballroom.

After the Coronation itself the ball on 12 May was the social event of the year. Victoria, twelve days away from her nineteenth birthday, wore a white satin gown with the badge and ribbon of the Order of the Garter and a headdress of roses. Her royal relations wore court dress or military uniform and they were joined by 600 guests, including twelve dukes led by Wellington, the hero of Waterloo.

Strauss followed his usual practice of creating a piece especially for the occasion. This time it was a waltz, 'Hommage à la Reine d'Angleterre', which incorporated elements of 'Rule, Britannia!' in its introduction and 'God Save the Queen' in waltz tempo in its coda. Victoria was delighted with it. She danced every quadrille he played and requested he repeat the Parisian and Venetian Galop. Besides Strauss's popularity with the Queen, the following day's newspapers were fixated on whom the unwed monarch danced with, headed by her first cousin, Prince George of Cambridge. There were also detailed descriptions of the New Palace, which the former Buckingham House was labelled in the late 1830s, when Victoria became the first British head of state to live there since its restoration.

In her journal account of the ball, Victoria wrote that earlier in the day she'd talked to her Prime Minister, Lord Melbourne, 'of the disorder the House is in, on account of tonight's ball'.

'At ½ p.10,' she continued:

the doors were opened and I went through the Saloon into the other Ball-room next to the Dining-room in which was Strauss's band. I felt a little shy in going in, but soon got over it, and went and talked to the people.

She danced a 'valse' between each quadrille and noted excitedly:

I never heard anything so beautiful in my life as Strauss's band … I did not leave the ball-room till 10 m. to four!! and was in bed by ½ p.4, – the sun shining. It was a lovely Ball, so gay, so nice, – and I felt so happy and so merry; I had not danced for so long and was so glad to do so again![2]

Not all the balls were a success. Victoria attended one hosted by her uncle the Duke of Cambridge at his mansion on the north side of Piccadilly, where once again the Strauss orchestra provided the musical accompaniment. 'The House is ill adapted for a Ball,' noted the Queen, 'and the whole was not half as well arranged or ½ so gay as at Gloucester House. The heat was awful, and what was dreadful, all the candles melted and covered everybody, as well as the floor, with wax.'[3]

The final State Ball of the Coronation summer was held at Buckingham Palace on 26 July. The Queen noted, 'I cannot say how grieved I was to think this was my last Ball this (very pleasant, gay) season.' It was also the composer's final performance before returning to Vienna, as Victoria was obviously aware: 'I instantly went into the other Ball-room (where Strauss played delightfully the whole evening, alas! for the last time this year!)'[4]

By the time of his second tour of Britain in the spring and summer of 1849 Victoria and Albert had been married for nine years and had six children. The Queen still danced the polka, 'valse' and quadrilles, but her youthful exuberance seems to have worn off as the royal couple never stayed later than 2 a.m. Nevertheless, Strauss was invited to play five times at Buckingham Palace between 30 April and 19 June. At the first of these, a State Ball for 1,600 people, Strauss introduced the 'Alice Polka', named after the Queen's second daughter, who had celebrated her sixth birthday five days before.

After the composer and his orchestra entertained them at a private party on 11 May, Victoria noted:

> Strauss played in the Throne Room & we danced. It was really a most enjoyable evening, for he played so beautifully, – The most charming Francaises, Valses, &c. – also Marches, – all with such a spirit & precision. The whole was over by a little after 12.[5]

Once again Strauss's tour of Britain was exacting, with forty-six concerts performed – approximately five a week for ten weeks. The composer died two months after his return home, on 25 September 1849, having contracted scarlet fever from one of his illegitimate children. He was 45.

Family involvement in the Strauss orchestra continued under Johann's three sons – Johann II, Josef and Eduard. The latter managed the orchestra from 1870 until he disbanded it in 1901.

In the spring of 1895 Queen Victoria heard that Eduard and his musicians were performing in London and she requested they play for her at Windsor on 17 May. This meant the Austrians had to cancel their appearance at the Imperial Institute, scheduled for the same evening, and ticket holders had to make do with the replacement Royal Hungarian Band.

Eduard played two of the most recognisable works by his brother, Johann II: the overture from the operetta *Die Fledermaus* and the 'Pizzicato Polka'. The orchestra also played compositions by Liszt, Tchaikovsky and Mendelssohn as well as some of Eduard's own work.

Afterwards the music-loving Prince Alfred, Duke of Edinburgh, presented Eduard to the Queen, who presented him with a silver writing outfit 'with the request that he should make use of it in penning his next composition'.[6] In a letter of thanks, Eduard described the concert at Windsor as 'one of the most beautiful and memorable of my artistic career ... I and my family will always remember Her Majesty and the Royal Family with undying veneration.'[7]

In her journal entry the Queen reflected on the fact that she'd seen the first Strauss orchestra play in its heyday almost sixty years before:

> We afterwards went to St. George's Hall, where Strauss's band played beautifully, chiefly waltzes & compositions of his own & his brothers, & one of Liszt's Hungarian Rhapsodies. This Strauss (Edward) is the son of the one who played here in the year 1838, at the time of my coronation.[8]

Notes

1   Bloomfield, Georgiana Lady: *Reminiscences of Court and Diplomatic Life*: Kegan Paul: 1883: p.19

2   RA VIC/MAIN/QVJ (W) Thursday 10 May 1838 (Lord Esher's typescripts). Retrieved 11 May 2018

3   RA VIC/MAIN/QVJ (W) Friday 13 July 1838 (Lord Esher's typescripts). Retrieved 11 May 2018

4   RA VIC/MAIN/QVJ (W) Thursday 26 July 1838 (Lord Esher's typescripts). Retrieved 11 May 2018

5   RA VIC/MAIN/QVJ (W) Friday 11 May 1849 (Princess Beatrice's copy). Retrieved 11 May 2018

6   Kemp, Peter: *The Strauss Family*: Omnibus Press: 1989: p.82

7   Ibid.: p.83

8   RA VIC/MAIN/QVJ (W) Friday 17 May 1895 (Princess Beatrice's copy). Retrieved 11 May 2018

24

'NEARER MY GOD TO THEE'
THE QUEEN, GILBERT AND SULLIVAN

Arthur Sullivan.

ALTHOUGH VICTORIA never met W.S. Gilbert, she was a great admirer of Arthur Sullivan, more for his 'serious' choral music than his comic operas. He composed a 'Jubilee Hymn' to mark the Queen's sixty years on the throne and she bestowed honours on him from a knighthood to membership of the Royal Victorian Order.

One afternoon, more than twenty years into her widowhood, the elderly Queen summoned her Groom-in-Waiting, Alick Yorke, and announced that after lunch he and she would sing duets. While another courtier sat down at the piano to play the accompaniment, Victoria propped up on the table a copy of Gilbert and Sullivan's comic opera *Patience* and found her place.

'Now Mr Yorke, you begin,' she instructed. The groom obediently sang to her, 'Prithee, pretty maiden, will you marry me?' Then in a very clear soft voice she sang, 'Gentle Sir, although to marry I'm inclined.' Clearly pleased with her performance, she stopped mid-verse and threw in the non-sequitur, 'You know Mr Yorke, I was taught singing by Mendelssohn.'[1]

It wasn't the Queen's first documented foray into G & S. On New Year's Eve 1881 she recorded:

After the gentlemen had left, we had some amusing singing, out of 'Patience' by Sullivan, that aesthetic piece, which is very pretty, & very comical. Beatrice played and she, Leopold & Capt. Bigge, sang the solos, the words of which are so very funny. Louise, Mary Ponsonby & Bettie, and also I, joining in the chorus.[2]

The 'so very funny' words were of course penned by the librettist W.S. Gilbert, who would never meet the monarch face to face, whereas the composer Arthur Sullivan became a firm favourite at court and a close friend of three of Victoria's children.

Sullivan first encountered the Queen when he was an ambitious boy chorister at the Chapel Royal, St James's Palace, for three years from Easter 1854. 'It means everything to me,' he said at the time of his appointment, and within a few weeks he was one of 1,700 performers in front of the entire Royal Family at the reopening of the Crystal Palace at its new site of Sydenham on 17 June. Afterwards he wrote to his mother, 'I cannot tell you by letter of the grandeur of the scene.'

On 16 June 1857 the Queen's ninth and youngest child was baptised in the Private Chapel at Buckingham Palace. The Chapel Royal choir sang 'Halleluja' from Beethoven's *Christ on the Mount of Olives*, and Sullivan would have heard when the baby was christened, 'to our horror Beatrice Maria (instead of Mary) Victoria Feodore & though the Archbishop had the names written down he christened her so.'[3]

Aged 14, Sullivan won a scholarship to the Royal Academy of Music and he began composing while still in his teens. The royal wedding of Albert Edward, Prince of Wales to Princess Alexandra of Denmark in 1863 gave him the opportunity to write 'Bride From the North' and a commercially successful 'Royal Wedding March'. He was even allowed to dedicate the latter to the Prince of Wales.

What brought the composer into the royal fold was his 'serious' work rather than his comic operas. This suited Sullivan, who once wrote, 'My sacred music is that on which I base my reputation as a composer. These works are the offspring of my liveliest fancy, the children of my greatest strength.'

In this category he is best remembered today for composing the music to 'Onward Christian Soldiers', which was adopted as the Salvation Army's favourite processional hymn. He also created two versions of 'Nearer My God to Thee', one of which, 'Propior Deo', composed in 1872, is usually accepted to have been played by the ship's string ensemble during the sinking of RMS *Titanic*. What may well have brought him to the Queen's attention was his hugely popular *Festival Te Deum*, which was composed to celebrate the Prince of Wales's recovery from a near fatal bout of typhoid fever in December 1871. It was played at Crystal Palace on Thanksgiving Day, 1 May, in front of an audience of 30,000, including the Prince's siblings Princess Louise and the Duke of Edinburgh.

An impressed Victoria asked him to send her a full set of his works, and to edit her own more than sacred works: Prince Albert's amateur compositions. The royal couple had passed on their love of music to all their children and Sullivan became especially close to Bertie and Prince Alfred, Duke of Edinburgh. The Queen might have been less impressed if she'd known just how easily Sullivan slipped into the Prince of Wales's 'fast' set thanks to his love of racing, card games, gambling in the casinos of Monte Carlo, London clubs and house parties.

Sullivan dined at the Wales's London residence, Marlborough House, and stayed with them at Sandringham, their country estate in Norfolk. During one visit he took a phonograph – then still a novelty voice recorder – to entertain Bertie's five children. In return the composer hosted more intimate gatherings for the royal brothers at his rooms in London's Victoria Street. Both princes were there to celebrate the composer's forty-first birthday on 13 May 1883 and, after giving the host an enamel match-box, Bertie declared, 'Never has Sullivan given a more successful dinner!'

That was before the highlight of the evening. Sullivan had persuaded the entire Savoy Theatre company to show up at the theatre, despite the fact that it was Whit Sunday and a non-performance evening. Then, having already had the telephone installed at his rooms and linked to the theatre, the birthday boy rang the Savoy, handed the receiver to the Prince of Wales, and let the excited royal listen to a performance of selections from Sullivan's *Iolanthe* from the comfort of an armchair.

Sullivan even holidayed with the princes. In the spring of 1889 the composer was offered a lift in the royal train by the Prince of Wales, as well as passage on a special boat to Calais. Here they parted – HRH to Cannes, Sullivan to Monte Carlo – but a diary note tells us, 'February 21st – P. of Wales came from Cannes to stay at "Le Nid" and wished me to go with him after the Casino to Ciro's. Brought him into the hotel to have a look at the ball.'[4]

Eight years earlier there had been another royal sea journey, this time with Prince Alfred, who asked Sullivan to join him on HMS *Hercules* for a jolly around the Baltic. Firstly they docked at Copenhagen, where the King of Denmark revealed his orchestra had everything Sullivan had ever composed. This 'princely swanning', as the composer dubbed it, continued in St Petersburg, where the Emperor of Russia hosted a gala at the Winter Palace, with his Imperial Chapel Choir dressed in scarlet and gold and ready to perform for them. The Duke of Edinburgh said to his shipmate, 'Doesn't it remind you of when you were in the Chapel Royal?' and presumably it did.

The final stop of the voyage was at Kiel where Prince Wilhelm – later Kaiser Wilhelm II – bowed to Sullivan and sang 'He polished up the handle of the big front door' from HMS *Pinafore*. Sullivan recorded, 'I burst out laughing and so did everyone else. It was too funny.'[5]

Back in England, a shared love of music meant he was a frequent guest of the Duke of Edinburgh and his wife Marie, daughter of Tsar Alexander II of Russia. The composer played duets with Marie at the Edinburghs' country home, Eastwell Park in Kent. In May 1882, at a charity fundraiser for the Royal College of Music, Sullivan played Gounod's 'Ave Maria' accompanied by Prince Alfred on the violin. Although Prince Alfred was a keen violinist, he had little skill. At a dinner party given by the Prince of Wales, he was persuaded to play.

Victoria's Private Secretary, Sir Henry Ponsonby, wrote, 'Fiddle out of tune and noise abominable.'[6]

Victoria's fourth daughter, Princess Louise, was another Sullivan admirer and a regular royal guest at his parties. In February 1880 he stayed with Louise and her husband Lord Lorne, when the latter was Governor General of Canada, at Rideau Hall, their official residence in Ottawa. Here the two men composed a new national anthem for the country based on Lorne's words. Entitled 'God Bless our wide Dominion, Our Fathers' chosen land', it fell flat in the 'wide Dominion' and was never adopted. It did have one fan though – the Queen of Canada herself. During the Christmas festivities at Osborne in 1880 she noted that she, Louise, Beatrice and Leopold sang 'very successfully' the Dominion hymn, 'Charlie is My Darling' and 'Auld Lang Syne'. How those long winter evenings must have flown by for the courtiers who were obliged to listen or perform.

Today's Royal Collection still has a photograph of a fur-wrapped Sullivan dressed for that Canadian spring of 1880. Signed and dated by the composer, it was acquired by Victoria for her photo albums.

By then he was firmly in the ascendant where the Queen was concerned. She described his second oratorio in glowing terms: '*The Light of the World* is destined to uplift British music' – a remark, according to one biographer, that 'assured Sullivan's position as the laureate of the English "serious" music'.[7] In May 1883 he was knighted by the Queen at Windsor alongside his old friend George Grove, best remembered today for his *Dictionary of Music and Musicians*. Two years later she bought a Rosewood baby grand piano on his recommendation, after he'd awarded it a Gold Medal at the 1885 Commonwealth and India Exposition. Today it is still on display in the Waterloo Chamber at Windsor Castle.

Two landmark royal anniversaries occupied Sullivan in 1887. In March he was in Berlin to perform his new cantata, *The Golden Legend* (regarded by many as the greatest of his 'serious' works), at the ninetieth birthday celebrations for Emperor Wilhelm I. Much to his annoyance the 'fun' compositions always intruded. When Victoria's daughter, the Crown Princess of Germany, asked him to play excerpts of *The Mikado* while she posed in a tableau dressed as Yum-Yum, he had no choice but to comply.

Back in England his old friend the Prince of Wales asked him to compose a 'Jubilee Ode' to mark the fiftieth anniversary of the Queen's accession, which again found favour with the Royal Family.

The following spring the Queen made a rare foray into London society to hear a Sullivan piece performed with a full accompaniment. 'At ½ p. 3,' she noted on 8 May 1888:

> went to the Albert Hall, with Lenchen, Helen & Victoria S.H. Louise & Christian meeting me there, where Sullivan's 'Golden Legend' was most beautifully given. The Hall was very full & it was very hot. The Choir of the Royal Albert Hall Choral Society, sang the choruses. Albani sang exquisitely & the music is lovely.

Afterwards she asked to meet 'Sir A. Sullivan, whom I complimented very much. There was a great crowd outside, who cheered very much.'[8] Sullivan's own diary account of the meeting mentions a virtual command from the Queen: 'Her first words were: "At last I have heard the 'Golden Legend' Sir Arthur!" Later she said: "You ought to write a grand opera, you would do it so well."'[9]

The result was *Ivanhoe*, another solo Sullivan project, which premiered at the opening of the ill-fated Royal English Opera House on 31 January 1891, and which he dedicated to the Queen. The Prince and Princess of Wales attended with two of their daughters and the Edinburghs. Afterwards the two princes adjourned to Sullivan's room to congratulate him and to smoke cigarettes until the early hours of the morning. *Ivanhoe* lasted for 155 performances – quite good going for grand opera – but after it was finally taken off, there were no new productions to succeed it, and the Opera House was sold off. Today the red-brick building at Cambridge Circus survives as the Palace Theatre.

Victoria didn't see the opera but sent her congratulations via Princess Louise:

> The Queen wishes me to write and tell you with what pleasure she sees in the papers of today that your opera met with such a success on Saturday. It is a particular satisfaction to her, as she believes it is partly owing to her own instigation that you undertook the great work.[10]

Five weeks later she opted to see a typical G & S comic opera instead. This time the singers and musicians came to Windsor and later the Queen noted:

At 9, we went over to the Waterloo Gallery, where all the seats were filled by the & the Ladies & Gentlemen of the Household. All the Princes & Princesses sat with me in the front row. The 'Gondoliers', the last of Sir A. Sullivan's comic operas was performed by D'Oyly Carte's company of the Savoy Theatre, & lasted about 2 hours & ½. The music, which I know & am very fond of, is quite charming throughout & was well acted & sung.

As always with the Queen's accounts of theatre and opera performances, no detail escaped her eye:

The opening scene with the Contadine singing & binding flowers, with a lovely view of Venice & the deep blue sea & sky, was really extraordinarily pretty. The dancing which often comes in was very graceful & pretty. The Dialogue is written by Gilbert & very amusing. The Grand Inquisitor (Mr Denny) was excellent & most absurd, also Mr Rutland Barrington, who is very fat, as one of the Gondolieri. Miss Jesse Bond is a clever little actress & sings nicely. The dresses are very gay & smart, & the whole ensemble brilliant & well put on the stage. In the last scene there were 90 people on the stage, which for an extemporised one was wonderful. I really enjoyed the performance very much.

Neither Gilbert nor Sullivan was present, though the impresario responsible for nurturing their collaboration – Richard D'Oyly Carte – was in attendance and the Queen complimented him on the fine production.[11]

Hoping to watch a similar triumph, Victoria commanded D'Oyly Carte to bring one of his travelling companies to Balmoral to perform *The Mikado*. 'Dined earlier on account of the performance of Sullivan's Operette, the "Mikado",' the Queen wrote in her journal on 5 September:

At ½ p. 9, we went down to the Ball Room. There were many neighbours invited, & some of the servants & tenants. The stage had been a little widened. The Orchestra as well as the whole company came. The music is gay, but to my thinking inferior to the Gondoliers & though there are witty remarks & amusing topical allusions, the story is rather silly. The Operette was well put on the stage, & 40 people took part in it.

Once again the Queen's critical eye for detail is evident:

> The Japanese dresses were very correct. The Choruses were very
> good, the women good looking. The part of the High Executioner
> was taken by a very funny little man of the name Thorne, who
> jumped about wonderfully. Mr Billington, the 'Ld High Everything',
> a tall fat man, did his part very well. The Tenor, a Mr Charles sang
> very nicely.

Victoria was interested to learn that 'One of the 3 Ladies, Miss Alice
Pennington is Sullivan's niece'. Despite not liking the production as
much as *The Gondoliers* she ended on a positive note: 'We were much
amused & Arthur's [her third son] darling Children were delighted with
the Japanese costumes, much the same as they had worn in the Tableaux.'[12]

During the summer of 1891 Sullivan suffered a recurrence of the kidney
disease that had affected him since he was diagnosed with kidney stones at
the age of 30. He took a villa in Monte Carlo the following New Year but
his health worsened during the spring and at one point he was slipping in
and out of a coma. Regular bulletins appeared in *The Times* and the Queen
telegraphed for news of him. The Prince of Wales visited him and sent a
highly recommended surgeon to confer with Sullivan's local doctor. The
Prince was in Cannes recovering from the death of his eldest son Prince
Albert Victor, who had succumbed to pneumonia aged 28 in January.
Sullivan's funeral anthem 'Brother thou art gone before' was played at the
young Prince's funeral and was often chosen by Victoria for the annual
Mausoleum Day service to mark Prince Albert's death on 14 December.

Victoria's relationship with Sullivan, like her reign itself, reached its
zenith in 1897, the year she celebrated her Diamond Jubilee. The composer received a royal command to create a celebratory piece to mark
the historic occasion. In April he went to Cimiez, near Nice, where the
Queen was holidaying, to discuss the project with Sir Arthur Bigge, the
Private Secretary:

> He told me that the Queen thought it desirable to have well-known
> tunes sung outside St Paul's, so that people could join in ... but that
> as the real Thanksgiving service would be on the 20th June, it would
> be better I should write a special tune for that day, which might be
> sung in every church of the Empire.

Ten days later, while both of them were still in the south of France, he received a telegram from the Queen asking him to play the organ for her on Easter Day. (To be accurate, he'd met up with Prince Alfred in Cimiez the day before and offered his services, so the latter had obviously informed his mother.)

A clearly chuffed Sullivan recorded:

> Easter Sunday: Lovely morning. Drove to Regina Hotel, Cimiez, to play the organ at service in the Chapel by the Queen. Saw Princess Beatrice for a few minutes before service to arrange hymns. Queen came into the Chapel at 11 (whilst I played a voluntary) ... Self and Lord Rowton only outsiders ... Queen sent me a lovely pocket-book as a souvenir of the day.[13]

The Queen's journal entry was more matter of fact: 'Service at 11, performed by Mr Mossan from Cannes. Sir Arthur Sullivan, at his own request, played the Harmonium.'[14]

The royal command prompted a surge of energy in the composer. While supervising a Jubilee ballet at the Alhambra called *Victoria and Merrie England*, he composed the official Queen's Jubilee Hymn, 'O King of Kings'. The words by the Bishop of Wakefield were reverential, loyal, totally banal but unlikely to offend the Queen or her Saviour:

> Thou hast been mindful of Thine own
> And lo! we come confessing –
> 'Tis Thou hast dower'd our Queenly throne
> With sixty years of blessing.

To thank the composer the Queen made him a Member of the newly inaugurated Royal Victorian Order (MVO) which is conferred by the monarch without ministerial advice on those who have performed service for the sovereign.

In December of this Jubilee year, Sullivan journeyed to Windsor once more to conduct an anthem the Queen had commissioned for Mausoleum Day, entitled 'Wreaths for our Graves'. Unremittingly downbeat, it hit the right note with Victoria, who demanded an immediate encore. He conducted the choir of St George's Chapel in St George's Hall and a Lady-in-Waiting noted, 'The Queen enjoyed it all to the full,

I have never seen anyone more worthy of music and moved by it than she is.'[15]

The following April Sullivan was back playing the harmonium in Cimiez and this time was asked back to join the royal party after dinner. Around this time he was sent a signed photo of the Queen which he placed in prime position in his Drawing Room. Since the background was very sombre she used a change of ink to sign her name. Handing it to a courtier to convey to Sullivan, she said naively, 'Mind you tell him that I wrote my name in white ink so that he could be sure of it.'[16]

At the end of 1899 he had a final request from the Queen. The Boer War had recently started in South Africa and the *Daily Mail* asked Sullivan to set Rudyard Kipling's patriotic 'The Absent-Minded Beggar' to music. It was the first charitable song for war and was an instant hit, with its tub-thumping chorus, 'pass the hat for your credit's sake and pay-pay-pay!' The barrel organs in flag-waving cities went into overdrive and thousands of copies were sold in aid of soldiers' dependants. Sales of the poem and/or the sheet music raised a total of more than £250,000 (around £30 million at today's rate). Once again the Queen asked Sullivan to send her a copy.

During the late 1890s Sullivan grew increasingly concerned about the health and well-being of his friend the Duke of Edinburgh. A surviving letter from the composer to Princess Louise refers obliquely to the Duke's unhappy marriage to Marie of Russia and his increasing dependence on alcohol. The fact that Sullivan felt able to write so openly to one member of the family about another is testament to the strength of his relationship with the royals.

The letter marked 'Very Private' tells Louise, 'years ago even, before he was married, I have tried to check the evil tendency which was manifesting itself' (i.e. Alfred's drinking problem). He goes on to say, 'I have often neglected important work ... to be with him by night or by day ... to keep him at home – to prevent his going out into society injurious to his health and reputation.' After the Duke's marriage Sullivan felt:

> there was a distinctly *hostile element* risen up against me ... *I got no help* whatever from one to whom I desired to be a faithful servant and ally [in other words, Marie]. I have seen things – witnessed little scenes – heard words which have pained me dreadfully.[17]

In January 1899, Alfred and Marie's only son, also named Alfred, died under mysterious circumstances. The commonly held theory is that he shot himself at his parents' silver wedding party over an affair with an aristocratic woman whom some historians believe he married. Whatever the circumstances, the Prince died two weeks after the celebrations. Alfred senior died from throat cancer on 30 July 1900 – the third of Victoria's nine children to die in her lifetime. Arthur Sullivan went to Clarence House, the Duke's London home, to leave a message of condolence.

Sullivan didn't survive his royal friend for very long. He died of heart failure following an attack of bronchitis at his London apartment on 22 November 1900. The Queen telegraphed her condolences and it is often suggested she commanded what amounted to a semi-state funeral at St Paul's Cathedral, followed by internment in the crypt, even though Sullivan had asked to be buried with his mother and the family grave had already been opened. Victoria, with her sentimental attitude to death, would never have ignored a son's wish to be buried with his mother. She would undoubtedly, however, have been asked to approve the first part of the service which took part at the Chapel Royal, St James's Palace, where Sullivan had been a chorister over forty years before. Here her representative, Sir Walter Parratt, Master of the Queen's Musick, placed a wreath on the coffin. It bore the inscription:

a mark of sincere admiration
for his great musical talents
Victoria Regina

Notes

1. Benson, E.F.: *As We Were*: Longmans: 1930: p.29
2. RA VIC/MAIN/QVJ (W) Saturday 31 December 1881 (Princess Beatrice's copies). Retrieved 14 February 2018
3. RA VIC/MAIN/QVJ (W) Tuesday 16 June 1857 (Princess Beatrice's copies). Retrieved 14 February 2018
4. Sullivan, Herbert: *Sir Arthur Sullivan*: Cassell & Co.: 1927: p.192
5. Brahms, Caryl: *Gilbert and Sullivan*: Weidenfeld and Nicolson: 1975: p.106
6. Rose, Kenneth: *King George V*: Weidenfeld and Nicolson: 1983: p.41
7. Baily, Leslie: *Gilbert & Sullivan and Their World*: Thames and Hudson: 1973: p.40
8. RA VIC/MAIN/QVJ (W) Tuesday 8 May 1888 (Princess Beatrice's copies). Retrieved 14 February 2018
9. Sullivan: Op. Cit.: p.177
10. Brahms: Op. Cit.: p.210

11 RA VIC/MAIN/QVJ (W) Friday 6 March 1891 (Princess Beatrice's copies). Retrieved 14 February 2018
12 RA VIC/MAIN/QVJ (W) Friday 4 September 1891 (Princess Beatrice's copies). Retrieved 14 February 2018
13 Brahms: Op. Cit.: pp.236–7
14 RA VIC/MAIN/QVJ (W) Sunday 18 April 1897 (Princess Beatrice's copies). Retrieved 14 February 2018
15 Mallet, Victor: *Life With Queen Victoria*: John Murray: 1968: p.121
16 von Zedlist, M.A.: 'Interviews with Eminent Musicians No. 3 – Sir Arthur Sullivan': *Strand Musical Magazine* 1.3 (March 1895): pp.169–74
17 Longford, Elizabeth: *Darling Loosy*: Weidenfeld and Nicolson: 1991: p.242

25

Three Degrees of Separation — Queen Victoria and Oliver Reed
Meeting Sir Henry Beerbohm Tree

Sir Henry Beerbohm Tree. (Library of Congress)

IN SEPTEMBER 1894, the 75-year-old monarch was entertained at Balmoral by the actor/manager Sir Henry Beerbohm Tree and his Haymarket Theatre Company of actors, including Mrs Tree and their daughter Viola. It was the only time the Queen saw the legendary thespian and she thought him 'a wonderful actor'.

On the same occasion the Queen met one of the most successful members of the company, Tyrone Power II (father of the Hollywood heartthrob and namesake), having already in her youth been a fan of his grandfather Tyrone Power I.

During the first two decades of her reign, Victoria visited the theatre as often as her duties permitted, sometimes two or three times a week. Following the death of the Prince Consort she never set foot in a theatre again, though in the autumn of 1881, twenty years into her widowhood, she was invited to watch a professional production at Abergeldie Castle, a carriage drive away from Balmoral. In the remaining two decades of her life she herself commanded actors or companies to perform for her at either Balmoral or Windsor, including the Beerbohm Tree event in 1894.

Born in 1852, Tree began performing as a character actor in the late 1870s. He came to the notice of Genevieve Ward, an American-born opera singer and actress, who was now in management. She encouraged his early London-based career, including a charity performance of Émile Augier's *L'Aventurière* in the presence of the Prince of Wales. According to a reviewer from *The Times*, it was the Prince who suggested Miss Ward should 'organize this somewhat bold venture' of having an all-British cast perform it in French. After lambasting this 'not very intelligible undertaking', the critic does however single out Tree for playing the part of Monte-Prade 'really very cleverly'.[1]

A few weeks later he again acted in front of the Prince. He and Ward performed *La Pluie et le Beau Temps* at the home of the French-born writer Hamilton Aïdé. At dinner Bertie sat between his latest squeeze Lillie Langtry and the Polish actress Helena Modjeska, the latter astonishing Tree by defying convention and smoking a cigarette.[2]

After several years as a jobbing actor, in 1887, aged 34, he took over management of London's Haymarket Theatre, where he produced and appeared in some thirty plays over the next decade. These included new productions such as Oscar Wilde's *A Woman of No Importance* as well as several Shakespeare plays. His portrayal of Hamlet was critically acclaimed, though the librettist W.S. Gilbert bitchily commented, 'I never saw anything so funny in my life and yet it was not in the least vulgar.'[3]

Periodically the Haymarket company toured the provinces and it was during an arduous visit to Scotland and Ireland that Tree received the command (it was never 'an invitation') to perform for the Queen. Tree and the entire company of more than fifty members were on the Edinburgh leg of the tour when a telegram reached the actor at 6 p.m. on Friday 21 September informing him of the royal summons to act at Balmoral three days later. The timing couldn't have been worse since the company was giving two performances in Edinburgh on Saturday and then had to take themselves and their stage set to Dublin to perform on Monday.

Having cancelled the latter, Tree and the Royal Household had to decide which plays should be performed. Since even the Ballroom, the largest venue available at the castle, was deemed too small to stage *Hamlet*, the final choice was *The Red Lamp* by Sir Walter Pollock and William Outram Tristram's *The Ballad-Monger*. The next problem was the scenery, since the vast amount lugged from London again wouldn't fit, so there was no alternative but for stage hands to create two sets in exactly twenty-four hours to fit the schedule.

On Sunday Beerbohm Tree and his wife left Edinburgh for Royal Deeside, with Mr Shelton, the stage-manager, and Mr Watson, the acting assistant manager. The four travelled ahead in order to be at the castle first thing on Monday to supervise the erecting of the set and make other preparations. The rest of the company took the train from Edinburgh to Ballater, the nearest village to Balmoral, where they were taken in a procession of brakes to the estate. Here they were met by Victoria's Private Secretary, Sir Henry Ponsonby, and given a one-hour tour of the grounds as well as dinner.

Meanwhile the Queen, with her affection for her estate workers and her morbid fascination with everything to do with death, was watching the funeral of Mrs Stuart, the mother of one of her 'wardrobe women'. Mrs Stuart had also been the widow of a retainer from nearby Birkhall, and as she was interred in Crathie churchyard Victoria observed the event from her carriage outside the gate.

The company players went to see the Ballroom, which, like most of the other rooms, had suffered from an outbreak of 'tartanitis' with carpet, curtains and upholstery all decorated with Balmoral plaid. Over the heads of the visitors were the antlered heads of slaughtered stags staring morosely down at the proceedings, which included seating for an audience of about a hundred.

The Queen's journal entry testifies to her never-waning exuberance for theatrical performances, even in later life:

Dined early with the Dss of Atholl, Ct Hahn, Mr Fowler (come today) & Sir F. Edwards, besides ourselves. — Afterwards went down to the Ball Room, where 2 Plays 'the Red Lamp' & the 'Ballad Monger' were performed by Mr Beerbohm Tree & his wife, with the Haymarket Company. The performance was admirable. The 'Ballad Monger' was given first. It is in one act. of the period of Louis Xith of France. Mr Tree took the principal part of 'Gringoire' (a ballad monger), & Mr Holman Clark that of Louis XI. Mrs Tree acted the part of the King's god daughter 'Loyse', very gracefully. The 2nd Play is very exciting & somewhat terrible, a little in the style of 'Diplomacy'. It is in 4 short acts. Mr Tree is most won-derfully disguised as a fat old man of the Russian Secret Police & acted admirably. Mrs Tree as 'Pss Claudia Morakoff' acted extremely well, & all the parts were well done. The scenery was extremely good. It was a most excellent & interesting performance & the 2nd piece very exciting. We went at once to the Drawingroom, where I received all the invited guests & then the actors & actresses came in. Mr Tree I should have never recognised, he looks so different on the stage.[4]

The following day she wrote to Vicky:

> ... in the evening we had a beautiful theatrical performance by Bierbaum [sic] Tree and his wife and company. He is of Dutch descent, educated in Germany, then came to England. He took to the stage and is a wonderful actor ...[5]

She would no doubt have thought him less 'wonderful' if she'd known that by the time of his visit he'd begun a very lengthy affair with one Beatrice May Pinney, with whom he eventually had six children. These included the film director Sir Carol Reed, born in 1906, and known for films including *The Third Man*, and also his younger brother, sports journalist Peter Reed, the father of the legendary hell-raiser Oliver Reed, who became a star after playing Bill Sykes in his uncle's Academy Award-winning movie, *Oliver!*

As her journal describes, some of the key players were presented to her. These included Tyrone Power II, descendant of the first Earl of Tyrone, a supporter of Catholic James II, and the father of the legendary Hollywood actor of the same name.

Power was in England to launch a play he'd written himself – *The Texan* – which premiered at the Princess's Theatre in the Strand. It proved to be a dismal failure, opening on 21 June 1894 and closing ten days later. Critics, searching for anything positive to write, praised the scenery, and one said Power's make-up was 'quite a work of art'. So with time on his hands Power joined the Haymarket company and at last received some critical acclaim. The *Glasgow Herald* noted that he 'acted with the necessary force and dignity' when he played General Morokoff in *The Red Lamp*, while another reviewer praised his 'pleasant, well-modulated voice'.

We have no idea if the Queen, when she greeted Power, told him that she'd been a huge fan of his grandfather's in her youth, though both would have been aware that Tyrone Power I had also been working with the same theatre company as his grandson. (William Gratton) Tyrone Power (1797–1841) was an Irish-born actor and comedian. Shortly before Christmas 1838, the 19-year-old monarch noted that her Prime Minister and father-figure, 'my truly excellent Lord Melbourne', was going 'to see Power in the *Irish Ambassador* at the Haymarket'.

Lord M must have given the Queen a favourable report since a few weeks later we learn:

> At 20 m. to 8 I went ... to the Haymarket, where I had never been before. We came in before the 2nd act of the Irish Ambassador, in which Power acted inimitably; this was followed by 'O'Flanigan and the Fairies', a burletta in 3 acts, in which Power as Phelim O'Flanigan, an Irish peasant, was quite delightful; his acting, his speaking, his dancing, his face, – all was perfect; his acting when he was drunk, and during his dream, was excellent; it is a very lively piece ... After O'Flanigan, they called for me, and I was obliged to appear and come forward. Came home at 20 m. to 12. Told Mr. Webster, the Manager, as I left the Theatre, that I was very much pleased.[6]

Three months later we hear:

> At a ¼ to 8 I went ... to the Haymarket. We came in just after the 1st Piece was over. The first Piece we saw was called 'Born to Good Luck' or 'An Irishman's Fortune', in which Power as Pandeen O'Rafferty was beyond everything; I never saw him act better; he kept us in fits the whole time. After this came 'The Irish Liver' in one act, in which Power as Tim Moore was also very good; but I thought the 1st Piece the best.[7]

Finally in August of the same year, Victoria was once again being entertained at the Haymarket:

> We came in while the 1st piece was concluding, which was followed by 'The Village Doctor' in 2 acts, in which Farren as the Doctor acted delightfully – with great humour and great feeling, and so natural; Miss Taylor (now Mrs. W. Lacy) also acted very well. This was followed by 'Teddy the Tiler', in which Power was very funny.[8]

Power's life ended tragically at the age of only 43. On Thursday 11 March 1841 he set sail from New York on the SS *President*, the largest steamer then afloat, bound for Liverpool. They hit a storm on the night of the 12th which raged the whole of the next day. By daybreak on the Sunday the ship had sunk without trace. There were 123 people on board. No wreckage, bodies or survivors were ever found.

It took several weeks for the news to filter through. On 15 April the Queen noted:

> Ld Melbourne ... talked of the unfortunate ship, the 'President', which left New York, 34 days ago & ought to have arrived a fortnight or 3 weeks ago. Poor Fitzroy Lennox, & Power, the actor were on board. There are still hopes that the ship maybe at Halifax or Bermuda. The poor Duke & Dss of Richmond [parents of 20-year-old Fitzroy] must be in a terrible state of suspense about the wretched ship.[9]

An eventful, though thankfully not tragic, journey awaited the Haymarket company. After the Queen withdrew for the night, they were all given a hasty supper before leaving Balmoral at 1.30 a.m. on Tuesday morning. A 590-mile journey by land and sea to Dublin and the prospect of performing on stage there that night lay ahead.

First they had to drive 10 miles to Ballater to catch the specially laid-on train. This was an hour late departing due to the difficulty of transporting the scenery and other properties, which could only be driven at a snail's pace through the dark country lanes. Although they were an hour and a half behind schedule by the time they crossed the border near Carlisle, they reached the port of Holyhead on Anglesey at five minutes past four. All the men in the company shifted the baggage and sets on to the specially chartered steamer. The ship was spotted in Dublin Bay at 7.22 p.m. and by 7.40 p.m. the actors, fully changed into their costumes, were being driven hell for leather through the Irish capital. A large crowd cheered Tree and his party as they headed into the theatre. Amazingly the curtain rose at the advertised time of 8.30 p.m.

Immediately after he arrived at the theatre, Tree sent the following telegram to Balmoral: 'In accordance with her gracious Majesty's request, I have great pleasure in informing Sir Fleetwood Edwards [Groom-in-Waiting, only remembered today for the death of a zebra given to Victoria and left in his care; it was buried at Windsor] that we have accomplished the journey just in time to appear in the Gaiety Theatre, Dublin, having broken the record for the distance.'[10]

Tree received the following reply from Edwards on behalf of the Queen:

Your telegram on arrival last evening received. The Queen is anxious to know if you had a fine and smooth crossing, and hopes that you and Mrs Tree and the rest of the company were not too tired after the long journey. Her Majesty is glad you all arrived in time.[11]

Being one of the very few who had the chance to perform for the Queen in her later years was perfect publicity for Tree and his company. Details of the plays seen by the Queen and a full cast list featured in the Court Circular at a time when even local newspapers featured this daily account of the Queen's activities.

Back in London, a prospering Tree opened a new theatre in the Diamond Jubilee year of 1897 and loyally named it Her Majesty's Theatre (renamed His Majesty's after the accession of Edward VII in 1901). Bertie graced the opening night, objecting loudly that the flunkeys in attendance were wearing the same royal livery as their Buckingham Palace equivalent. Then, while he was still in the foyer, there was an electricity cut, plunging the royal party into darkness.

Over the following two decades until his death in 1917 Tree staged approximately sixty plays, ranging from classics such as *The School for Scandal* (1909) to the London première of Bernard Shaw's *Pygmalion* (1914). Her/His Majesties also became noted for popularising the works of Shakespeare. Tree also embraced cinematography. His *King John* was the first of the Bard's work to appear on film. The year before his death he also acted in *Macbeth*, filmed in California by D.W. Griffith.

Tree maintained his contact with the British court. In 1909, the same year he was knighted by Edward VII, he played Svengali in an adaptation of George du Maurier's novel *Trilby* during the state visit of 20-year-old King Manuel II of Portugal.

Tree wasn't the only member of his family with links to the court. The caricaturist Max Beerbohm was a younger half-brother (from their father's second marriage). In 1921 he produced a series of eight caricatures of Edward VII, from youth to old age, in which Bertie is seen growing increasingly corpulent and always with a different stylish woman in the background. When the images were included in an exhibition of Max's work in 1923, it caused a scandal, especially when he mischievously captioned them *Proposed Illustrations for Sir Sidney Lee's Forthcoming Biography*. Lee's two-volume official biography of Edward VII was magisterial in its style, reverential towards its subject matter and as far removed from humour as could be. Such was the furore generated that Beerbohm felt obliged to remove them from show.

Twenty years later they were shown to the Royal Librarian, Sir Owen Morshead, by the director of the bookshop Bumpus, who was worried about selling such sensitive material. Morshead told Queen Elizabeth (later the Queen Mother), who thought it all hilarious and purchased them for the Royal Library, where they still reside.[12] There is no evidence the Royal Collection has an even more famous Max cartoon entitled 'The rare and rather awful visits of Albert Edward, Prince of Wales, to Windsor Castle'. It depicts a grief-stricken Victoria, dressed in black and clutching a handkerchief, while behind her the well-rounded Prince of Wales stands facing the corner of the room, like a naughty child. Like his other Bertie cartoons it has more than a grain of truth, and neatly sums up the Queen's constant reproach of her wayward son.

Another item that never found its way into the Royal Collection is Max's copy of Victoria's *More Leaves from a Journal of Our Life in the Highlands*, which he embellished with a mock inscription apparently in the Queen's hand: 'For Mr Beerbohm – the never-sufficiently-to-be-studied writer whom Albert looks down on affectionately, I am sure – From his Sovereign Victoria R.I. Balmoral 1896.'[13]

Sadly Tyrone Power II's theatrical career didn't peak as much as Tree's after the Balmoral performance. The next time we hear of him in 1894 he was in pantomime at Liverpool playing Admiral Torpedo in *The Fair One with the Golden Locks* at the Royal Alexandra Theatre. Like all good pantos it took a pop at contemporary issues. According to a review in the *Liverpool Mercury* this included 'numerous amusing allusions to the Manchester Ship Canal [opened by Queen Victoria the previous May], to the Mersey Docks Board, to Home Rule, to the Abolition of the House of Lords, to the imposition of taxes, to football, to socialism …'[14]

The end of the First World War heralded a new realism in the theatre and Power's rhetorical delivery was out of place in the Roaring Twenties. He returned to the United States and starred in several silent pictures directed by the likes of D.W. Griffith, Henry King and Raoul Walsh. He was beginning to adapt to sound movies when, on 30 December 1931, he collapsed and died in the arms of his 17-year-old son, the future matinee idol, Tyrone Power Jnr.

There is even a Victoria link with the latter. On 30 October 1950 Power, who was in London to play the title role in the play *Mister Roberts* at the Coliseum, met the future Elizabeth II with her sister Princess Margaret and their parents at the Royal Film Performance. The movie chosen was *The Mudlark*, a fictional account of a boy who breaks into Windsor Castle to try to meet Queen Victoria.

Notes

1   *The Times*: 12 May 1880: p.10
2   Bingham, Madeleine: *The Great Lover – The Life and Times of Herbert Beerbohm Tree*: Hamish Hamilton: 1973: p.15
3   Pearson, H.: *Beerbohm Tree – His Life and Laughter*: 1956: p.214
4   RA VIC/MAIN/QVJ (W) Tuesday 25 September 1894 (Princess Beatrice's copy). Retrieved 15 June 2018
5   Ramm, Agatha (ed.): *Beloved and Darling Child – Last Letters Between Queen Victoria and her Eldest Daughter 1886–1901*: Alan Sutton: 1990: p.170
6   RA VIC/MAIN/QVJ (W) Tuesday 15 January 1839 (Lord Esher's typescripts). Retrieved 15 June 2018
7   RA VIC/MAIN/QVJ (W) Tuesday 2 April 1839 (Lord Esher's typescripts). Retrieved 15 June 2018
8   RA VIC/MAIN/QVJ (W) Thursday 13 August 1839 (Lord Esher's typescripts). Retrieved 15 June 2018
9   RA VIC/MAIN/QVJ (W) Thursday 15 April 1841 (Lord Esher's typescripts). Retrieved 15 June 2018
10 *The Era* (London): 29 September 1894
11 Ibid
12 Owens, Susan: *Watercolours and Drawings from the Collection of Queen Elizabeth The Queen Mother*: Royal Collection: 2005
13 Longford, Elizabeth: *Victoria R.I.*: Weidenfeld and Nicolson: 1964: p.453
14 *Liverpool Mercury*: Monday 24 December 1894

26

HITTING THE RIGHT NOTE
QUEEN VICTORIA AND RICHARD WAGNER

Richard Wagner.

THE QUEEN and Richard Wagner (1813–83) met twice. She was intrigued by his conducting style and thought his *Tannhäuser* 'wonderful'. He was bowled over by her charm and thought it ironic that the Queen of England should happily receive a man dubbed as a revolutionary.

By the time of his visit to London in 1855, Wagner had composed three of his most famous works – *The Flying Dutchman*, *Tannhäuser* and *Lohengrin* – begun a tempestuous marriage to Christine Wilhelmine 'Minna' Planer, fled Russia with crippling debts and had a warrant issued for his arrest as a revolutionary in Dresden following the May uprising of 1849. He was to spend the next twelve years in dire financial straits, exiled from Germany.

In the spring of 1855 he agreed to perform eight concerts in London with the London Philharmonic Society for a fee of around £200. He took rooms at 22 Portland Terrace to the north of Regent's Park, where he soon discovered that he was making little money after allowing for the daily cab fare to Hanover Square, rent, formal dress hire, food and the high cost of living in the capital.[1]

To add to his woes, the list of pieces he was required to perform was challenging – all of Beethoven's symphonies, five Weber overtures, pieces by Mendelssohn, Haydn, Spohr, Cherubini, Chopin and Hummel, plus some of his own pieces. On 16 May he wrote to Liszt:

> I am living here like a damned soul in hell!! I did not think I should ever again be obliged to sink so low! I cannot describe how wretched I am in having to put up with conditions so utterly repugnant to me, and I realize it was no less than a sin and a crime to accept this London invitation which must, even at the best, have led me far out of my true path.

His sole delight, he told his wife, was being able to read Buddhist literature.[2]

Such was Wagner's frame of mind when it was announced that the Queen and Prince Albert would attend the seventh of his eight concerts on 11 June. Albert's brother Ernest II, Duke of Saxe-Coburg and Gotha, was a great Wagnerian, and the royal couple were keen to see the composer for themselves.

Afterwards the Queen noted in her journal:

> We dined early with Feodore [Victoria's half-sister], her girls, our Boys, & all the Ladies & Gentlemen, going to the Philharmonic where a fine concert was given, under the directions of the celebrated composer Herr Richard Wagner. He conducted in a peculiar way, taking Mozart's & Beethoven's Symphonies in quite a different time,

to what one is accustomed. His own Overture to 'Tannhäuser' is a wonderful composition, quite overpowering, so grand, & in parts wild, striking & descriptive. We spoke to him afterwards. He is short, very quiet, wears spectacles & has a very finely developed forehead, a hooked nose, & projecting chin. He must be 3 or 4 & 30.[*3]

The following day it was an altogether more exuberant Wagner who wrote to Minna about the encounter with the royals, joking that they had asked him all about his pets. 'First she asked me how was Peps? Then, if Knackerchen was well-behaved?' etc. Like Victoria in her account, the composer gave a physical description of the other person:

The Queen of England had a very long conversation with me. Further, I can assure you that she isn't fat, but very short and not at all pretty, alas with a slightly red nose; still, she has something un-commonly kind and familiar about her, and even if she isn't precisely imposing, she is pleasing and amiable.

Then to Victoria's musical tastes:

She doesn't care for instrumental music, and when she attends a long concert like this – which is by no means the case every year – she does it simply for her husband's sake, who goes in more for music and is fond of German instrumental music. This time, however, she really appears to have received an impression. Sainton, who kept her in eye the whole time from his desk, declared she followed my con-ducting and the pieces with unwanted and increasing interest, whilst she and Prince Albert quite warmed at the Tannhäuser in particular. So much is certain: when I faced about at the close of that overture, both of them applauded me most heartily, and looked towards me with a friendly smile; of course the audience did not leave them in the lurch, but honoured me this time with very decided, universal and prolonged applause.[4]

Wagner was summoned to meet the royal party during the interval and he recalled the Queen's first words to him in a letter to William Fischer,

_____

[*] Not a bad guess: Wagner was 32 at the time.

one of his Dresden associates, on 15 June: 'I am delighted to make your acquaintance, your composition has enraptured me.'[5]

Back to the music conversation and Wagner told Minna that there:

> ensued a lengthy conversation about my operas, in which Prince Albert – a very handsome man ! – joined with most gratifying interest. To the Queen's opinion that my things might perhaps be translated into Italian, to be given at the Italian Opera here, the Prince quite intelligently replied that probably my texts would not be suited for it, and certainly Italian singers would not know how to sing them. Upon that said the Queen very naively 'But most of the singers at the Italian Opera now, you see, are Germans; consequently they would only need to sing in their mother-tongue.' We were obliged to laugh, and I then replied that unfortunately the German singers also had much deteriorated, and – if I wanted one day to produce the big work I now was working at – I should seriously have to think of first training my people.[6]

In the same letter to Minna (signed 'Thy Knight of the Order of the Garter'), Wagner also jokingly mentioned the Queen's admiration for his satin trousers: 'I'm having to send them to the palace for her, so that she can have a pair made for Prince Albert.'[7]

'You have probably heard how charmingly Queen Victoria behaved to me,' he wrote to Franz Liszt:

> She attended the seventh concert with Prince Albert … I really seemed to have pleased the Queen. In a conversation I had with her after the first part of the concert, she was so kind that I was really quite touched. These two were the first people in England who dared to speak in my favour openly and undisguisedly, and if you consider that they had to deal with a political outlaw, charged with high treason and wanted by the police, you will think it natural that I am sincerely grateful to both.

Five years after the meeting Wagner, clearly thinking he was still well thought of at the British court, wrote to his friend, the poet Mathilde Wesendonck (whom he was infatuated with), to tell her that Victoria:

has taken it into her head to want to hear my *Lohengrin* this winter; the director of Covent Garden Theatre has looked me up, and the Queen wants Lohengrin in English. It would have to be in February, but I know nothing more precise about it, nor even if I shall be able to entertain it. It would be droll, though, were I to hear this work in English for my own first time![8]

In the event, the final illness and death of Victoria's mother, the Duchess of Kent, the following spring, followed by the calamitous death of Prince Albert several months later, put paid to that idea. Plunged into grief, the Queen put all thoughts of entertainment out of her mind. She did, to the surprise of her family and courtiers, agree to a holiday in Switzerland in 1868. Travelling as the Countess of Kent she took with her two cooks, a carriage, ponies (with their attendants) and her own bed. Travelling by the Emperor of France's Imperial train this massive royal caravan arrived at the Villa Wallace in Lucerne. The Queen enjoyed the mountain air, trips on the steamer *Winkelreid* across the lake, and 'the great composer Wagner's Villa, not far from Lucerne, was pointed out to us'.[9]

As so often happened in their forty-year correspondence, the Queen and her eldest daughter clashed when it came to artists, musicians and writers. Vicky's approach was usually cerebral, while her mother's was passionate and from the heart. On 10 April 1869 the Princess wrote to the Queen, 'If you want to read anything perfectly cracked you should see Richard Wagner's new pamphlet called "Jewish Influence in Music". I never read anything so violent, conceited or unfair. It is very much talked about here in Germany.'[10] This attack on the Jews, written in 1850, was reprinted by Wagner to counteract the hostile press he received, which he said was in the hands of the Jews. It was of course this anti-Semitic viewpoint which generations later appealed to Hitler and the Nazi party.

Wagner's beliefs may have coloured Vicky's hostile attitude to his music. Writing to her mother on 8 May 1881 she reports:

I have been the last two evenings to hear Wagner's celebrated trilogy and have already [illegible] *Rheingold* and *Valkyrie*. It is impossible to imagine anything more dull and tiresome and heavy – and fatiguing to listen to – though there are snatches of melody in the orchestral part – the whole is one long recitation from beginning to end. I own I could hardly stand it …[11]

In her reply, written three days later, the Queen concedes, 'Wagner's trilogy must have been rather overpowering and so noisy.'[12]

Her comment came four years after her second and last meeting with the composer. Once again facing financial ruin, Wagner came to London to conduct six concerts at the Albert Hall for a fee of £1,500 which was reduced to £700 due to a lack of profit at the box office. Socially it was successful, with both the Prince of Wales and the Duke of Edinburgh attending more than once.

Finally on 17 May 1877 he travelled to Windsor to see the Queen. 'After luncheon,' noted Victoria:

> the great composer Wagner, about whom the people in Germany are really a little mad was brought into the Corridor by Mr Cusins. I had seen him with dearest Albert in 55, when he directed at the Philharmonic Concert. He has grown old & stout & has a clever, but not pleasing countenance. He was profuse in expressions of gratitude, & I expressed my regret at having been unable to be present at one of his Concerts.[13]

The Queen's last recorded mention of the composer was to the young Henry Wood, who came to Windsor in November 1898 with an orchestra of 106 from the Queen's Hall to play, among other pieces, the Good Friday music from *Parsifal*, which she 'thought most impressive'.[14] Unable to resist impressing the young man by name-dropping, she told him, 'I knew Richard Wagner quite well', which was not strictly true, adding that as she was now too old to travel to the composer's concert house at Bayreuth, she hoped he would come again to play some more extracts from the piece.[15]

What she didn't tell Wood was that the previous day she had driven 'with Vicky & Louischen to the Shaw Farm' where they'd seen 'dear Fritz's old horse, Parsifal'.[16]

Notes

1 Watson, Richard: *Richard Wagner – A Biography*: Dent: 1979: p.141
2 Ibid.: p.143
3 RA VIC/MAIN/QVJ (W) Monday 11 June 1855 (Princess Beatrice's copy). Retrieved 2 July 2018
4 Ellis, William Ashton (translator): *Richard to Minna Wagner – Letters to his First Wife*, Vol. I: H. Grevel & Co.: 1909: p.257

5 Sessa, Anne Dzamba: *Richard Wagner and the English*: Associated University Presses Inc.: 1979: p.24

6 Ellis: Op. Cit.: p.258

7 Christian, Rupert: *The Visitors – Culture Shock in Nineteenth Century Britain*: Chatto and Windus: 2000

8 Ellis, William Ashton (translator): *Richard Wagner to Mathilde Wesendonck*: H. Grevel & Co.: 1905: p.251

9 RA VIC/MAIN/QVJ (W) Tuesday 11 August 1868 (Princess Beatrice's copies). Retrieved 2 July 2018

10 Fulford, Roger (ed.): *Your Dear Letter*: Evans Brothers: 1971: p.232

11 Fulford, Roger (ed.): *Beloved Mama*: Evans Brothers: 1981: p.101

12 Ibid.: p.102

13 RA VIC/MAIN/QVJ (W) Thursday 17 May 1877 (Princess Beatrice's copies). Retrieved 2 July 2018

14 RA VIC/MAIN/QVJ (W) Thursday 24 November 1898 (Princess Beatrice's copies). Retrieved 2 July 2018

15 St Aubyn, Giles: *Queen Victoria*: Sinclair-Stevenson: 1991: p.498

16 RA VIC/MAIN/QVJ (W) Wednesday 23 November 1898 (Princess Beatrice's copies). Retrieved 2 July 2018

27

THE LOVE THAT DARE NOT SPEAK ITS NAME

OSCAR WILDE'S FASCINATION WITH QUEEN VICTORIA

Oscar Wilde. (Library of Congress)

DESPITE THE fact that Queen Victoria signed the Criminal Law Amendment Act of 1885, which was used to send Oscar Wilde to prison ten years later, Wilde never lost his respect and affection for her. On his release from gaol, and living in impecunious exile, he even threw a party for local children to mark her Diamond Jubilee. He once memorably said that the three great personalities of the nineteenth century were Napoleon, Victor Hugo and Queen Victoria.

Oscar Fingal O'Flahertie Wills Wilde was born in Dublin in 1854, the second of three children of William Wilde, an eye and ear specialist, and his wife Jane, a writer and Irish nationalist. In 1863 Wilde Snr was made Surgeon Oculist to Queen Victoria – quite a cushy post since she never set eyes on him or his country during his tenure in the post, though she did make him a knight in 1864.

His only royal contact appears to have been an alleged one. Some Wildean biographers recount the rumour that he operated on the eye of the future King Oscar of Sweden. While the Prince was temporarily blinded, Wilde Snr is then supposed to have seduced his wife. The two parties did meet in the Swedish city of Uppsala, but there is no documented evidence that Wilde took care of either the Prince or his wife. Nevertheless, on a visit to Dublin years later the royal couple's heir, Prince Gustav, waggishly joked that he was Oscar Wilde's half-brother.[1]

Wilde settled in London in 1879 after five years at Oxford, where he studied classics and had rooms in Magdalen College. He rapidly became a recognisable figure in the artistic life of the capital and he managed to befriend the three great beauties of the generation, Ellen Terry, Lillie Langtry and Sarah Bernhardt. His foppish dress of knee-breeches, elaborate bow-ties and flamboyant hats ensured he was noticed when he attended first nights, society parties or his (now London-based) mother's literary salons.

He soon crossed paths with the Prince of Wales, himself famed for his sartorial taste as well as his taste for Terry, Langtry and Bernhardt. In fact the Prince, intrigued by what he'd heard about Wilde, asked to see him. Bertie even tried, but failed, to emulate the Irish wit, with what he clearly thought was a Wildean epigram: 'I do not know Mr Wilde, and not to know Mr Wilde is not to be known.'[2]

When they did meet in 1881 the future playwright was staying at the recently built home of Frank Miles, who earned a living painting pastel portraits of society ladies. Number 1 (later renumbered 44) Tite Street, Chelsea, was the venue for an extraordinary event: a private séance for the Prince, attended by, among others, Lillie Langtry, Lady Mandeville (American-born heiress, later Duchess of Manchester and another beauty Bertie admired), the artist James Whistler and his patron Lady Archibald Campbell.

Wilde and Miles had invited the American 'stage mentalist' Walter Irving Bishop to entertain the Prince. The previous year he had published a book called *Second Sight Explained*. His main party piece was to ask someone in the audience to hide an object in the room, and then by holding their hand or wrist he would ask them to think of the location. He then claimed to read their mind and, hopefully, to find the item.

Bishop came to an unfortunate end eight years after the royal show. He was performing at an event in Manhattan when he became unconscious and was carried upstairs to a room where he remained in a coma until he died the next day. An autopsy was performed hours later at the funeral home. His wife and mother claimed he suffered from cataleptic fits, and could remain in a trance for many hours. He was even supposed to carry a card on his person asking eager pathologists to wait at least forty-eight hours before carrying out their procedure. Bishop's mother Eleanor sued the physicians, but a hung jury meant they were not charged and we will never know if Bishop suffered death by autopsy.

Two months after the séance, Wilde sent a copy of his recently published book of poetry to the Prince, with the inscription:

H.R.H The Prince of Wales
loyauté
homáge
de l'auteur.[*]
August 81.

He also added, again in his own hand:

I have marked in the index a few [poems] which I should like to think might interest your Highness. One of them 'The Garden of Eros' being my attempt, how weak and inadequate no one feels more than myself, to express the meaning and value of this modern artistic movement, a movement in England, a movement which, when it has passed out of the extravagance of its youth, will I know produce noble and serious work in art and in song. Your Highness's faithful servant, Oscar Wilde.

Bertie seems to have treasured it and it was given his personal library bookplate as both Prince and King, and that also of his successor,

---

[*]   loyalty / homage / from the author.

George V. The latter presented it to the Royal Library in 1930. (It is difficult to imagine George sharing his father's fondness for Wilde. In 1931 when William Lygon – 7th Earl Beauchamp, the Liberal leader in the House of Lords, Knight of the Garter, and bearer of the Sword of State at George's Coronation – was 'outed' as homosexual, the shocked George said, 'I thought that men like that shot themselves!'[3])

The posturing of 'this modern artistic movement', especially amongst the flamboyant aesthetes of Tite Street, was ripe for ridicule. *Punch* in particular satirised Wilde, and its verdict on the book of poems was that 'The poet is Wilde but his poetry's tame'. Despite this it went into a second print run the same year it was published.

There was more lampooning in a new play, *The Colonel*, with the character Lambert Stryke appearing as a typical Wildean aesthete. The Prince of Wales was so amused by it he persuaded the actor manager Edgar Bruce and his company from the Prince of Wales's Theatre to put on a special performance at Abergeldie Castle, Bertie's residence near Balmoral. On 4 October 1881 the Queen drove the short distance from the castle. It was twenty years since she had been to see a theatre production. She was warmly cheered by the audience, and from her journal entry clearly enjoyed the evening:

> Went to Abergeldie, where a theatrical performance was given in the coach house. At the end of it, a small stage was erected, & beautifully arranged with plants & flowers. Bertie & Alix, received us at the door. The room was very full, Bertie having invited everyone from here, I should think more than 200, including the servants & tenants ... The piece given, was the 'Colonel' in 3 acts, a very clever play, written to quiz & ridicule, the foolish aesthetic people, who dress in such an absurd manner, with loose garments, large puffed sleeves, great hats, & carrying peacock's feathers, sun flowers & lilies. It was very well acted ... It was the first time I had seen professionals act a regular play, since March 61. Mr Bruce presented me with a nosegay & play bill, before we went in, & spoke to him at the conclusion of the performance. We got home shortly before 12, having been very much amused.[4]

In May 1887, Wilde took over as editor of *The Lady's World – A Magazine of Fashion and Society*. He decided to rebrand it as *The Woman's World*, relegated fashion to the back pages and sought out pieces on the education of women, women's suffrage and the like. Fired up by his new status, he aimed for the top and wrote to the Queen asking for leave 'to copy some of the poetry written by the Queen when young'. An exasperated Victoria sent a minute to her Private Secretary, Sir Henry Ponsonby, dated 8 April 1888: 'Really what will people not say and invent. Never c^d the Queen in her whole life write <u>one line of poetry</u> serious or comic or make a Rhyme even. This is therefore all <u>invention</u> & <u>a myth</u>.'[5]

Since he couldn't coerce Victoria into contributing, he included her in a poem called 'Historic Women' written by his mother. A copy was sent to the Queen, and her Lady-in-Waiting Lady Churchill wrote back to say Her Majesty had liked it very much.[6]

Oscar and his new wife Constance, whom he had married in May 1884, continued to be on the edge of royal circles over the next decade. In May 1887 Constance was presented at court at one of the Queen's Drawing Rooms. The Princess of Wales presided over the event and guests included Victoria's daughter Princess Helena and Princess Victoria Mary of Teck, later the consort of George V.

In his last years, following his release from prison, Oscar gave an account of the only time he saw the Queen. He told the story while staying in Dieppe at the home of the Norwegian painter Fritz Thaulon and his wife. Another guest, and a fellow Norwegian, Christian Krohg, left a record of the conversation in a memoir, *Four Portraits*.

The topic of conversation at the Thaulons' dining table turned to the recent Diamond Jubilee. The host said that the response from the people had been so enthusiastic 'because she represents the nation's greatness'. Wilde disagreed: 'No! Because of her personality. She is a personality. She is a woman. Through and through. And distinguished.'

Asked by Thaulon if he had ever met her, Wilde replied, 'Yes at a garden party given by the Prince of Wales. I shall never forget it. She passed through the garden on the Prince's arm. She has the most graceful walk.' At this point the writer used his hands on the tablecloth to imitate a swaying motion.

Wilde went on to describe her as 'a ruby framed in jet', adding, 'she's quite small,' and that she 'has the most beautiful hands and the loveliest wrists'. He told the captive audience, 'I stood there together with Bastien Lepage. He was overcome with enthusiasm. "I must paint that woman."' Lepage asked Wilde to seek out the Prince of Wales to see if this was feasible. The Prince said it was 'impossible' and Lepage 'was inconsolable'.[7]

There is no other reference to this meeting, or to Wilde attending a garden party, but Victoria was present at one on Tuesday 13 July 1880 and Jules Bastien-Lepage is among the names of overseas visitors present. Wilde may well be one of the 'and many more' at the end of the coverage in *The Times*. Certainly he was in London at the time and 'there's a letter from OW to Mrs Alfred Hunt dated 15 July 1880 in the *Complete Letters* which, while proving nothing, seems to give the impression that OW was throwing himself into the social round'.[8] Bastien-Lepage, who sketched Bertie dressed in Elizabethan clothing in 1879 (the original is now in the British Museum; the Royal Collection has a photograph of it), had been dead thirteen years by the time of the Thaulon lunch. Since having met Victoria is a much better postprandial anecdote than not having met her, it's always possible that Wilde 'lifted' it from Bastien-Lepage's account of the day.

Certainly Wilde's other anecdote about the Queen is hard to imagine. The writer recounted for the dinner guests that Victoria was about to leave for the State Opening of Parliament when her Lady-in-Waiting, the Duchess of Sutherland, couldn't be found. Eventually she arrived ten minutes late by carriage, and speechless with embarrassment knelt before the Queen, who apparently said, 'It seems to me that your watch, Duchess, is out of working order. Allow me!' At which point the Queen hung a costly gold watch chain, bearing her initials picked out in diamonds, over the bowed head of the Duchess.[9] Certainly Harriet, Duchess of Sutherland, was Mistress of the Robes four times between 1837 and 1861, and as the holder of this prestigious post would have been present at the State Opening. However, since she was in-waiting, and therefore based at whichever residence the Queen was occupying at the time, it is doubtful she would be late at such an important event.

Separating fact from fiction isn't easy with figures as iconic as Victoria and Wilde. When it comes to the two of them together it is virtually impossible. The much-respected Elizabeth Longford's *Victoria R.I.* repeats an oft-quoted anecdote about Wilde being sent by *The Telegraph* to cover a memorial service for the late Emperor of Germany (and father-in-law of Vicky). William I. Longford asserts that Wilde arrived at Windsor on 16 March 1888 to report events: 'Much annoyed at this intrusion, she nevertheless allowed him to see the Chapel. According to Ponsonby, "he was most affected".'[10] Wilde's grandson Merlin Holland disputes this:

This has been the subject of lengthy correspondence between the editors of Wilde's journalism, a number of academics and the Royal Archives. There is nothing in the Royal Archives about it at all. The original story seems to have been invented (or just repeated without a proper source) by A.L. Rowse. It was first thought that it might have referred to Willie Wilde who wrote regularly for the *Telegraph*, but not even that seems to have been the case.[11]

Mr Holland similarly dismisses another Wildean rumour – that the author was in receipt of a post-imprisonment pension from the Queen – as '1930s sensationalist French rubbish'.[12]

What is beyond dispute is that the Prince of Wales was a huge admirer of Wilde's plays. In February 1892 he was one of the first to see *Lady Windermere's Fan* and told the playwright how much he enjoyed it. A year later he witnessed the second performance of *A Woman of No Importance* at the Haymarket Theatre, taking with him his mother's cousin Princess Mary of Teck, known for her resonating laugh. 'Do not alter a single line!' urged Bertie, to which Wilde rejoined, 'Sire your wish is my command.' Afterwards, still on a post-performance high, Wilde exclaimed, 'What a splendid country where princes understand poets.'[13] Bertie returned two weeks later to see it again with his heir, Prince George.

The year 1895 is of course Wilde's 'annus horribilis', beginning on a positive note with the critical successes of *An Ideal Husband* at the Haymarket followed by *The Importance of Being Earnest* at St James's Theatre. Bertie went to see both. Meanwhile Wilde was publicly flaunting his affair with Lord Alfred Douglas, third son of the 9th Marquess of Queensbury, known to friends and adoring mother as 'Bosie'. The brutish Marquess memorably left his calling card bearing the handwritten message, 'For Oscar Wilde, posing as a Somdomite [sic]' at the writer's club. Wilde sued for criminal libel, then abandoned the case, but incriminating evidence that came to light in cross-examination led to Wilde being arrested for homosexual offences. He was eventually found guilty, sentenced to two years' hard labour and became bankrupt. (Even such adversity brought a typical Wildean quip: 'If this is how Queen Victoria treats her prisoners she doesn't deserve to have any.') Most devastating to Wilde was that the man who had rubbed shoulders with royalty was now a social pariah. After two years in prison he spent his last three years in a relatively penurious exile in France.

Curiously, Bertie himself had a run-in with the dyspeptic Queensbury who, fittingly, gave his name to the Marquess of Queensbury rules – the code of generally accepted rules in the sport of boxing. Queensbury's heir, Lord Drumlanrig, was employed as Private Secretary to Lord Rosebery, Prime Minister for a year from 1894 and widely rumoured to be homosexual. Fearing that he would turn his son in that direction and hearing that Rosebery was on holiday at the popular spa town of Bad Homburg, Queensbury hot-footed it to Germany with a horse whip for some gay-lashing. By chance the Prince of Wales was there taking the waters. He urged the Marquess to calm down, the police were called in and Queensbury was forced to leave. Back in England he had already sent abusive letters about the 'relationship' to Victoria, Gladstone, Rosebery and his own son.[14]

In October 1894 Drumlanrig was killed during a shooting party. His unexplained death – officially 'accidental' but rumoured to have been either suicide or murder – combined with Bosie's very public fling with Wilde only stoked Queensbury's fury. In a letter he let rip that 'Snob Queers like Rosebery' had corrupted his sons and he believed the PM was indirectly responsible for Drumlanrig's death.[15]

Not all the Queensburys came to blows with the Royal Family. The pugilistic Marquess's father, Archibald Douglas, 8th Marquess, held the senior post of Comptroller of the Household at Victoria's court for three years from 1853. Like his grandson Drumlanrig, he too met a sticky end, again possibly suicide, from an exploding shotgun, dying in 1858 on the hunting field aged 40.

Less to Victoria's liking was Archibald's eccentric daughter – and Bosie's aunt – Florence. A nonconforming tomboy, she wore her hair cropped, rode astride her horses like a man, and for her presentation to the Queen wouldn't wear the conventional lace and feathers, much to the annoyance of the Lord Chamberlain. Even more upsetting for Victoria was the news that Florrie's pet panther brought back from her recent trip to Patagonia had escaped into Windsor Great Park and killed several of the royal deer.[16]

Bosie himself saw the Queen at a distance several times when he attended Lambrook School, based in a large country house at Winkfield near Windsor, which, at the time, catered for fewer than two dozen boys. Lord Alfred was a contemporary of two of the Queen's grandsons, Princes Christian Victor and Albert of Schleswig-Holstein, who lived at Cumberland Lodge in the Great Park. Victoria would occasionally drive to Lambrook to watch the boys playing cricket.[17] Christian Victor (known to the family as 'Chrystle') went on to play the game at a first class level and in 1887 scored 35 against W.G. Grace's team at a match in Scarborough. He died of enteric fever in South Africa in October 1900 during the Boer War. Recent Lambrook alumni include the rugby players Max and Thom Evans and the actor Alex Pettyfer.

Bosie used the family connection to petition the Queen regarding Oscar's prison sentence: 'I appeal to you to exercise your power of pardon in the case of Oscar Wilde the poet and dramatist who now lies in prison …' A disapproving Private Secretary hoisted it out of the royal in-tray and Victoria never saw it. Instead it was forwarded to the government and the Home Secretary issued a formal letter of rejection.[18]

Wilde was released from prison on 18 May 1897. He immediately set sail for France and never returned to Britain. He adopted the name Sebastien (from the martyred St Sebastien) Melmoth (from *Melmoth the Wanderer*, a Gothic novel written by his great-uncle Charles Maturin).

Wilde initially stayed with his friend Robert Ross in the northern coastal village of Berneval-le-Grand. It was here he wrote *The Ballad of Reading Gaol*. Any bitterness for his homeland and its establishment clearly excluded Queen Victoria. He celebrated her Diamond Jubilee with a party for local children, as he proudly told Bosie in a letter written the following day:

My fête was a huge success: fifteen *gamins* were entertained … I had a huge iced cake with *Jubilé de la Reine Victoria* in pink sugar … Every child was asked beforehand to choose his present: they all chose instruments of music!
6 accordions
5 trompettes
4 clarons.

… They sang the *Marseillaise* and other songs and danced a *ronde*, … I gave the health of *La Reine d'Angleterre!!!* … and finally I gave *Le Président de la République*, I thought I had better do so. … It was an amusing experience as I am hardly more than a month out of gaol.[19]

Ross was in London for the celebrations and on the eve of Jubilee Day an envious Wilde sent greetings on a postcard:

> Dear Robbie, Just a line to wish you a very happy Jubilee, and many of them. I fear I cannot hope to live long enough to see more than five or six more myself, but with you it is different. I don't know the exact route of the procession, but I suppose the dear Queen passes by Upper Phillimore Gardens and will look up and see you waving the flags of no nations. Of course we are having 'Queen's weather' here. It began today.[20]

He cut out a portrait of Victoria from the *New Review*. It was a copy of a woodcut showing the Queen walking her dog. In a letter to Ross he praised it as 'wonderful. I am going to hang it on the wall of the chalet. Every poet should gaze at the portrait of his Queen all day long.'[21]

Sadly for Wilde his Jubilee party did not have the positive long-term benefit he'd hope for, as one of the boys present that day later recounted:

> People began to gossip … First of all, why had he only invited the boys and not the girls and their schoolmistresses? … Then one day – it's unclear how – we learned that Mr Sebastien Melmoth was … Oscar Wilde … whose prison sentence was still fresh in people's minds … Parents forbade their children to have anything to do with a man hiding under an alias and attempting to smother a recent scandal.[22]

After a brief reunion with Bosie in Naples the fallen Oscar Wilde returned to France, where he spent his last months in the dingy Hôtel d'Alsace in Saint-Germain-des-Prés. Here he became increasingly confined to his room and memorably quipped, 'My wallpaper and I are fighting a duel to the death. One of us has to go.' He died from meningitis on 30 November 1900 at the age of 46, just over seven weeks before the death of the Queen.

One of his later visitors, the American writer Vincent O'Sullivan, recalled Wilde telling him not long before his death, 'The three women I have most have admired are Queen Victoria, Sarah Bernhardt and Lily [sic] Langtry. I would have married any of them with pleasure.'[23]

Notes

1 Ellman, Richard: *Oscar Wilde*: Hamish Hamilton: 1987: p.11

2 Ibid.: p.123

3 Paula Byrne (9 August 2009): 'Sex scandal behind Brideshead Revisited': *The Times*: Retrieved 25 June 2018

4 RAVIC/MAIN/QVJ (W) Tuesday 4 October 1881 (Princess Beatrice's copies). Retrieved 15 June 2018

5 Ponsonby, Arthur: *Henry Ponsonby – His Life From His Letters*: Macmillan: 1942: p.50

6 Ellman, Op. Cit.: p.277

7 Krohg, Christian (Jennifer Lloyd, translator): *Fire Portretter/Four Portraits*: Lysaker Geelmuyden Kiese: 1999: p.81ff

8 Merlin Holland: email to the author: 5 July 2018

9 Krohg: Op. Cit.: p.85ff

10 Longford, Elizabeth: *Victoria R.I.*: Weidenfeld and Nicolson: 1964: p.505

11 Merlin Holland: email to the author: 13 December 2017

12 Ibid.

13 Ellman: Op. Cit.: p.358ff

14 Ibid.: p.381

15 Lord Queensbury to Alfred Montgomery: 1 November 1894. Quoted in Murray, Douglas: *Bosie – A Biography of Lord Alfred Douglas*: Hodder and Stoughton: 2000

16 Hyde, H. Montgomery: *Lord Alfred Douglas*: Methuen: 1984: p.4

17 Ibid.: p.16

18 Ibid.: p.91ff

19 Hart-Davis, Rupert (ed.): *The Letters of Oscar Wilde*: Harcourt, Brace and World Inc.: 1962: p.617

20 Ibid.: p.615

21 Ibid.: p.610

22 Frankel, Nicholas: *Oscar Wilde – The Unrepentant Years*: Harvard University Press: 2017: p.112

23 Hart-Davis: Op. Cit.: p.65n

28

I WAS KAISER BILL'S GRANDMA
QUEEN VICTORIA AND KAISER WILHELM II

Kaiser Wilhelm II. (Library of Congress)

QUEEN VICTORIA has been dubbed the Grandmother of Europe. Harald V of Norway, Carl XVI, Gustaf of Sweden, Felipe VI of Spain, Margrethe II of Denmark and, of course, Elizabeth II of Great Britain are all direct descendants of the Queen Empress. The most infamous of her descendants was her eldest grandson, Kaiser Wilhelm II of Germany. While his relationship with his mother and England, the land of her birth, was volatile, he rarely wavered in his love and admiration for his grandmother. When she died at Osborne House in January 1901 she did so cradled in his arms.

Victoria, Princess Royal, the Queen's eldest child, was betrothed at the age of 16 to Prince Frederick of Prussia. Although it was a dynastic union, backed by Albert and Victoria, to help create a liberal Prussia that would lead Germany to unification, it was also a great love match.

A year into her marriage and aged just over 18, Vicky gave birth to a son, the future Kaiser Wilhelm II, on 27 January 1859. Queen Victoria, whose ninth child Princess Beatrice was born less than two years earlier, was ecstatic.

'After luncheon,' she wrote in her journal:

> came the welcome eagerly expected news, in a telegram from Sir J. Clark: 'All is happily over. The Princess as well as can be, the young Prince also.' Called all the Children in, & ran along to the Rubens Room, where Albert was sitting to Mr Boxall, to bring him the blessed news! Such joy! All the Household, servants, everyone delighted. Ran back to send numberless telegrams, to Berlin & to relations, &c … Children in extacies [sic] at Uncle- & Aunt-ship, Arthur shouting out 'I'm an uncle.' General rejoicing, ringing of bells, & illuminations in the town.[1]

Ironically, given what fate had in store, the Queen prayed the baby would 'be a blessing to his country!':

> I delight in the idea of being a grandmama; to be that at 39 (D.V.) and to look and feel young is great fun, only I wish I could go through it for you, dear, and save you all the annoyance. But that can't be helped. I think of my next birthday being spent with my children and grandchild. It will be a treat.[2]

The baby was named Frederick William Albert Victor and the Queen was thrilled to be asked to be a godparent until she realised that she was one of a total of forty-two, which she found 'most alarming'. She was slightly mollified when she was informed by Vicky that the four grand-parents had the distinction of being the child's 'peculiar sponsors'.

It was only when a detailed medical report was sent to her that Victoria found out the Princess had had the kind of traumatic labour she herself had never had. It was a breech birth, mishandled by the team of doctors, and at one point the lives of both mother and child were despaired of.

Something she wasn't aware of was that William's arm had been dislocated at the brachial plexus during the delivery, which injured the nerves in his arm. Initially the parents and doctors were hopeful it would respond to treatment, but it eventually became clear it would fail to develop normally. When he became an adult this left arm would remain 15cm shorter than the right, something William became adept at disguising in public and in photographs.

Vicky decided to break the news of the arm to her parents in person, so it wasn't until May 1859 that they found out, as the Queen noted in her journal the day mother and daughter were reunited: 'Vicky only began to cry when she talked of her poor little boy's left arm being so weak, which it has been from his birth, having been injured in being brought into the world.'[3] The topic of William's arm would be the first of so many shared concerns, mostly about his personality and behaviour, between mother and daughter over the next four decades.

The Queen was a sympathetic bystander quick to offer support to Vicky as William was subjected to a succession of 'cures' for his paralysed limb, from hours spent in an 'arm-stretching machine' to electrolysis. She was even amused by one of the more barbaric treatments on offer in Berlin. 'Baby has had 2 "Animalische Bäder" for his arm, such a nasty, horrid idea,' wrote Vicky to her mother on 11 August 1859. 'They put his arm into a warm just killed animal (a hare) and keep it there for an hour. It is supposed to strengthen.' The Queen passed on the anecdote to her personal physician, and reported back to Vicky, 'When I told Clark about these wonderful Animalische Bäder he laughed very much & said, "Well it can do no harm."'[4]

William was over a year and a half old before his British grandparents met him for the first time. In September Victoria and Albert travelled to Coburg for the event. The Queen was delighted with her first 'darling grandchild' and wrote to her mother, the Duchess of Kent, that William was 'such a fine, darling Child – very fat and fair – very intelligent'.[5] The Prince Consort, belying his dour image, tossed him in the air. In her journal the Queen continued to wax lyrical about the meeting:

Our darling grandchild was brought in, such a little dear. He came in walking, holding his nurse Mrs Hobbs's hand & was very good. He is a fine fat child, with a beautiful white soft skin. We felt so happy to see him at last.[6]

In June 1861 Vicky and Fritz arrived at Buckingham Palace with William and his sister Charlotte, born the previous summer. 'This happy meeting, seeing our dear 1rst born so happy with her good husband & 2 pretty little children,' wrote Victoria in her journal.[7]

Family life had changed radically by the time of William's next meeting with the Queen. Aged 4 he arrived at Windsor to attend the wedding of his uncle, the Prince of Wales, to Alexandra of Denmark. In an early attempt to rile the British, the young prince threw his aunt Beatrice's muff out of the carriage window, then chucked the cairngorm from his dirk across the floor of St George's Chapel before sinking his teeth into the bare knees of his kilted uncles. He addressed his grandmother as 'duck', which amused her and was one of the only light moments in a wedding that resembled a funeral thanks to the Queen's intense mourning over the death of Prince Albert fifteen months earlier.

William proved to be a useful distraction for the grieving Victoria. In July 1864 he arrived at Osborne with his nurse at the invitation of the Queen to try to strengthen his arm by bathing in the sea: 'He is looking very nice & so grown, and seemed so pleased to see me!'[8] The fact that 'the dear child remembers his dear grandpapa' also meant he soared in her estimation. At the same time she warned Vicky that she thought he was developing an arrogant streak. The young mother admitted she'd been aware of this for a while but that he was thoroughly spoilt by the servants.[9]

Curing her grandson of his arrogance was the theme of a letter to Vicky marking William's twelfth birthday. She warned her daughter of the dangers of his living an isolated life in palaces with no contact with people of different backgrounds: 'It is terribly difficult and a terrible trial to be a Prince. *No one* having the courage to tell them the truth or to accustom them to those rubs and knocks which are so necessary to Boys and Young Men.'[10]

Concern over William increased the close bond between mother and daughter. 'Why does Willy always sign himself "William, Prince of Prussia"?' an exasperated Victoria asked her daughter in 1878. 'His father never does.' She suspected the real reason was Prussian arrogance, gradually being instilled in him by the Chancellor, Otto von Bismarck, and the boy's German grandparents, who combined to steer William away from the liberal influence of Fritz and Vicky.[11]

Occasionally Victoria found in dealing with Willy that the role of grandson was at odds with his position as a future German Emperor. When he reached his eighteenth birthday in January 1877, the Queen proposed to give him the Order of the Bath, which is prestigious but not the most senior order. Vicky felt that this would be regarded by the Berlin court as a slight. Her mother sought advice from Prime Minister Benjamin Disraeli and Foreign Minister Lord Derby. Like Vicky both urged her to bestow the Order of the Garter, the highest British order. The Queen acquiesced and the decision was widely welcomed:

> Dear Willie of Prussia's 18th birthday. Received most delighted & astonished telegrams about my intention of giving him the Garter. It is a rare thing that 3 members of the same family & the 3 generations should have it at the same time. May God long bless, protect & guide dear Willie.[12]

'Dear Willie' was more than delighted. He was 'quite speechless with astonishment' at receiving 'the highest order in Christendom', as he wrote to his grandmother on the day after his birthday, mindful that 'this highest mark of distinction is conferred by You only on sovereigns'. He was still glorifying in the honour a year later when he wrote to congratulate Victoria on her fifty-ninth birthday in May 1878. He told her he was 'proud of beeing [sic] Your grandson & as Knight of the Garter also Your subject. Yes on that day I feel a thorough Englishman & am glad to say it, I am also a Briton!' Pandering to William's enormous ego and insecurities clearly worked in making him loyal and deferential to the British throne, as Victoria would realise again when she made him an Admiral of the Fleet and a British general.[13]

In welcoming her grandson to adulthood, Victoria also took pains to emphasise his filial duty to '*never* show a want of respect' to his parents. In this she was on a less sure footing than when bestowing the Garter. Relations between Fritz and Vicky and their eldest son declined sharply during the 1880s as the younger Prince allied himself more and more with his reactionary grandfather Kaiser Wilhelm I and his court. He was also becoming more anti-British. Victoria admonished him for not congratulating her on her army's victories in Egypt and for opposing the marriage of her daughter (and his aunt) Beatrice to Prince Henry of Battenberg. The latter's father, Prince Alexander of Hesse-Darmstadt, had morganatically married a countess, which meant their sons were deprived of their Hessian rank. The morally rigid Prussian court disapproved of the Battenbergs and the royal marriage. William exacerbated the rift between his English-born mother and his grandmother by opposing the marriage of another Battenberg brother – Alexander (known as 'Sandro') – to his own sister Victoria. The Queen exploded with rage to Vicky about 'the extraordinary impertinence and insolence, and I must add, great unkindness of Willie' as well as his 'foolish' new wife Augusta of Schleswig-Holstein ('Dona' to her family), whom she dubbed 'a poor, little, insignificant Princess'.[14]

Victoria exacted her revenge during her Golden Jubilee celebrations in 1887. William had sent, she told his mother, an 'impertinent letter' that had given her a 'great shock'. He told his grandmother that he had asked the Kaiser if he could represent him at the festivities, which would be an obvious snub to his parents, the Crown Prince and Princess. Fortunately for the Queen she already knew of Vicky and Fritz's plans to attend and so she bluntly telegraphed William: 'Am delighted dear Papa is quite able to come. You will therefore only bring 2 gentlemen.'

William was incensed at his grandmother's snub. During a hunting expedition with the Eulenburg family in early June he fumed that it was 'high time the old woman died ... She causes trouble, more than one would think. Well, England should look out when I have something to say about things.'[15]

At one point Victoria toyed with the idea of not inviting William at all, but Vicky, mindful of how this snub would be interpreted at her father-in-law's court, said he should be invited as the eldest grandchild:

> He need only stay for a very few days. He has behaved very badly to you – and to us – but I fear it would only do harm in every way to appear to take more notice of his behaviour than it is worth! It is well *not* to give him a handle for saying he is ill-treated! ... He fancies himself of immense importance & service to the State.[16]

In the end the Prince and his wife did attend but were treated more or less the same as any other grandchild and partner, much to the Prince's fury. 'Pr. W and the Princess were received with exquisite coolness, with bare courtesy,' commented a German Lady-in-Waiting. 'He only saw his grandmother a couple of times, at Court functions. *She* was always placed behind the black Queen of Hawaii!! Both returned not in the best of tempers.'[17]

Tragically for Fritz and Vicky, not only did the Emperor Wilhelm I live until two weeks short of his ninety-first birthday but by the time of his death and the accession of the Crown Prince as Frederick III, the latter was suffering from incurable throat cancer. Far from ushering in a new era of liberal ideals, his reign of just ninety-nine days was merely a brief interlude between the first reactionary Kaiser Wilhelm and the second.

During the brief reign the younger William was the usual thorn in the side of his parents. The Queen advised her daughter to 'send William and his odious ungrateful Wife, to travel & find his level'.[18] In April 1888 she hammered home this message in person, by travelling to Berlin to say an emotional farewell to her son-in-law. She took the opportunity to summon Bismarck for an interview, during which she voiced her concerns about William's inexperience. The Chancellor agreed the Prince was inexperienced in civil affairs but 'should he be thrown into the water, he would be able to swim'.[19] After the meeting the Iron Chancellor emerged mopping his brow and exclaiming, 'That was a woman. One could do business with her.'

Although the Queen was extremely agitated about her grandson's continual snubs to his parents, which she lambasted as 'wicked and horrid!', the expected showdown with William never occurred. The Queen had been so incensed she sent excerpts of her daughter's letters outlining William's behaviour to her Prime Minister, Lord Salisbury. The latter feared that with the accession of the Crown Prince likely at any time soon, what was essentially a major family rift could become an international crisis between the two super-powers. 'She is very unmanageable about her conduct to her relations,' Salisbury wrote to the Duke of Rutland, the government minster accompanying the royal party. 'She will persist in considering William only as her grandson. But the matter has become political and very grave and she must listen to advice.'[20] The Queen must have done since, according to the British Ambassador in Berlin, she was 'extraordinarily gracious' to William 'and vice versa'.[21]

On 15 June 1888 William succeeded Fritz as Emperor. One of his first acts was to telegraph the news of his father's death to the Queen at Balmoral. She replied, 'I am broken-hearted. Help and do all you can for your poor dear Mother and try to follow in your best, noblest, and kindest of father's footsteps.'[22]

William failed on both counts. He followed in his grandfather's reactionary footsteps and as for his mother, he took her two main residences from her, leaving her feeling insecure and ill. The Queen wrote to her daughter in October, 'If I do not speak of William's shameful conduct it is because I feel too furious, too indignant, too savage also to trust myself.'[23]

Once again Lord Salisbury urged the Queen to mollify William for the sake of Anglo-German relations. She invited him to Britain on an official visit in the summer of 1889. Victoria was at Osborne House on the Isle of Wight, and as his yacht berthed off Spithead on 2 August, William, dressed in her gift of an Admiral of the Fleet uniform, was ebullient: 'Fancy wearing the same uniform as St Vincent and Nelson; it is enough to make one quite giddy.'[24]

No matter how she felt about her bumptious 30-year-old grandson as a wayward member of the family, she treated him with all the respect due to a visiting head of state, quite literally rolling out the red carpet for the Emperor of Germany. 'All on the "qui vive" [alert] for William's arrival which had been expected at 5,' she wrote in her journal that evening:

> The Guard of Honour with the Band was drawn up, & waited & waited. At length, at near ½ p. 7 he appeared. I received him at the door … Ld Salisbury was also there. We took William, who was in British Admiral's uniform, into the Drawingroom, & then he went to his rooms downstairs. He was very amiable & kissed me very affectionately on both cheeks, on arriving. We dined in the big tent … William led me in, & I sat between him & Henry … We were in all 40. All the gentlemen were in uniform. The Household all came in after dinner, & William presented all his people. The Marine Band played during & after dinner.[25]

Two years later there was a state visit from the Emperor and Empress to Windsor. Again the Queen detailed the deference she, and her court, showed to a fellow monarch:

> I went down to the Grand Hall, where all the Household were assembled. William was received in the same way as all other Sovereigns. As the carriages drove up I went to the door to greet William who drove with 3 Uncles, & was in Prussian uniform. He embraced me, & then I waited for the 2nd carriage in which drove

Dona, Alix, Lenchen & Beatrice. There was a general 'embrassade' & presentation of people, after which William went out in the Quadrangle to inspect the Guard of Honour, & we Ladies went into the Throne Room.

The Queen herself 'took Dona to her rooms (the state ones)'.[26]

Two days later the German delegation attended the wedding of another of Victoria's grandchildren, Princess Marie Louise, to Prince Aribert of Anhalt at St George's Chapel, Windsor. Once again due deference was paid to the Kaiser by the Queen, who noted in her journal that on her arrival at the Chapel, 'I bowed to William & Dona, who stood to my right'. At the wedding breakfast later in the day the guests sat at numerous small tables. The Queen's was made up of the bride and groom, their four parents and William. It was a far cry from the Golden Jubilee dinner four years earlier when William and Dona were seated well below the salt.

The previously fraught relationship between Victoria and her eldest grandson was replaced with mutual respect now the Prince had joined the exclusive monarchs club. They exchanged gifts. Some, such as the Queen's present of a silver statuette of the Prince Consort conquering sin, could be taken on two levels. She was amused when one of her birthday gifts from him included the message, 'May God preserve our revered belovedest Colleague for the benefit of Europe, its nations and their peace.' 'I think the colleague will amuse you,' Victoria wrote to Vicky.

William was fond of recalling a rarely glimpsed facet of his grandmother's personality: her earthy sense of humour. Once she invited the elderly Admiral Foley for dinner to report on the tragic sinking of HMS *Eurydice* with a loss of 317 lives off the Isle of Wight in March 1878. 'After she had exhausted this melancholy subject,' recalled the Kaiser in his memoirs:

> my grandmother, in order to give the conversation a more cheerful turn, inquired after his sister, whom she knew well, whereupon, the Admiral, who was hard of hearing and still pursuing his train of thought about the *Eurydice,* replied in his stentorian voice, 'Well, Ma'am, I am going to have her turned over and take a good look at her bottom and have it well scraped.' The effect of this answer was stupendous. My grandmother put down her knife and fork, hid her face in her handkerchief and shook and heaved with laughter till the tears rolled down her face.[27]

So enjoyable were his visits to England as Emperor that William invited himself four years running. Before the fourth visit, Victoria told him that there was no room for him at Osborne and he would have to stay on his yacht. This failed to deter him, so she asked the British Ambassador in Berlin to strongly 'hint that these regular annual visits are not quite desirable'. William remained undeterred, arrived for the Cowes Regatta, won the Queen's Cup and kept his grandmother waiting for dinner the following evening.

The rapprochement was too good to last, and William's clumsy attempts to assert himself on the international stage led to conflict with his grandmother and her countrymen. At the end of 1895, Dr Jameson, Administrator of Rhodesia, led a few hundred mounted police in a night-time dash into the Transvaal in a revolt against President Kruger. Known as the 'Jameson Raid', it ended with failure when the Boers captured the attackers. Captured papers pointed to a conspiracy between Cecil Rhodes and his South Africa Company as well as Britain's Colonial Office, and it would eventually result in the Boer War.

The Kaiser sent a telegram, thereafter dubbed 'the Kruger Telegram', to the President congratulating him on preserving his 'independence' against 'attacks from without'. On 3 January 1896 an exasperated Victoria wrote in her journal, 'The papers are full of very strong articles against William, who sent a most unwarranted telegram to President Kruger congratulating him, which is outrageous, and very unfriendly towards us.'[28]

Two days later she sent a restrained letter to her grandson in which she spoke of her 'deep regret at the telegram' and said that it had made 'a very painful impression here'. While acknowledging that the Jameson raid was 'very wrong and totally unwarranted … I think it would have been far better to have said nothing.'[29]

At the beginning of 1897 the Kaiser again came into conflict with Britain, this time about the Greek and Turkish argument over control of Crete. Victoria labelled her grandson's involvement 'so fearfully & senselessly violent'. She determined it would not be wise to invite him to that summer's Diamond Jubilee marking her sixty years as monarch: 'She asked her Private Secretary to inform the Prince of Wales: that there is *not* the slightest fear of the Queen's giving way about the Emperor William's coming here in June. It would *never* do.'[30]

By 1899 Anglo-German relations had once again improved enough for the Queen to agree to another visit from William and Dona at the start of the Boer War. 'William came to me after tea,' Victoria noted later:

> I had a long interesting conversation with him on all subjects. We first spoke about his dear Mama's health, which is not satisfactory [Vicky was dying of inoperable cancer of the spine, though her mother was unaware of the true nature of her illness], then of the shocking tone of the German press & the shameful attacks on England, as well as monstrous misrepresentation & lies about the war, which he greatly deplores ... William himself wishes for a better understanding with us.

That night there was a banquet for 144 in St George's Hall. Bertie proposed the health of William and Dona. The Kaiser proposed the health of the Queen.[31]

William made one final, poignant, visit to see his grandmother when he hurried to Osborne where her family had gathered at her deathbed. As the end approached the Bishop of Winchester said prayers for the dying and Dr Reid, the royal physician, administered oxygen. Meanwhile her daughters kept telling the Queen who was beside her, as she was now too blind to see. One name they omitted was the Kaiser's. Reid whispered to the Prince of Wales, 'Wouldn't it be well to tell her that her grandson the Emperor is here too?' The Prince replied, 'No it would excite her too much.'

Later in the day, the Prince relented and Reid took the Emperor in, and asked the maids to leave the bedroom. Leaning over the Queen the doctor told her, 'Your Majesty, your grandson the Emperor is here; he has come to see you as you are so ill.' Reid noted, 'she smiled and understood. I went out and left him with her five minutes alone. She said to me afterwards, "The Emperor is very kind."'

Queen Victoria died at 6.30 p.m. on 22 January 1901. In her last hour she was supported by Dr Reid at her right side and by Kaiser William 'who knelt at her left side with his arm around her'.[32]

The Queen's body was carried downstairs in a coffin, covered by a white satin pall. It was placed in the dining room, which was used for the time being as a mortuary chapel, filled with the scent of tuberoses and gardenias. Eight enormous candles lit the room and four soldiers from the Grenadier Guards with reversed arms stood at each corner of the coffin. Above them hung a solitary Union flag. Afterwards the Kaiser asked if he could keep it. He always maintained it was his most valued possession.[33]

Notes

1 RA VIC/MAIN/QVJ (W) Thursday 27 January 1859 (Princess Beatrice's copies). Retrieved 3 May 2018

2 Fulford, Roger (ed.): *Dearest Child*: Evans Brothers: 1964: p.120

3 RA VIC/MAIN/QVJ (W) Thursday 27 January 1859 (Princess Beatrice's copies). Retrieved 3 May 2018

4 Röhl, John: *Young Wilhelm*: Cambridge University Press: 1998: p.26

5 Ibid.: p.67

6 RA VIC/MAIN/QVJ (W) Tuesday 25 September 1860 (Princess Beatrice's copies). Retrieved 3 May 2018

7 RA VIC/MAIN/QVJ (W) Wednesday 26 June 1861 (Princess Beatrice's copies). Retrieved 3 May 2018

8 RA VIC/MAIN/QVJ (W) Tuesday 12 July 1864 (Princess Beatrice's copies). Retrieved 3 May 2018

9 Röhl: Op. Cit.: p.77

10 Ponsonby, Sir Frederick (ed.): *Letters of the Empress Frederick*: London: 1928: pp.123ff

11 Longford, Elizabeth: *Victoria R.I.*: Weidenfeld and Nicolson: 1964: p.423ff

12 RA VIC/MAIN/QVJ (W) Saturday 27 January 1877 (Princess Beatrice's copies). Retrieved 3 May 2018

13 Röhl: Op. Cit.: p.254

14 Fulford, Roger (ed.): *Beloved Mama*: Evans Brothers: 1981: p.178ff

15 Röhl: Op. Cit.: p.679

16 Hibbert, Christopher: *Queen Victoria*: HarperCollins: 2000: p.382

17 Ibid.: p.383

18 Longford: Op. Cit.: p.505

19 Hibbert, Christopher: *Queen Victoria in her Letters & Journals*: John Murray: 1984: p.311

20 Röhl: Op. Cit.: p.807

21 Ibid.: p.808

22 Hibbert: *Queen Victoria in her Letters & Journals*: Op. Cit.

23 Bennett, Daphne: *Vicky*: Constable: 1983: p.283

24 Longford: Op. Cit.: p.508

25 RA VIC/MAIN/QVJ (W) Friday 2 August 1889 (Princess Beatrice's copies). Retrieved 3 May 2018

26 RA VIC/MAIN/QVJ (W) Saturday 4 July 1891 (Princess Beatrice's copies). Retrieved 3 May 2018

27 William II, Former Emperor of Germany: *My Early Life*: Methuen: 1926: p.65

28 RA VIC/MAIN/QVJ (W) Friday 3 January 1896 (Princess Beatrice's copies). Retrieved 3 May 2018

29 Hibbert: *Queen Victoria in her Letters & Journals*: Op. Cit.

30 Longford: Op. Cit.: p.546

31 RA VIC/MAIN/QVJ (W) Tuesday 21 November 1899 (Princess Beatrice's copies). Retrieved 3 May 2018

32 Reid, Michaela: *Ask Sir James*: Hodder and Stoughton: 1987

33 Hibbert: *Queen Victoria*: Op. Cit.

BIBLIOGRAPHY

BOOKS

Aga Khan, His Highness the: *Memoirs of the Aga Khan – World Enough and Time*: Simon and Schuster: 1954

Aronson, Theo: *Grandmama of Europe*: John Murray: 1973

Aronson, Theo: *Princess Alice, Countess of Athlone*: Thistle Publishing: 2014

Baily, Leslie: *Gilbert and Sullivan and their World*: Thames and Hudson: 1973

Baker, E.C.: *Sir William Preece F.R.S – Victorian Engineer Extraordinary*: Century Benham: 1976

Barkeley, Richard: *The Road to Mayerling*: Macmillan: 1958

Barnum, Phineas T.: *Struggles and Triumphs*: Warren, Johnson & Co.: 1872

Bartholdy, Paul Mendelssohn (ed.): *Letters of Felix Mendelssohn Bartholdy*: London: 1863

Basler, Roy (ed.): *Collected Works of Abraham Lincoln, Volume 4*: Rutgers University Press: 1953

Basler, Roy (ed.): *Collected Works of Abraham Lincoln, Volume 5*: Rutgers University Press: 1953

Bennett, Daphne: *Vicky*: Constable: 1983

Benson, E.F.: *As We Were*: Longman: 1930

Bingham, Madeleine: *The Great Lover – The Life and Times of Herbert Beerbohm Tree*: Hamish Hamilton: 1973

Bloomfield, Georgiana Lady: *Reminiscences of Court and Diplomatic Life*: Kegan Paul: 1883

Bostridge, Mark: *Florence Nightingale*: Penguin: 2009

Brahms, Caryl: *Gilbert and Sullivan*: Weidenfeld and Nicolson: 1975

Bruce, Robert V.: *Bell – Alexander Graham Bell and the Conquest of Solitude*: Gollancz: 1973

Burke, John: *Buffalo Bill*: Cassell: 1974

Carley, Lionel: *Edvard Grieg in England*: Boydell: 2006

Casals, Pablo: *Joys and Sorrows*: MacDonald: 1970

Christian, Ian: *Discovering Classical Music – Liszt: His Life, The Person, His Music*: Pen and Sword Books: 1991

Christian, Rupert: *The Visitors – Culture Shock in Nineteenth-Century Britain*: Chatto and Windus: 2000

Cornwallis-West, Mrs George: *The Reminiscences of Lady Randolph Churchill*: The Century Co.: 1908

Davies, Clara Novello: *The Life I Have Loved*: Heinemann: 1940

Duff, David: *Victoria Travels*: Frederick Muller Ltd: 1970

Dunraven, the Earl of: *Past Times and Pastimes*: Hodder and Stoughton: 1922

Ellis, William Ashton (translator): *Richard to Minna Wagner – Letters to his First Wife, Volume I*: H. Grevel & Co.: 1909

Ellis, William Ashton (translator): *Richard Wagner to Mathilde Wesendonck*: H. Grevel & Co., London: 1905

Ellman, Richard: *Oscar Wilde*: Hamish Hamilton: 1987

Elton, George: *General Gordon*: Collins: 1954

Fitzsimons, Raymund: *Barnum in London*: Geoffrey Bles Ltd: 1969

Frankel, Nicholas: *Oscar Wilde – The Unrepentant Years*: Harvard University Press: 2017

Fraser, Rebecca: *Charlotte Brontë*: Vintage: 2003

Fulford, Roger (ed.): *Beloved Mama – Private Correspondence of Queen Victoria and the Crown Princess of Prussia, 1878–1885*: Evans Brothers: 1981

Fulford, Roger (ed.): *Darling Child – Private Correspondence of Queen Victoria and the Crown Princess of Prussia, 1871–1878*: Evans Brothers: 1976

Fulford, Roger (ed.): *Dearest Child – Letters Between Queen Victoria and the Princess Royal, 1858–1861*: Evans Brothers: 1964

Fulford, Roger (ed.): *Your Dear Letter – Private Correspondence of Queen Victoria and the Crown Princess of Prussia, 1865–1871*: Evans Brothers: 1971

Gallop, Alan: *Buffalo Bill's British Wild West*: The History Press: 2009

Gaskell, Elizabeth: *The Life of Charlotte Brontë*: Cosimo Inc.: 2008

Guerin, Winifred: *Charlotte Brontë – The Evolution of Genius*: Oxford University Press: 1987

Hardy, Alan: *Queen Victoria Was Amused*: John Murray: 1976

Harman, Claire: *Charlotte Brontë – A Life*: Viking: 2015

Hart-Davis, Rupert (ed.): *The Letters of Oscar Wilde*: Harcourt, Brace and World Inc.: 1962

Hibbert, Christopher: *Queen Victoria – A Personal History*: HarperCollins: 2000

Hibbert, Christopher: *Queen Victoria in her Letters and Journals*: John Murray: 1984

Housman, Laurence: Florence Nightingale: in H.J. Massingham and Hugh Massingham (eds): *The Great Victorians*: Nicholson and Watson: 1932

Johnson, Edgar: *Charles Dickens – His Tragedy and Triumph*: Viking: 1977

Judtmann, Fritz: *Mayerling – The Facts Behind the Legend*: Harrap: 1971

Kasson, J.S.: *Buffalo Bill's Wild West*: Hill and Wang: 2000

Kemp, Peter: *The Strauss Family*: Omnibus Press: 1989

Kirk, H.L.: *Pablo Casals*: Hutchinson & Co.: 1974

Kuhn, William M: *Henry and Mary Ponsonby*: Duckworth: 2003

Lamont-Brown, Raymond: *Royal Poxes and Potions*: The History Press: 2009

Lennie, Campbell: *Landseer – The Victorian Paragon*: Hamish Hamilton: 1976

Leslie, Anita: *Jennie*: Hutchinson: 1969

Lloyd, Jennifer (translator): Krohg, Christian: *Fire Portretter/Four Portraits*: Lysaker Geelmuyden Kiese: 1999

Longford, Elizabeth: *Darling Loosy*: Weidenfeld and Nicolson: 1991

Longford, Elizabeth: *Victoria R.I.*: Weidenfeld and Nicolson, 1964

Lyon Playfair (1818–1898): doi:10.1093/ref:odnb/22368

McDonald, Lynn (ed.): *The Collected Works of Florence Nightingale Volume 5 – Florence Nightingale on Society and Politics, Philosophy, Science, Education and Literature*: Wilfred Laurier University Press: 2003

McKay, James: *Sounds of Silence*: Mainstream: 1997

Magnus, Philip: *King Edward VII*: John Murray: 1964

Malet, Victor: *Life With Queen Victoria*: John Murray: 1968

Marie Louise, Princess: *My Memories of Six Reigns*: Penguin: 1956

Marsden, Philip: *The Barefoot Emperor*: HarperCollins: 2007

Martin, Ralph: *Lady Randolph Churchill*: Cassell: 1969

Maylunas, Andrei: *A Lifelong Passion*: Weidenfeld and Nicolson: 1996

Montgomery Hyde, H.: *Lord Alfred Douglas*: Methuen Ltd: 1984

Murray, Douglas: *Bosie – A Biography of Lord Alfred Douglas*: Hodder and Stoughton: 2000

Nelson, Michael: *Queen Victoria and the Discovery of the Riviera*: I.B. Tauris: 2001

Ormond, Richard: *Sir Edwin Landseer*: Thames and Hudson: 1981

Owens, Susan: *Watercolours and Drawings from the Collection of Queen Elizabeth The Queen Mother*: Royal Collection Enterprises Ltd: 2005

Pearson, H.: *Beerbohm Tree – His Life and Laughter*: Methuen & Co.: 1956

Ponsonby, Arthur: *Henry Ponsonby – His Life From His Letters*: Macmillan: 1942

Ponsonby, Sir Frederick (ed.): *Letters of the Empress Frederick*: MacMillan & Co.: 1928

Ponsonby, Sir Frederick: *Recollections of Three Reigns*: Eyre and Spottiswode: 1951

Ramm, Agatha (ed.): *Beloved and Darling Child – Last Letters Between Queen Victoria and Her Eldest Daughter, 1886–1901*: Alan Sutton: 1990

Rappaport, Helen: *Four Sisters*: Macmillan: 2014

Rappaport, Helen: *Magnificent Obsession*: Windmill Books: 2012

Rappaport, Helen: *Queen Victoria – A Biographical Companion*: ABC-Clio: 2003

Redhouse, J.W.: *Diary of H.M. The Shah of Persia During his Tour Through Europe in AD 1873*: John Murray: 1874

Reid, Michaela: *Ask Sir James*: Hodder and Stoughton: 1987

Ridley, Jane: *Bertie – A Life of Edward VII*: Chatto and Windus: 2012

Röhl, John: *Young Wilhelm*: Cambridge University Press: 1998

Rose, Kenneth: *King George V*: Weidenfeld and Nicolson: 1983

Russell, Don: *The Lives and Legends of Buffalo Bill*: University of Oklahoma Press: 1973

St Aubyn, Giles: *Queen Victoria*: Sinclair-Stevenson: 1991

Sebba, Anne: *Jennie Churchill*: John Murray: 2007

Sessa, Anne Dzamba: *Richard Wagner and the English*: Associated University Presses Inc.: 1979

Short, Michael (ed. and translator): *Correspondence of Franz Liszt and the Comtesse Marie d'Agoult*: Pendragon Press: 2013

Shorter, Clement K.: *Charlotte Brontë and her Circle*: Hodder and Stoughton: 1896

Skinner, Cornelia Otis: *Madame Sarah*: Houghton-Mifflin, 1966

Smith, Margaret (ed.): *The Letters of Charlotte Brontë, Volume 1, 1829–1847*: Oxford University Press: 1995

Stanley, H.M.: *Coomassie and Magdala*: Sampson Low: 1874

Storey, Graham (et al.): *The Letters of Charles Dickens – Volumes 1–12*: Oxford University Press: 1965–2002

Sullivan, Herbert: *Sir Arthur Sullivan*: Cassell & Co.: 1927

Surtees, Virginia: *Charlotte Canning*: John Murray: 1975

Vicinus, Martha and Nergaard, Bea: *Ever Yours, Florence Nightingale – Selected Letters*: Virago: 1989

Walker, Alan: *Franz Liszt, Volume 3 – The Final Years, 1861–1886*: Faber and Faber: 1997

Warwick, Christopher: *Ella – Princess, Saint and Martyr*: Wiley: 2006

Watson, Richard: *Richard Wagner – A Biography*: Dent: 1979

Weintraub, Stanley: *Victorian Yankees at Queen Victoria's Court*: University of Delaware Press: 2011

Weybright, V. and Sell, H.: *Buffalo Bill and the Wild West*: Hamish Hamilton: 1956

William II, Former Emperor of Germany: *My Early Life*: Methuen: 1926

Wohl, Janka: *Francois Liszt – Recollections of a Compatriot*: Ward and Downey: 1887

Woodham-Smith, Cecil: *Florence Nightingale*: Constable: 1950

Zeepvat, Charlotte: *Prince Leopold*: Sutton Publishing Ltd: 1999

NEWSPAPERS and MAGAZINES

Daily Express (London, England)
East London Observer (London, England)
The Era (London, England)
Isle of Wight Observer (Ryde, England)
Liszt Society Journal
Liverpool Mercury (Liverpool, England)
Llangollen Advertiser (Llangollen, Wales)
Lloyd's Weekly Newspaper (London, England)
The Morning Post (London, England)
The Musical Standard (London, England)
Nottinghamshire Guardian (Nottingham, England)
The Pall Mall Gazette (London, England)
Reynolds's Newspaper (London, England)
The Strand Musical Magazine (London, England)
The Sunday Telegraph (London, England)
The Times (London, England)
The York Herald (York, England)

WEBSITES

www.bbc.co.uk/news/uk-england-york-north-yorkshire
Oxford Dictionary of National Biography: Oxford University Press: 2004; online
    edn: www.oxforddnb.com
www.treorchymalechoir.com

INDEX

IF YOU ENJOYED THIS, YOU MIGHT LIKE ...

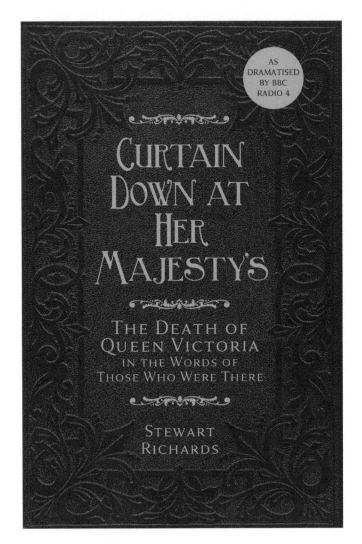

978 0 7509 9062 2